Hannah Adams

# An alphabetical compendium of the various sects : which have appeared in the world from the beginning of the Christian aera to the present day. With an appendix, containing a brief account of the different schemes of religion

Hannah Adams

**An alphabetical compendium of the various sects : which have appeared in the world from the beginning of the Christian aera to the present day. With an appendix, containing a brief account of the different schemes of religion**

ISBN/EAN: 9783337263645

Printed in Europe, USA, Canada, Australia, Japan

Cover: Foto ©Lupo / pixelio.de

More available books at **www.hansebooks.com**

A N

# ALPHABETICAL COMPENDIUM

OF THE VARIOUS

# S E C T S

Which have appeared in the World from the beginning of the
Christian Æra to the present Day.

WITH AN

# A P P E N D I X,

Containing a brief Account.

Of the different Schemes of

# R E L I G I O N

Now embraced among Mankind.

The whole collected

From the best Authors, ancient and modern.

## BY HANNAH ADAMS.

*"Prove all things, hold fast that which is good."*
Apostle Paul.

<hr>

B O S T O N:
Printed by B. EDES & SONS, Nº 42, Cornhill,
M,DCC,LXXXIV.

IT will be easily perceived, that the compiler of the following work has, with great labour and pains, ransacked the treasures of ecclesiastical history, ancient and modern, to bring into view what is here presented to the public.

She claims no other merit than that of having honestly and impartially collected the sense of the different sects, as it is given by the authors to whom she refers; nor was it a vain ambition of appearing as an author, that put her upon writing; her own satisfaction and amusement being the only object. Having yielded however to its publication, at the desire of several judicious friends, she has also done violence to her own inclination, by prefixing her name.

The world has been absurdly accustomed to entertain but a moderate opinion of female abilities, and to ascribe their pretended productions to the craft and policy of designing *men*; either to excite admiration or screen their weakness from censure: whereas unbiased reason must allow, if an invidious comparison between the sexes is in any respect justifiable, it cannot be grounded upon a defect of natural ability, but upon the different, and perhaps faulty mode of female education; for under similar culture, and with equal advantages, it is far from being certain that the female mind would not admit a measure of improvement, that would at least equal, and perhaps in many instances eclipse, the boasted glory of the other sex.

There have been female writers, and historians, who have been deservedly honored in the literary world.—The celebrated Mrs. Maccauley Graham, who has lately honored our country with her presence, is a living example. The

The writer of this compendium having been from her youth fond of books, has made herself acquainted with the Greek and Latin tongues, which may sufficiently account for so frequent a use of terms in those languages.

However the volume may be received by those who are vers'd in the historic page, it may at least be useful and entertaining to those who have neither leisure nor opportunity to peruse the numerous volumes from which the whole is collected—With regard to many of the ancient sects, it is well known little has been preserved, and therefore little can be here expected.—With respect to others, such as desire further information, are directed by references to the volumes, and generally to the pages, where their inquisitive minds may be satisfied

It is truly astonishing that so great a variety of faith and practice should be derived with equal confidence of their different abettors, from one and the same revelation from heaven : but while we have the lively oracles, we are not to adopt any of the numerous schemes of religion, further than they have a manifest foundation in the sacred pages. To the law and to the testimony ; if they speak not according to this word, however specious their systems may appear, " there is no light in them."

With cordial wishes for the divine illumination of the holy spirit, by which the sacred scriptures were indited, and a universal prevalence of the knowledge and practice of pure and undefiled religion before God and the Father :

I am the readers most obedient humble servant,

THOMAS PRENTISS.

*Medfield, September 2d,* 1784.

# ADVERTISEMENT.

THE reader will pleaſe to obſerve, that the following rules have been carefully adhered to through the whole of this performance.

1. To avoid giving the leaſt preference of one denomination above another : omiting thoſe paſſages in the authors cited, where they paſs their judgment on the ſentiments of which they give an account : conſequently the making uſe of any ſuch appellations as *Hereticks, Schiſmaticks, Enthuſiaſts, Fanaticks,* &c. is carefully avoided.

2. To give a few of the arguments of the principal ſects, from their own authors, where they could be obtained.

3. To endeavour to give the ſentiments of every ſect in the general collective ſenſe of that denomination.

4. To give the whole as much as poſſible in the words of the authors from which the compilation is made, and where that could not be done without too great prolixity, to take the utmoſt care not to miſrepreſent the ideas.

*Medfield, September* 2, 1784.

AN

# ALPHABETICAL COMPENDIUM, &c.

❖❖❖❖❖❖❖❖❖❖❖❖❖❖❖❖❖❖❖❖

## A C E

ABRAHAMIANS, A fect in the ninth century; fo called from their founder, Abraham.
They received the doctrines of the Paulicians,
and are faid to have employed the crofs in the moft
fervile offices.  [See Paulicians.]

*Dictionary of Arts and Sciences, vol. 1. p. 10.*

ABYSSINIAN-CHURCH, *that* eftablifhed in
the empire of Abyffinia : they maintain that the *two
natures* are *united* in Chrift without either *confufion* or
*mixture* ; fo that though the nature of our Saviour be
really *one*, yet it is at the fame time *two-fold and
compound*.

The Abyffinian church embraced thefe tenets in
the feventh century.  They difown the Pope's fupremacy, and moft points of the Popifh doctrines.

*Mofheim's Ecclefiaftical Hiftory, vol. 2 p. 172. vol. 3 p. 492.
Dictionary of Arts and Sciences, vol. 1. p. 15.*

ACEPHALI, i. e. headlefs.  The word is compounded of the privative [a] and [kephale] *a bead.*
They were a branch of the Eutichians, who, by the
fubmiffion of Mongos, had been deprived of their chief.
This fect was afterwards divided into three others,

who

who were called Anthopomorphites, Parfanaphites, and Efaianites. [See Eutychians.]

Mofheim's Ecc' efiaftical Hiftory, vol. 1. p. 418.

ADAMITES, A fect in the fecond century; who affumed this title from their afferting that fince their redemption by the death of Chrift, they were as innocent as Adam before the Fall, and confequently went naked in their affemblies. The author of this denomination was Prodicus, a difciple of Carpocrates. It was renewed in the fifteenth century by one Picard, a native of Flanders.

Broughton's Hiftorical Library, vol. 1. p 14.

ADESSENARIANS, A branch of the *Sacramentarians*, fo called from the Latin *Adeffe, to be prefent* ; becaufe they believed the prefence of Chrift's body in the *euchariff;* though in a manner different from the Romanifts. They were fubdivided into thofe who held that the body of Jefus Chrift is in the bread; whence they were likewife *Impanatores* ; thofe who hold that it is *about* the bread ; thofe who faid it is *with* the bread ; and thofe who maintained that it is *under* the bread.

Broughton, ibid, p. 15.

ADIAPHORISTS. [See Lutherans ]

ADOPTIANS, Followers of Felix of Urgel, an Elipand of Toledo ; who, towards the end of the eighth century, taught that JefusChrift, with refpect to his human nature, was not the natural, but adoptive Son of GOD.

Dictionary of Arts and Sciences, vol. 1. p 49.

AERIANS, A fect which arofe about the year 342 ; fo called from one Aerius, a Prefbyter, Monk, and Semi-arian.

Semi-arian. One of his principal tenets was, that there is no diftinction, founded in fcripture, between a Prefbyter and a Bifhop. He built his opinion chiefly on the paffage in the firft epiftle to Timothy, in which the *apoftle* exhorts him not to neglect *the gift he had received by the laying on the hands of the Prefbytery.* Aerius condemned prayers for the dead, ftated fafts, the celebration of Eafter, and other rites of the like nature.

*Mofheim's Ecclefiaftical Hiftory,* vol 1 *p.* 314.
*Broughton's Hiftorical Library,* vol. 1 *p* 22.

AETIANS, A fect which appeared about the year 336, fo called from Aetius, a Syrian. Befides the opinions which the Aetians held in common with the Arians, they maintained that *faith* without *works* was fufficient to falvation, and that no fin, however grievous, would be imputed to the faithful. Aetius moreover affirmed, that what GOD had concealed from the *apoftles,* he had revealed to him.

*Broughton, ibid, p.* 24.

AGINIANS, A fect which appeared about the end of the feventh century. They condemned the ufe of certain meats and marriage.—They had but few followers, and were foon fuppreffed.

*Broughton, ibid, p.* 26.

AGNOITES, A fect which appeared about the year 370. They were followers of Theophronius, the Capadocian, who called in queftion the omnifcience of GOD; alledging that he knew things paft only by memory, and things future only by an uncertain prefcience.

There arofe another fect of the fame name about the year 535, who followed the fentiments of



Themifticus.

Themifticus, deacon of Alexandria, who held that Chrift knew not when the day of judgment fhall be. He founded this opinion on a paffage of St. Mark : *Of that day and hour knoweth no man ; no not the angels who are in heaven, nor the ſon, but the Father only.*

This fect derive their name from the Greek *agnoein*, to be ignorant.

*Broughton, ibid, p. 26 27:*

ALBANENSES, A fect which commenced about the year 796. They held with the Gnoftics and Manichæans, two principles, the one of good, the other of evil. They denied the *divinity*, and even the *humanity* of Jefus Chrift, afferting that he was not truly man ; did not fuffer on the crofs, die, rife again, nor really afcend into *heaven*. They rejected the doctrine of the *refurrection* ; affirmed that the general judgment was paft ; and that hell torments were no other than the evils we feel and fuffer in this life. They denied *free-will*, did not admit *original fin* ; and never adminiftered *baptifm* to infants. They held that a man can give the holy fpirit of himfelf, and that it is unlawful for a chriftian to take an oath.

This *fect* derived their name from the place where their fpiritual ruler refided. [See Manichæans and Chatharifts.]

*Brough·n ibid p* 31.<br>*Mofheim's Ecclefiaftical Hift vol* 2 *p* 445.

ALBANOIS, A fect which fprung up in the eighth century, and renewed the greateft part of the Manichæan principles. They alfo maintained that the world was from eternity. [See Manichæans.]

*Collier's Hiftorical Dictionary, vol.* I. [*See Albanois* ]

ALBIGENSES,

ALBIGENSES, So called from their firſt increaſe in Albi and Albigeos.  A denomination remarkable for their oppoſition to the diſcipline and ceremonies of the church of Rome.  Their opinions are ſimilar with the Waldenſes.  [See Waldenſes]

*Perrin's Hiſtory of the Waldenſes p 3.*

ALMARICIANS, A ſect which aroſe in the thirteenth century.  They derived their name from Almaric, profeſſor of loic and theology at Paris, who taught that *every chriſtian was obliged to believe himſelf a member of Jeſus Chriſt, and that without this belief none could be ſaved.*  His followers aſſerted that the *power* of the *Father* had continued only during the Moſaic diſpenſation; that of the *Son* twelve hundred years after his entrance upon earth; and that, in the thirteenth century, the *age of the Holy Spirit* commenced, in which the ſacraments and all external worſhip were to be aboliſhed; and that every one was to be ſaved by the internal operations of the Holy Spirit alone, without any external act of religion.

*Moſheim's Eccleſiaſtical Hiſtory Note [c] vol iii. p 129 133.*

ALOGIANS, [in Latin Alogi] A ſect in Aſia-Minor, in the year 171; ſo called, becauſe they denied the divine *logos,* or word, and the goſpel and writings of St. John, attributing them to Cerinthus.

One Theodore of Byzantium, by trade a currier, was the head of this denomination.

*Broughton's Hiſtorical Library vol 1 p. 33.*

AMMONIANS, So called from Ammonius Saccas, who taught with the higheſt applauſe in the Alexandrian ſchool, about the concluſion of the ſecond century. This learned man attempted a general reconciliation of all *sects*, whether *philosophical* or *religious*. He maintained, that the great principles of all *philosophical* and *religious truth* were to be found equally in all sects ; and they differed from each other only in their method of expressing them, and in some opinions of little or no importance ; and that by a proper interpretation of their respective sentiments, they might easily be united in one body.

AMMONIUS, Supposed that true philosophy derived its origin and its consistence from the Eastern nations ; that it was taught to the Egyptians by Hermes ; that it was brought from them to the Greeks, and preserved in its original purity by Plato, who was the best interpreter of Hermes and the other Oriental sages. He maintained that all the different religions which prevailed in the world, were in their original integrity, conformable to this ancient philosophy ; but it unfortunately happened that the symbols and fictions, under which, according to the Eastern manner, the ancients delivered their precepts and doctrines, were, in process of time, erroneously understood both by priests and people in a literal sense ; that in consequence of this, the invisible beings and dæmons, whom the supreme Deity had placed in the different parts of the universe as the ministers of his providence, were, by the suggestions of superstition, converted into Gods, and worshiped with a multiplicity of vain ceremonies. He therefore insisted, that all the religions of all nations should be restored to their primitive standard, viz. *the ancient philosophy of the East* ; and he asserted that his project was agreeable to the intentions of Jesus Christ (whom he acknowledged to be a

most

moſt excellent man, the friend of GOD) and affirmed that his ſole view in deſcending on earth, was to
ſet bounds to the reigning ſuperſtition, to rem ve
the errors which had crept into the religion of all
nations, but not to aboliſh the ancient theology,
from whence they were derived.

Taking theſe principles for granted, Ammonius
aſſociated the ſentiments of the Egyptians with the
doctrines of Plato ; and to finiſh this conciliatory
ſcheme, he ſo interpreted the doctrines of the other
*philoſophical* and *religious ſects* by art, invention, and
allegory, that they ſeemed to bear ſome reſemblance
of the *Egyptian* and *Platonic* ſyſtems.*

With regard to moral diſcipline, Ammonius permitted the people to live according to the law of
their country and the dictates of nature ; but a more
ſublime rule was laid down for the wiſe,—they were
to raiſe above all terreſtrial things by the towring efforts of holy contemplation, thoſe ſouls whoſe origin was celeſtial and divine. They were ordered
to extenuate by hunger, thirſt, and other mortifications, the ſluggiſh body which reſtrains the liberty
of the immortal ſpirit ; that in this life they might
enjoy communion with the *Supreme Being*, and aſcend after death, active and unencumbered, to the
Univerſal Parent, to live in his preſence forever.

*Moſheim's Eccleſiaſtical Hiſtory, vol.* 1. *p.* 137 to 144.

**AMSDORFIANS, A** ſect of Proteſtants in the
ſixteenth century, who took their name from Armſ-
dorf their leader.                                    It

* Ammonius left nothing behind him in writing ; nay, he im-
poſed a law upon his diſciples not to divulge his doctrines among
the multitude, which law, however, they made no ſcruple to
neglect and violate.

It is said they maintained that good works were not only unprofitable, but even opposite and pernicious to salvation.

*Dictionary of Arts and Sciences, vol. 1. p. 131.*

**ANABAPTISTS,** [See Baptists.]

**ANGELITES,** A sect which sprung up about the year 494 ; so called from Angelium, a place in the city of Alexandria, where they held their first meetings. They were called likewise Serverites, from one Serverus, who was the head of their sect ; as also Theodosians, from one among them named Theodosius, whom they made Pope at Alexandria.

They held that the Father, Son, and Holy-Ghost, are not the same ; that none of them exists of himself, and of his own nature ; and that there is a common Deity exifting in them all ; and that each is GOD, by a participation of this Deity.

*Broughton's Historical Library, vol. 1 p 49.*

**ANOMOEANS,** A name by which the pure Arians were diftinguished in the fourteenth century, in contradiftinction to the Semi-Arians. The word is taken from the Greek [anomoios] different, diffimilar.    [See Arians.]

*Broughton. ibid p 51.*

**ANTHROPOMORPHITES,** A sect in the tenth century : so denominated from [anthrœpos] man, and [morphæ] shape. In the diftrict of Vicenza, a confiderable number, not only of the illiterate vulgar, but also of the facerdotal order fell into the notion, that the Deity was cloathed with an human form, and feated like an earthly monarch,

upon

upon a throne of gold, and that his angelic ministers were men arrayed in white garments, and fur-
nished with wings to render them more expediti-
ous in executing their sovereign's orders. They
take every thing spoken of God in scripture in a literal sense, particularly that passage in Genesis, in
which it is said that *God made man after his own
image.*

Broughton. ibid. p. 55.<br>Mosheim's Ecclef Hist. vol. 3 p.227.

ANTINOMIANS, They derive their name
from the Greek [anti] *against* and [nomos] *law.*
In the 16th century while Luther was eagerly employed in censuring and refuting the Popish doctors,
who mixed the *law* and *gospel* together, and repre-
sented eternal happiness as the fruit of legal obedience, a new teacher arose whole name was John
Agricola, a native of Aisleben, and an eminent doctor in the Lutheran church. His fame began to
spread in the year 1538, when from the doctrine of
Luther, now mentioned, he took occasion to advance sentiments which were interpreted in such a
manner, that his followers were distinguished by
the title of Antinomians. *

The principal doctrines which bear this appellation, together with a short specimen of the arguments made use of in their defence, are comprehended in the following summary.

I. That the *law* ought not to be proposed to the
people as a rule of manners, nor used in the church

as

---

* Agricola held, that repentance was not to be taught from
the decalogue; and opposed such as maintained that the gospel
was not to be preached to any but such as were humbled by the
law.

as a means of inftruction ; and that the *gofpel* alone was to be inculcated and explained, both in the churches and in the fchools of learning.

For the fcriptures declare, that *Chrift is not the law-giver,* as is faid, *The law was givin by Mofes ; but grace and truth came by Jefus Chrift.* Therefore, the minifters of the *gofpel,* ought not to teach the *law.* Chriftians are not ruled by the *law,* but by the fpirit of regeneration, according as it is faid, *ye are not under the law, but under grace.* Therefore the *law* ought not to be taught in the church of Chrift.

II. That the *juftification* of *finners,* is an immanent and eternal act of God, not only preceding all acts of fin ; but the exiftence of the finner himfelf. †

For nothing new can arife in God, on which account he calls things that are not as though they were ; and the apoftle faith, *who hath bleffed us with all fpiritual bleffings in heavenly places in Chrift Jefus, before the foundation of the world.——* Befides, CHRIST was *fet up from everlafting,* not only as the head of the church, but as the furety of his people ; by virtue of which engagement the Father decreed never to impute unto them their fins. See 2d. of Cor. iv. 19.

III. That juftification by faith, is no more than a manifeftation to us of what was done before we had a being.

For

---

† This is the opinion of moft, who are ftiled Antinomi ns, though fome fuppofe, with Dr. Crifp, that the elect were juftified at the time of Chrift's death.

For, it is thus expreſſed in Hebrews xi. i. *Now faith is the ſubſtance of things hoped for, the evidence of things not ſeen.* We are juſtified only by Chriſt; but by *faith* we perceive it, and by *faith* rejoice in it, as we apprehend it to be our own.

IV. That men ought not to doubt of their faith, nor queſtion whether they believe in Chriſt.

For, we are commanded to *draw near in full aſſurance o faith.* Hebrews x. 22. *He that believeth on the Son of GOD hath the witneſs in himſelf.* 2d of John v. 10. i. e. he has as much evidence as can be deſired.

V. That GOD ſees no ſin in believers, and they are not bound to confeſs ſin, mourn for it, or pray that it may be forgiven.

For GOD has declared, Heb. x. 17. *Their ſins and iniquities I will rememb. rſto more:* and in Jer. l. 20. *In thoſe days, and in that time, ſaith the Lord, the iniquity of Iſrael ſhall be ſought for, and there ſhall be none; and the ſins of Judah, and they ſhall not be found: for I will pardon them whom I reſerve.*

VI. That GOD is not angry with the elect, nor doth he puniſh them for their ſins.

For Chriſt has made ample ſatisfaction for their ſins, ſee Iſaiah liii. 5. *He was wounded for our tranſgreſſions, he was bruiſed for our iniquities,* &c. And to inflict puni.hment once upon the ſurety, and again upon the believer, is contrary to the juſtice of GOD, as well as derogatory to the ſatisfaction of Chriſt.

VII. That by GOD's laying our iniquities upon *Chriſt,* he became as completely *ſinful as we,* and we as completely *righteous as Chriſt.*

C

For

For *Chriſt* repreſents *our perſons* to the *Father ;* *we* repreſent the *perſon* of *Chriſt* to *him* : the lovelineſs of Chriſt is transferred to us ; on the other hand, all that is hateful in our nature is put upon *Chriſt,* who was forſaken by the *Father* for a time ; ſee 2d of Cor. v. 21. *He was made ſin for us, who knew no ſin ; that we might be made the righteouſneſs of GOD in him.*

VIII. That *believers* need not fear either their own ſins or the ſins of others, ſince neither can do them any injury.

See Rom. viii, 33, 34. *Who ſhall lay any thing to the charge of GOD's elect ?* &c.   The apoſtle does not ſay that they never tranſgreſs ; but triumphs in the thought that no curſe can be executed againſt them.

IX. That the new covenant is not made properly with us, but with Chriſt for us ; and that this covenant is all of it a promiſe, having no conditions for us to perform ; for faith, repentance, and obedience, are not conditions on our part, but Chriſt's ; and he repented, believed, and obeyed for us.

For the covenant is ſo expreſſed, that the performance lies upon the Deity himſelf, *For this is the covenant that I will make with the houſe of Iſrael after thoſe days, ſaith the Lord ; I will put my laws into their mind, and write them in their hearts ; and I will be to them a GOD, and they ſhall be to me a people.* Hebrews viii. 10.

X. That *ſanctification* is not a proper evidence of *juſtification.*

For thoſe who endeavour to evidence their juſtification by their ſanctification, are looking to their
                                                                own

own attainments and not to Chrift's righteoufnefs for hopes of falvation.

Mofheim's Ecclef. Hift  vol 4 p. 33.
Clark's Lives  p 142.
Urfinus'. Body of Divinity, p. 620.
Spiritual Magazine, vol 2 p 171.
Chrifp's Sermons, vol 1. p 24 29 136. 137, 143,
      281, 298 :30. vol. 2 p. 144. 155.
Saltmarfh of Free Grace, p. 92,
Eaton's Honey-comb, p 446.
Town's Affertions. p 96.
Difplay of GOD's fpecial Grace. p. 102:

ANTITACTES, Of [antitaktö] to oppofe, A fect of Gnoftics who held that GOD the creator of the univerfe, was good and juft ; but that one of his creatures had created evil, and engaged mankind to follow it in oppofition to GOD ; and that it is the duty of mankind to oppofe this author of evil in order to avenge GOD of his enemy.

Bailey's Dictionary, vol. 2. [See Antitgctes ]

ANTITRINITARIANS, A general name given to all thofe who deny the doctrine of the Trinity, and particularly to the *Arians* and *Socinians*.

Dictionary of Arts and Sciences, vol. 1  p. 167:

APELLÆANS, A fect in the fecond century, fo called from Apelles, a difciple of Marcion. They affirmed that Chrift, when he came down from Heaven, received a body, not from the fubftance of his mother, but from the four elements ; which, at his death, he rendered back to the world, and fo afcended into Heaven without a body. With the Gnoftics and Manichees, they held two principles, a good and a bad God. They afferted that the prophets contradicted each other ; and denied the refurrection of the body.

C 2

They

They erafed that paffage of St. John, which fays *every fpirit that confeffeth not that Jefus Chrift is come in the flefh, is not of GOD.*

*Broughton's Hiflorical Library,* vol. 1 p 58.

**APHTHARTODOCITES,** A fect in the fixth century, fo called from the Greek [aphthartòs] *incorruptible,* and [dòkèò] *to judge,* becaufe they held that the body of JESUS CHRIST was incorruptible, and not fubject to death. They were a branch of the Eutychians. See Eutychians.

*Broughton, ibid. p.* 58.

**APOCARITÆS,** A fect in the third century, fprung from the Manicheans. They held that the foul of man was of the fubftance of God.

*Broughton, ibid. p.* 60.

**APOLLINARIANS,** A fect in the fourth century, who were the followers of Apollinaris, bifhop of Laodicea. He taught that Chrift's perfon was compofed of a union of the true divinity and a human body, endowed with a fenfitive foul, but deprived of the reafonable one, the divinity fupplying its place. He added, that the human body united to the divine fpirit, formed in Jefus Chrift one entire divine nature.

*Formey's Ecclef. hift. vol* 1, p. 79.

**APOSTOLICS,** A fect in the twelfth century, who had at their head one Gerard Saggarel, of Parma. They were fo called, becaufe they profeffed to exhibit in their lives and manners the piety and virtues of the holy apoftles. They held it unlawful

lawful to take an oath ; renounced the things of this world, and prefered celibacy to wedlock.

*Mosheim's Ecclef. hift. vol. 2 p. 457*
*Dufrefnoy's Chronological Tables, vol 2 p. 239.*

**AQUARIANS,** A fect in the fecond century ; who under pretence of abftinence, made ufe of water inftead of wine, in theEucharift. See Encratites.

*Dictionary of Arts and Sciences, vol. 1, p. 178.*

**ARABICI,** So called becaufe they fprung up in Arabia, in the year 207. It is uncertain who was their author. They denied the immortality of the foul, believed that it perifhed with the body ; but maintained at the fame time that it was to be again recalled to life with the body, by the power of God.

*Mosheim's Ecclef. Hift. vol. 1. p. 249.*
*Broughton's Hiftorical Library, vol 1, p. 73.*

**ARCHONTICKS,** A fect which appeared about the year 175, fo called becaufe they held that *archangels* created the world. They denied the refurrection of the body ; they maintained that the God of Sabaoth exercifed a cruel tyranny in the feventh heaven ; that he engendered the Devil, who begot Abel and Cain of Eve.

Thefe tenets they defended by books of their own compofing, ftiled, *The revelation of the prophets,* and the *Harmony.*

*Echard's Ecclef. hift. vol. 2. p. 542.*

**ARIANS,** A denomination in the fourth century, which owed its origin to Arius, a man of a fubtil turn, and remarkable for his eloquence. He maintained that the *Son* was totally and *effenti-ally* diftinct from the *Father* ; that he was the *firft*
and

and *noblest* of thofe beings whom God the Father had created out of nothing, the inftrument by whofe fubordinate operation the *Almighty Father* formed the univerfe, and therefore inferior to the *Father* both in *nature* and in *dignity.* * He added that the holy fpirit was of a different nature from that of the Father, and of the Son ; and that he had been created by the *Son.* However, during the life of Arius, the difputes turned principally on the divinity of Chrift.

To prove their fundamental doctrine, the Arians alledge, that the apoftle ftiles Chrift, *The firft born of every creature.* Col. i. 15. Therefore he is only the firft and nobleft creature of God.

In the 1ft Cor. xv. 24, it is faid that *Chrift fhall deliver up the kingdom to God, even the Father ;* therefore he will be fubjected to him ; and confequently inferior.

John viii 24. v. 19. xiv. 10—28. Mark xiii. 33. Thefe texts with fome few others of like nature, are generally made ufe of by this denomination, as proofs of a fubordination of Jefus Chrift to God the Father.

The ARIANS were divided among themfelves, and torn into factions, which regarded each other with the bittereft averfion. Of thefe the ancient writers make mention under the names of Semiarians, Eufebians, Ætians, Eunomians, Æacians, Pfathyrians, and others : but they may all be ranked
with

---

* His followers deny that Chrift had any thing which could properly be called a *divine nature,* any otherwife than as any thing very excellent may by a figure be called divine, or his delegated dominion over the fyftem of nature might entitle him to the name of GOD.

with the utmoſt propriety into three claſſes ;—the firſt of theſe were the primitive and genuine Ariáns, who rejecting all thoſe forms and modes of expreſſions, which the moderns had invented to render their opinions leſs ſhocking to the Nicenians, taught ſimply, *That the Son was not begotton of the Father*, (i. e. produced out of his ſubſtance) *but only created out of nothing.* This claſs was oppoſed by the Semi-arians, who in their turn were abandoned by the Eunomians, or Anómæans, the diſciples of Ætius and Eunomius. The Semi-arians held, *that the Son was* [òmòròuſeòs] i. e. *ſimilar to the Father in his eſſence, not by nature, but by a peculiar privilege.* The Eunomians, who were alſo called Ætians, and Exucontians, and may be counted in the number of pure Arians, maintained *that Chriſt was* [ètèròòuſiòs] or [anòmòiòs] i. e. *unlike the Father in his eſſence as well as in other reſpects.*

Under this general diviſion many ſubordinate ſects were comprehended, whoſe ſubtleties and refinements have been but obſcurely developed by ancient writers.

*Moſheim's Eccleſ hiſt. vol.* I, *p.* 335, 342, 343.
*Formey's Eccleſ. hiſt. vol,* I, *p.* 76.
*Opera Zanchii, vol.* I, *tom.* I, *p* 492—494.
*Doddridge's Lectures, p* 401.
*Lowman's Tracts, p.* 253.

**ARMENIANS,** A diviſion of Eaſtern chriſtians, thus called from Armenia, a country they anciently inhabited.

The principal points in their doctrine are as follows, 1ſt. They aſſert, with the Greeks, the proceſſion of the Holy Ghoſt from the Father only. 2d. They believe that Chriſt, at his deſcent into

Hell,

Hell, freed the fouls of the damned from thence, and reprieved them till the end of the world, when they fhall be remanded to eternal flames. 3d. They believe that the fouls of the righteous fhall not be admitted to the beatific vifion till after the refurrection: notwithftanding which, they pray to departed faints, adore their pictures, and burn lamps before them. They ufe confeffion to the priefts; and adminifter the Eucharift in both kinds to the laity. In the facrament of baptifm, they plunge the infant thrice in water, and apply the chrifm with confecrated oil, in form of a crofs, to feveral parts of the body, and then touch the child's lips with the Eucharift.

They obferve a multitude of fafts and feftivals.

*Broughton's Hiftorical Library, vol 2. p. 329 330.*

ARMINIANS, They derive their name from James Arminius, who was born in Holland in the year 1560. He was firft paftor at Amfterdam; afterwards profeffor of divinity at Leyden, and attracted the efteem and applaufe of his very enemies, by his acknowledged candor, penetration and piety. They received alfo the denomination of Remonftrants, from an humble petition entitled their remonftrances, which they addreffed in the year 1610, to the ftates of Holland.

The principal tenets of the Arminians are comprehended in five articles, to which are added a few of the arguments they make ufe of in defence of their fentiments.

I. That the Deity has not fixed the future ftate of mankind, by an abfolute unconditional decree;

tree ; but determined from all eternity, to bestow salvation on those whom he foresaw would persevere unto the end in their faith in Jesus Christ ; and to inflict everlasting punishments on those who should continue in their unbelief, and resist unto the end his divine succours.

For, as the Deity is *just*, *holy*, and *merciful*, wise in all his counsels, and true in all his declarations to the sons of men, it is inconsistent with his *attributes*, by an antecedent *decree*, to fix our commission of so many sins, in such a manner, that there is no possibility for us to avoid them : and he represents GOD dishonorably, who believes, that by his *revealed will*, he hath declared he would have *all men* to be saved ; and yet, by an antecedent *secret will*, he would have the *greatest part* of them to perish. That he hath imposed a *law* upon them, which he requires them to obey, on penalty of his eternal displeasure, though he knows they cannot do it without his irresistable grace ; and yet is absolutely determined to withhold this grace from them, and then punish them eternally for what they could not do without his divine assistance.

II. That JESUS CHRIST, by his death and sufferings, made an atonement for the sins of *all mankind* in general, and of every individual in particular : that however, none, but those who believe in him, can be partakers of their divine benefit.

That is, the death of CHRIST put all men in a capacity of being justified and pardoned, upon condition of their faith, repentance, and sincere obedience to the laws of the new covenant.

For the scriptures declare, in a variety of places, that CHRIST died for the *whole world*. John iii.

16, 17. *GOD fo loved the world, that he gave his only begotten Son, that whofoever believeth on him might not perifh, but have everlafting life,* &c. 1ft of John, ii. 2. *He is the propitiation not only for our fins, but for the fins of the whole world.* And the apoftle expreffes the fame idea in Heb. ii. 9. when he fays, *CHRIST tafted death for every man.* Here is no limitation of that comprehenfive phrafe.

If CHRIST died for them that perifh, and for them that do not perifh, he died for *all.* That he died for them that do not perifh, is confeffed by all ; and if he died for any that may or fhall perifh, there is the fame reafon to affirm that he died for all that perifh. Now that he died for fuch, the fcripture fays exprefly, in 1ft of Cor. viii. 11. *And through thy knowledge fhall the weak brother perifh for whom Chrift died.* Hence it is evident Chrift died for them that perifh, and for them that do not perifh ; therefore he died for *all men.*

III. That mankind are not totally depraved, and that depravity does not come upon them by virtue of Adam's being their public head ; but that mortality and natural evil only are the direct confequences of his fin to his pofterity.

For, if all men are utterly difabled to all good, and continually inclined to all manner of wickednefs, it follows, that they are not moral agents. For how are we capable of performing duty, or of regulating our actions by a law commanding good and forbidding evil, if our minds are bent to nothing but what is evil ? Then fin muft be natural to us ; and if natural, then neceffary, with regard to us ; and if neceffary, then no fin : for what is natural to us, as hunger, thirft, &c. we can by no means hinder ; and

what

what we can by no means hinder, is not our fin : therefore mankind are not totally depraved.

That the fin of our firft parents is not imputed to us is evident ; becaufe, as the evil action they committed was perfonal, fo muft their real guilt be perfonal and belong only to themfelves : and we cannot, in the eye of juftice and equity, be punifhable for their tranfgreffion.

IV. That there is no fuch thing as irrefiftable grace, in the converfion of finners.

For, if converfion be wrought only by the unfruftrable operation of God, and man is purely paffive in it, vain are all the commands and exhortations to wicked-men *to turn from their evil ways :* Ifaiah i. 16. *To ceafe to do evil, and learn to do well :* Deut. x. 16. *To put off the old man, and put on the new :* Eph. iv. 22. And divers other texts to the fame purpofe. Were an irrefiftable power neceffary to the converfion of finners, no man could be converted fooner than he is ; becaufe, before this irrefiftable action came upon him he could not be converted, and when it came upon him he could not refift its operations, and therefore no man could reafonably be blamed that he lived fo long in an unconverted ftate : and it could not be praife-worthy in any perfon who was converted, fince no man can refift an unfruftrable operation.

V. That thofe who are united to Chrift by faith, may fall from their faith, and forfeit finally their ftate of grace.

For the doctrine of a poffibility of the final departure of true believers from the faith, is expreffed in Heb. vi. 4, 5, 6. *It is impoffible for them who were*



*once*

*once enlightened, &c.—If they shall fall away to re-
new them again to repentance ; seeing they crucify to
themselves the Son of God afresh, and put him to open
shame.* See also 2d. of Peter, ii. 18, 20, 21, 22,
and divers other passages of scripture to the same
purpose.

All commands to persevere and stand fast in the
faith, shew that there is a possibility that believers
may not stand fast and persevere unto the end. All
cautions to christians not to fall from grace, are
evidences and suppositions that they may fall, for
what we have just reason to caution any person
against, must be something which may come to pass
and be hurtful to him. Now such caution Christ
gives his disciples ; Luke xxi. 34, 36. To them
who had like precious faith with the apostles, St.
Peter saith, *Beware, left being led away by the error
of the wicked, you fall from your own steadfastness.* 2d.
of Peter, iii. 17. Therefore he did not look upon
this as a thing impossible : and the doctrine of perseverance renders those exhortations and motives in-
significant, which are so often to be found in scripture.

*Mosheim's Ecclef hift vol.* v. *p* 3 7 8
*Whitby, on the Five Points p.* 106, 107 120, 124, 134,
           231, 232 254 394 398
*Taylor, on Original Sin. p.* 13 125.
*Stackh use's Body of Divinity p* 155. 156.
*Collier's Historical Dictionary, vol.* i.     [*See Arminians* ]

ARNOLDISTS, A sect in the twelfth century,
which derive their name from Arnold, of Fresia.
Having observed the calamities that sprung from the
opulence of the *Pontiffs* and *Bishops*, he maintained,
that nothing was to be left to the ministers of the
gospel but a spiritual authority, and a subsistence
                                                drawn

drawn from tithes, and from the voluntary oblations of the people.

Mosheim's Ecclesiastical Hist vol. ii  p 50

ARTEMONITES, A sect in the second century, so called from Arteman, who taught, That the birth of the man CHRIST, a certain a energy, or portion of the divine nature, and ec to him.

Mosheim, ibid. vol. i.  p

ARTOTYRITES, A sect in the second century, who celebrated the Eucharist with bread and cheese, saying, that the first oblations of men were of the fruits of the earth, and of sheep.  The word is derived from the Greek of [artòs] bread, and [turòs] cheese.

The Artemonites admitted women to the priesthood and episcopacy.

Broughton's  Historical Library, vol. i.  p. 85.

ASCLEPIDOTÆANS,  A sect  in  the third century ;  so called from Asclepiodotus, who taught that Jesus Christ was a mere man.

Broughton, ibid. p. 88.

ASCODROGITES, A sect which arose in the year 181.  They brought into their churches bags, or skins, filled with new wine, to represent the new bottles, filled with  new wine, mentioned by Christ. They danced round these bags, or skins, and intoxicated themselves  with  the  wine.  They are likewise called Ascitæ, and both words are derived from the Greek of [askòs] a bottle, or bag.

Broughton, ibid, p. 88.

ASCODRUTES,

ASCODRUTES, A fect of Gnoftics in the fecond century ; who placed all religion in knowledge,
and afferted, that divine myfteries, being the images
of invifible things, ought not to be performed by
vifible things, nor incorporeal things by corporeal
and fenfible : therefore, they rejected *baptifm* and
the *Eucharift*.

*Broughton, ibid, p* 89.

ASSURITANS, A branch of the Donatifts, who
held that the Son was inferior to the Father ; and the
HolyGhoft to the Son : they re-baptized thofe who
embraced their fect ; and afferted that good men
only were within the pale of the church. [See
Donatifts]

*Dictionary of Arts and Sciences, vol.* i. *p.* 207.

AUDÆANS, A fect in the fourth century ; fo
called from Audæus, who was faid to have attributed to the Deity a human form.

*Mofheim's Ecclefiaftical Hiftory, vol.* i. *p.* 350.

AZYMITES, So called from the Greek [azu-
mòs] a name given by the Greeks in the eleventh
century, to the chriftians of the Latin church, becaufe they ufed unleavened bread in the *Eucharift.*

*Hiftorical Dictionary, vol.* i. *[See Azymitæ.]*

## B

BAPTISTS, or ANTIPÆDOBAPTISTS, This
denomination claim an immediate defcent from
the *apoftles* ; and affert, that the conftitution of their
churches is from the authority of JESUS CHRIST
himfelf, and his immediate fucceffors.

Many others indeed deduce their origin as a fect
from much later times, and affirm they firft fprang
up in Germany in the fixteenth century. The

The diſtinguiſhing tenets of the *Baptiſts* are as follow; to which are added a few of the arguments made uſe of in defence of their ſentiments.

I. That thoſe who actually profeſs *repentance* towards God, *faith* in, and *obedience* to our Lord Jeſus, are the only proper *ſubjects* of *baptiſm*; and that *immerſion* is neceſſary to the due *adminiſtration* of that *ordinance*.

For, ſay they, John the firſt adminiſtrator of that ordinance, preached the *baptiſm of repentance*, and required *repentance* previous to *baptiſm*. Mat. iii. 2, 5, 6, 8. See John iv. 1. Jeſus firſt made diſciples, and then baptized them, or ordered them to be baptized; and with his practice agrees the commiſſion he gave in Matt. xxviii. 19. with which compare Mark xvi. 16. See alſo Acts viii. 37. and other paſſages of ſcripture where *repentance* and *faith* are mentioned as neceſſary in order to *baptiſm*.

*Whoſoever are baptized* into *Chriſt*, *have put on Chriſt*, *have put on the new man*: but to put on the new man, *is to be formed in righteouſneſs, holineſs, and truth*; this whole argument is in the expreſs words of St. Paul: the major propoſition is poſitively determined, Gal. iii. 27. The minor in Epheſ. iv. 24. The concluſion then is obvious, that they who are not formed anew *in righteouſneſs, holineſs and truth*; they who remaining in the preſent incapacities cannot *walk in newneſs of li e*, have not been *baptized into Chriſt*, have not that *baptiſm which is the anſwer of a good conſcience towards God*, which is the only *baptiſm* which ſaves us:— and as this is the caſe of children, they are not proper ſubjects of that *ordinance*.

Reſpecting

Respecting the mode, they argue from the signification of the word *baptism*——from the phrase, *buried with him in baptism* ——from the first administrators repairing to rivers; and the practice of the primitive church after the *apostles.*

II. The *Baptists* in general refuse to communicate with other denominations.

For they suppose the mode of immersion essential to *baptism* ; and that *baptism* is necessary previous to receiving the *Lord's supper* : and that therefore it would be inconsistent for them to admit unbaptized persons (as others are in their view) to join with them in this ordinance.

This denomination all unite in pleading for *universal liberty of conscience.* For they alledge that *the sacred rights of conscience* are unalienable, and subject to no controul but that of the Deity. For it does not appear that God has given such authority to one man over another, as to compel any one to his religion. Nor can any such power be vested in the magistrate by the consent of the people ; because no man can so far abandon the care of his own salvation as blindly to leave it to the choice of any other, whether prince or subject, to prescribe to him what faith or worship he shall embrace.

*In the second place,* The care of souls cannot belong to the civil magistrate, because his power consists only in outward force, but true and saving religion consists in the inward persuasion of the mind, without which nothing can be acceptable to God. And such is the nature of the understanding, that it cannot be compelled to any thing by outward force.

From

From thefe and many other confiderations, they conclude that all the power of civil government relates only to mens civil intereft, is confined to the care of the things of this world, and has nothing to do with the world to come.

In confequence of this tenet, the *Baptifts* exclaim againft the civil authority compelling people to fupport minifters ; but they enjoin it on their churches as an incumbent duty, to afford their minifters a comfortable fupply.

The affociation of *Baptifts* in New-England call themfelves Calvinifts, with regard to doctrines ; and Independents, with referrence to church-government. [See Calvinifts and Independents]

The Englifh *Baptifts* have been divided into two parties ever fince the beginning of the Reformation, viz. thofe who have followed the *Calviniftical doctrines*, and, from the principal point in that plan, *perfonal election*, have been termed *particular Baptifts*; and thofe who profeffed the *Arminian tenets* ; and have alfo from the chief of thofe doctrines *univerfal redemption*, been ftiled *general Baptifts*.

For an account of the other denominations of *Baptifts*, fee Dunkers, Kethians, Mennonites, Sabbatarians, and Uckewallifts.

*Crofby's Hiftory of the Englifh Baptifts, vol. i, p. 23,*
173    *vol.* 4 *p* 165
*Hiftory of Religion, No.* 35 *p.* 193.
*Baptifts Confeffion of Faith. p.* 47 50.
*Gill on Baptifm p* 93 94 95.
*Taylor's Liberty of Prophefying, p* 329.
*Stillman's Election Sermon, p* 11. 23. 24.
*Affociation Minutes, for* 1777. *p.* 4.

E                    BARDESANISTES,

BARDESANISTES, A fect in the fecond century, they derived their name from Bardefanes a native of Edeffa, and a man of a very acute and penetrating genius.

The fum of his doctrine was as follows :

I. That there is a *Supreme* GOD, pure and benevolent, abfolutely free from all evil and imperfection ; and there is alfo a *Prince of Darknefs*, the fountain of all evil, diforder and mifery.

II. That the Supreme GOD created the world without any mixture of evil in its compofition ; he gave exiftence alfo to its inhabitants, who came out of his forming hand, pure and incorrupt, endued with fubtle ethereal bodies and fpirits of a celeftial nature.

III. That when the *Prince of Darknefs* had enticed men to fin, then the *Supreme* GOD permitted them to fall into fluggifh and grofs bodies, formed of corrupt matter by the *evil principle* ; he permitted alfo the depravation and diforder which this malignant being introduced both into the natural and moral world, defigning by this permiffion, to punifh the degeneracy and rebellion of an apoftate race ; and hence proceeds the perpetual conflict between reafon and paffion in the mind of man.

IV. That on this account JESUS defcended from the upper regions, cloathed not with a real, but with a celeftial and ærial body, and taught mankind to fubdue that body of corruption which they carry about with them in this mortal life ; and by *abftinence*, *fafting*, and *contemplation*, to difengage themfelves from the fervitude and dominion of that *malignant matter*, which chained down the foul to low and ignoble purfuits. ——————  V. That

V. That those who submit themselves to the discipline of this divine teacher, shall, after the dissolution of this terrestrial body, mount up to the mansions of felicity, cloathed with ætherial vehicles, or celestial bodies.

This denomination was a branch of the Gnostics. [See Gnostics]

*Mosheim's Ecclef. Hift. vol. i. p. 179, 180.*

**BARLAAMITES,** A sect in the sixteenth century, followers of Barliaam, he was by birth a Neopolitan, and Monk of the Order of St. Basil. He maintained that the light which surrounded Christ on mount Tabor was neither the Divine essence, nor flowed from it.*

*Broughton's Hiftorical Library, vol. i p. 127.*

**BASILIDIANS,** A sect in the second centur, so called from Baffilides, chief of the Egyptian Gnostics. He acknowledged the existence of one Supreme GOD, perfect in goodness and wisdom, who produced from his own substance seven beings, or *Æons* † of a most excellent nature. Two of these

E 2 *Æons*

---

* Barlaam was opposed by Palamas, Archbishop of Thesalonica, who asserted that the light seen upon Tabor, was an uncreated light, and co-eternal with GOD.

† The word [*Aïon, or Æon*] from expressing only the duration of beings, was by a *metonymy* employed to signify the beings themselves. Thus the Supreme Being was called [*Aïon, or Æon*] and the angels distinguished also by the title of *Æons.* All this will lead us to the true meaning of that word among the Gnostics. They had formed to themselves the notion of an invisible world, composed of *entities* or *virtues,* proceeding from the Supreme Being, and succeeding each other at certain intervals of time, so as to form an *eternal chain,* of which our world was the terminating link. To the beings which formed this eternal chain, the Gnostics assigned a certain term of duration and a certain sphere of action. Their *terms of duration* were, at first called [*Ai ni*] and they themselves were afterwards metonymically distinguished by that title.

*Æons* called *Dynamis* and *Sophia* (i. e *power and wif-dom*) engendered the angels of the higheft order. Thefe angels formed an Heaven for their habitation, and brought forth other angelic beings, of a nature fomewhat inferior to their own. Many other generations of angels followed thefe ; new Heavens were alfo created, until the number of angelic orders, and of their refpective Heavens, amounted to *three hundred and fixty-five*, and thus equalled the days of the year. All thefe are under the empire of an omnipotent Lord, whom *Bafilides* called *Abraxas*.

The inhabitants of the loweft Heavens, which touched upon the borders of the eternal, malignant, and felf-animated *matter*, conceived the defign of forming a world from that confufed mafs, and of creating an order of beings to people it. This defign was carried into execution, and was approved by the *Supreme* GOD, who, to the animal life, with which only the inhabitants of this new world were at firft endowed, added a reafonable foul, giving, at the fame time to the angels, the empire over them.

Thefe angelic beings advanced to the government of the world which they had created, fell, by degrees, from their original purity, and manifefted foon the fatal marks of their depravity and corruption. They not only endeavoured to efface in the minds of men the knowledge of the Supreme Being, that they might be worfhipped in his ftead, but alfo began to war againft one another, with an ambitious view to enlarge, every one, the bounds of his refpective dominion. The moft arrogant and turbulent of all thefe angelic fpirits, was that which prefided over the Jewifh nation. Hence the Supreme GOD, beholding with compaffion the miferable ftate of rational

beings,

beings, who groaned under the conteſt of theſe jar-
ring powers, ſent from Heaven his Son *NUS*, or
*CHRIST*, the chief of the *Æons*, that, joined in a
ſubſtantial union with the man JESUS, he might
reſtore the knowledge of the Supreme GOD, deſtroy
the empire of thoſe angelic natures which preſided
over the world, and particularly that of the arrogant
leader of the Jewiſh people. The God of the Jews
alarmed at this, ſent forth his miniſters to ſeize the
man JESUS and put him to death. They executed
his commands, but their cruelty could not extend to
CHRIST, againſt whom their efforts were vain.
Thoſe ſouls who obey the precepts of the Son of
GOD, ſhall, after the diſſolution of their mortal
frame, aſcend to the Father, while their bodies return to the corrupt maſs of matter from whence they
were formed. Diſobedient ſpirits, on the contrary,
ſhall paſs ſucceſſively into other bodies. [See Gnoſtics]

, *Moſheim's Eccleſ. Hiſt. vol.* i. *p.* 181, 182, 183.

BEHMENISTS, A ſect which aroſe in the ſeventeenth century, ſo called from Jacob Behman, a
Taylor at Gorlitz. He taught that the Divine grace
operates by the ſame rules, and follows the ſame methods, that the Divine Providence obſerves in the
natural world ; and that the minds of men are pur-
ged from their vices and corruptions in the ſame way
that metals are purified from their droſs.

This denomination was a branch of the Myſtics.
[See Myſtics]

*Moſheim's ibid, vol* iv. *p.* 476.

BERENGARIANS, A ſect in the eleventh century, which adhered to the opinions of Berengarius,
who aſſerted that the bread and wine in the Lord's
ſupper

ſupper is not really and eſſentially, but figuratively changed into the body and blood of Chriſt.

His followers were divided in opinion as to the *Euchariſt*. They all agreed, that the elements are not eſſentially changed, though ſome allowed them to be changed in effect; others admitted a change in part; and others an entire change, with this reſtriction, that to thoſe who communicated unworthily the elements were changed back again.

*Dictionary of Arts and Sciences, vol.* i. *p.* 289.

BERYLLIANS, So called from Beryllus, an Arabian, Biſhop of *Bozrah*, who flouriſhed in the third century. He taught that CHRIST did not exiſt before *Mary*, but that a ſpirit iſſuing from GOD himſelf, and therefore ſuperior to all human ſouls, as being a portion of the Divine nature, was united to him at the time of his birth.

*Moſheim's Eccleſ. Hiſt. vol.* i. *p.* 248.

BIDDELIANS, So called from John Biddele, who, in the year 1644, erected an independent congregation in London. The doctrines he taught were, in general, ſimilar with the Socinians. He admitted the perſonality of the Holy Ghoſt, but denied its divinity, aſſerting it to be no more than chief among the holy angels. [See Socinians]

*Hiſtory of Religion.* [*See Biddelians*]

BOGOMILES, A ſect in the twelfth century, which ſprung from the Maſſalians.

They derived their name from the *Divine mercy*, which its members are ſaid to have inceſſantly implored; for the word *Bogomites*, in the Myſian language, ſignifies *calling out for mercy from above*.

*Baſilius,*

*Basilius*, a Monk at Conftantinople, was the founder of this denomination. The doctrines he taught were fimilar with the Manicheans and Gnoftics. [See Gnoftics and Manicheans]

*Mofheim's Ecclefiaftical Hiftory vol.* ii. *p.* 444.

**BONOSIANS, A** fect in the third century; who followed the opinions of Bonofins, Bifhop of Sardica. Their fentiments were the fame with the Photinians, though they appear to have been different communions. [See Photinians]

*Broughton's Hiftorical Library, vol.* i. *p.* 169.

**BORRELLISTS, A** fect in Holland, fo called from their leader, one Adam Borreel, of Zealand, who had fome knowledge of the Hebrew, Greek, and Latin tongues. They reject the ufe of churches, of the *facraments, public prayer*, and all other external acts of worfhip. They affert that all the chriftian churches of the world have degenerated from the pure apoftolical doctrines.

They lead a very auftere life, and employ great part of their goods in alms and works of piety.

*Broughton. ibid, p.* 170.

**BORIGNONISTS, A** fect in the feventeenth century, which derive their name from the famous *Antoinette Bourignon de la Ponte*, a native of *flanders*, who pretended to be divinely infpired, and fet apart to revive the true fpirit of chriftianity that had been extinguifhed by theological animofities and debates.

The predominant principle which reigns through her productions, is as follows.

*That*

*That the christian religion neither confifts in knowledge nor in practice, but in a certain internal feeling and divine impulfe; which arifes immediately from communion with the Deity.* She allowed a general toleration of *all religions.*

*Dufrefnoy's Chronological Tables. vol ii p 253.*
*Mofheim's Ecclef. hift vol. v p 64 65.*

BRETHREN AND SISTERS OF THE FREE SPIRIT, A fect, which in the thirteenth century, gained ground imperceptibly, in Italy, France, and Germany.

They took their denomination from the words of St. Paul, Rom. viii. 2, 14, and maintained, that the true children of God were invefted with the privilege of a full and perfect *freedom* from the jurifdiction of the *law.* They were called by the Germans and Flemifh, *Begharas* and Beguttes ; which was a name given to thofe who make an extraordinary profeffion of piety and devotion.

The fentiments taught by this denomination, were as follow :

That all things flowed *by emanation* from God, and were finally to return to their divine fource :— That rational fouls were fo many *portions* of the Supreme Deity ; and that the univerfe, confidered as one great whole, was GOD :—That every man, by the power of contemplation, and by calling off his mind from fenfible and terreftrial objects, might be united to the Deity in an ineffable manner, and become one with the Source and Parent of all Things : and that they, who, by long and affiduous meditation, had plunged themfelves, as it were, into an *abyfs* of the Divinity, acquired thereby a moft glorious

and

and fublime liberty, and were not only delivered from the violence of finful lufts, but even from the common inftincts of nature.

From thefe, and fuch-like doctrines, the *Brethren* under confideration, drew this conclufion, viz. . That the perfon who had afcended to God in this manner, and was abforbed by contemplation in the abyfs of Deity, became thus a part of the God-head—commenced God—was the *Son of God* in the fame fenfe and manner that CHRIST was, and thereby raifed to a glorious independence, and freed from the obligation of all laws, human and divine.

In confequence of this, they treated with contempt the ordinances of the gofpel, and every external act of religious worfhip ; looking upon prayer, fafting, baptifm, and the facrament of the Lord's fupper, as the firft elements of piety, adapted to the capacity of children, and as of no fort of ufe to the *perfect man*, whom long meditation had raifed above all external things, and carried into the bofom and effence of the Deity.

They rejected with horror every kind of induftry and labour, as an obftacle to Divine contemplation, and to the affent of the foul towards the Father of Spirits.

*Mofheim's Ecclefiaftical Hiftory, vol. 3. p. 122 123. 124.*

BROWNISTS, A fect which fprung up in England towards the end of the fixteenth century. They derive their name from Robert Brown, a native of Northampton.

This denomination did not differ, in point of doctrine, from the church of England, or from the other Puritans ; but they apprehended, according to fcripture, that every church ought to be confined within the limits of a single congregation; and that the government should be democratical. They maintained the discipline of the church of England to be Popish and Antichristian, and all her ordinances and sacraments invalid. Hence they forbid their people to join with them in prayer, in hearing the word, or in any part of public worship; nay, they not only renounced communion with the church of England, but with all other churches, except such as were of the same model.

Mosheim, ibid. vol. 4. p 93<br>Neal's History of the Puritans, vol 1 p. 375, 377.

**BUDNEIANS,** A branch of the Socinians, which appeared in the year 1589; so called from Simon Budnœus, who maintained that Christ was not begotten by an extraordinary act of Divine power; but that he was born like other men, in a natural way, and that consequently he was no proper object of Divine worship and adoration. [See Socinians]

Mosheim's Eccles Hist. vol. 4 p. 199.

## C

**C**AINIANS, A sect which sprang up about the year 130, so called on account of their great respect for Cain. They pretended that the virtue which had produced Abel, was of an order inferior to that which had produced Cain, and that this was the reason why Cain had the victory over Abel and killed him; for they admitted a great number of Genii, which they called virtues, of different ranks and orders. They had a great veneration for the inhabitants of Sodom, Esau, Corah, Dathan and Abiram; and in particular for Judas,

under

under pretence that the death of JESUS CHRIST had faved mankind, and he betrayed him for that end ; they even made ufe of a gofpel of Judas to which they paid great refpect.

The morals of this denomination were the fame with thofe of the Carpocratians. [See Carpocratians.]

*Hiftorical Dictionary, vol.* i. [*See Cainians.*]
*Broughton's Hiftorical Library, vol.* i, *p.* 190.

CALIXTINS, A branch of the Huffites in Bohemia and Moravia in the fifteenth century. The principal point in which they differed from the church of Rome was the ufe of the Chalice, (Calix) or communicating in both kinds.

Calixtins, was alfo a name given to thofe among the Lutherans who followed the opinions of George Calixtus, a celebrated divine in the feventeenth century ; who endeavoured to unite the Romifh, Lutheran, and Calviniftical churches, in the bonds of charity and mutual benevolence. He maintained,

I. That the *fundamental doctrines of chriftianity,* by which he meant thofe elementary principles from whence all its truths flow, were preferved pure in all three communions, and were contained in that ancient form of doctrine that is vulgarly known by the name of the *Apoftles Creed.*

II. That the tenets and opinions which had been conftantly received by the ancient Doctors, during the firft five centuries, were to be confidered as of equal truth and authority with the exprefs declarations and doctrines of fcripture.

*Broughton, ibid, p.* 192.
*Mofheim's Ecclefiaftical Hift. vol.* 4. *p.* 450, 451.

F 2                    CALVINISTS,

CALVINISTS, They derive their name from John Calvin, who was born at Nogen, in Picardy, in the year 1509. He firſt ſtudied the civil law, and was afterwards made prefeſſor of divinity at Geneva, in the year 1536. His genius, learning, and eloquence, rendered him reſpeɕable even in the eyes of his very enemies.

The principal tenets of the Calviniſts are comprehended in five articles, to which are added a few of the arguments they make uſe of in defence of their ſentiments.

I. That GOD has choſen a *certain number* in Chriſt, unto everlaſting glory, before the foundation of the world, according to his immutable purpoſe, and of his *free grace* and *love*, without the leaſt foreſight of *faith*, good *works*, or any conditions performed by the creature : and that the reſt of mankind he was pleaſed to paſs by and ordain them to diſhonor and wrath for their ſins, to the praiſe of his vindiɕive juſtice.

For, as the *Deity* is infinitely perfeɕt and independent in all his aɕts, the manifeſtation of his eſſential perfeɕtions muſt be the ſupreme end of the Divine counſels and deſigns. Prov. xvi. 4.—*The Lord hath made all things for himſelf, &c.* Since GOD is omniſcient, it is evident that he foreſaw from everlaſting whatever ſhould come to paſs : but there can be no preſcience of future contingents ; for what is certainly foreſeen, muſt infallibly come to paſs, conſequently the preſcience of the Deity cannot be antecedent to his decrees.

The ſacred ſcriptures aſſert the doɕtrine of the Divine ſovereignty in the cleareſt terms. Rom. ix. 21.

21.--*Has not the Potter power over the clay of the same lump, to make one vessel unto honor, and another unto dishonor.* See from verse 11 to the end of the chapter. The same Divine author presents us with a golden chain of salvation in Rom. viii. 30. To the same purport see Eph. i. 4. Acts xiii. 48, and a variety of other passages in the sacred oracles.

II. That Jesus Christ, by his death and sufferings, made an atonement *only* for the sins of the *elect.*

That is, that redemption is commensurate with the Divine decree. Christ has absolutely purchased grace, holiness, and all spiritual blessings for his people.

For, if GOD really intended the salvation of all men, then no man can perish. *For the counsel of the Lord standeth forever.* Psalm xxxiii, 11. There are express texts of scripture which testify that Christ did not die for all men. John vi. 37, *All that the Father giveth me, shall come to me, &c.* and in John x. 11, Christ stiles himself, *The good shepherd, who lays down his life for his sheep.* This is also implied in our Saviour's limitation of his intercession. John xvii. 9.

To suppose that the death of Christ procured only a possibility of salvation, which depends upon our performance of certain conditions, is contradictory to those scriptures which assert that salvation is *wholly* owing to *free sovereign* grace. If Christ died for all, and all are not saved, the purposes of his death are in many instances frustrated, and he shed his precious blood in vain : to suppose this would be derogatory to the infinite perfections of the great *Redeemer* ; therefore he did not die for all, and all for whom he died will certainly be saved.

III. That

III. That mankind are *totally* depraved in confequence of the Fall ; and by virtue of *Adam*'s being their public head, the guilt of *his fin* was *imputed*, and a *corrupt nature* conveyed to *all* his pofterity : from which proceed all actual tranfgreffions : and that by *fin* we are made fubject to death, and all miferies, temporal, fpiritual and eternal.

For the infpired pages affert the original depravity of mankind, in the moft emphatical terms :— Gen. viii. 21. *The imagination of man's heart is evil from his youth.* Pfalm xiv. 2, 3. *The Lord looked down from Heaven upon the children of men, to fee if there were any that did underftand, and feek after GOD. They are all gone afide, they are altogether become filthy ; there is none that doeth good, no not one.* To the fame purport fee Rom. iii. 10, 11, 12, &c. And it is evident, that Adam's fin was imputed to his pofterity, from Rom. 5. 19. *By one man's difobedience many were made finners,* &c. The fcriptures alfo teach, that all fin expofes us to everlafting deftruction. See Gal. iii. 10. 2d of Cor. iii. 6, 7. And Rom. iv. 14.

The total depravity of human nature is alfo evident from the univerfal reign of death over perfons of all ages :—from the propenfity to evil which appears in mankind, and impels them to tranfgrefs God's law :—from the neceffity of regeneration :— the nature of redemption :—and the remains of corruption in the faints.

IV. That all whom God has predeftinated unto life he is pleafed in his appointed time *effectualiy* to *call* by his *word* and *fpirit*, out of that eftate of *fin* and *death*, in which they are by *nature*, to *grace* and *falvation* by JESUS CHRIST.      For

For an irrefiftable operation is evident from thofe paffages in fcripture, which exprefs the efficacious virtue of divine grace in the converfion of finners. Eph. i. 19. *And what is the exceeding greatnefs of his power towards us who believe*, &c.  Eph. ii. 1, 5. Phil. ii. 13. and divers other paffages.  If there was any thing in us which renders the grace of God effectual, we fhould have caufe for boafting ; but the facred pages declaim againft this in the moft emphatical terms. Rom. v. 27 : *Where is boafting then ? It is excluded*, &c. See Titus iii. 5.  1ft of Cor. i. 31. and a variety of other texts to the fame purport.

If the *free will* of man renders grace *effectual*, it may be made *ineffectual* by the *fame power*, and fo the creature fruftrate the defigns of his Creator, which is derogatory to the infinite perfections of that *omnipotent Being*, who *worketh all things according to the counfel of his will.*

V.   That thofe whom God has effectually called and fanctified by his fpirit, fhall never finally fall from a ftate of grace.

For this doctrine is evident from the promifes of perfevering grace in the facred fcriptures. Ifaiah liv. 10 : *For the mountains fhall depart, and the hills be removed, but my kindnefs fhall not depart from thee, neither fhall the covenant of my peace be removed, faith the LORD, that hath mercy on thee.* See alfo Jer. xxxii. 38—40.  John iv. 14.  vi. 39. x. 28.  xi. 26.  And the apoftle exclaims with triumphant rapture,—*I am perfuaded that neither life, nor death, &c. fhall be able to feparate us from the love of GOD, which is in Chrift Jefus our Lord.* Rom. viii. 38, 39.                           The

The *perseverance* of the *saints* is also evident from the immutability of the Deity ; his purposes and the reasons on which he founds them are invariable as himself ; *with him there is no variableness nor shadow of turning.* James i. 17. The faithfulness of the Deity is ever displayed in performing his promises : but the doctrine of falling from grace frustrates the design of the promises ; for if one saint may fall, why not another, and a third, till no sincere christians are left ? But the doctrine of *believers perseverance* remains firm as it is supported by the express tenor of scripture, the immutability of the Deity, and his faithfulness in performing his promises.

*Mosheim's Ecclesiastical History* vol 3. *p* 352. *vol.* 4. *p.* 70.
*Calvin's Institutions, p* 127.
*Assembly's Confession of Faith. p* 35, 36　48, 49, 67.
*Charnock's Works, vol.* 2. *p.* 1353, 1354.
*Twisse's Works, p.* 220.
*Doctor Edwards's Veritas Redux, p.* 56, 89　91, 92, 319　320.
　　321, 358　384　390. 450.
*Edwards on Original Sin, p.* 13, 40, 356　366.
*Broughton's Historical Library, vol.* 1 *p.* 195.

## CAMISARS.　　[See French Prophets]

CAPUTIATI, A sect which appeared in the twelfth century ; so called from a singular kind of cap which distinguish their party. They wore upon their caps a leaden image of the Virgin Mary, and declared publickly, that their purpose was to level all distinctions, to abrogate magistracy, and to remove all subordination among mankind, and to restore that primitive liberty, that natural equality, which were the inestimable privileges of the first mortals.

*Mosheim's Eccles. Hist. vol.* 2. *p.* 456, 457.

## CAROLOSTADIANS,

**CAROLOSTADIANS**, So called from Carolo-
ſtadt, a colleague of Luther's.   He denied the real
preſence in the *Euchariſt* ; and declaimed againſt
human learning.

*Moſheim's Eccleſ Hiſt vol 4 p. 28 30.*

**CARPOCRATIANS**, A ſect which aroſe towards the middle of the ſecond century ; ſo called
from Carpocrates, whoſe philoſophical tenets agreed
in general with thoſe of the Egyptian Gnoſtics.   He
acknowledged the exiſtence of a *Supreme* GOD;
and of the *Æons* derived from him by ſucceſſive generations.   He maintained the eternity of a *corrupt
matter*, and the creation of the world from thence
by angelic powers, as alſo the Divine origin of ſouls
unhappily impriſoned in mortal bodies; &c.   He af-
ſerted, that JESUS was born of *Joſeph* and *Mary*,
according to the ordinary courſe of nature, and was
diſtinguiſhed from the reſt of mankind by nothing
but his ſuperior fortitude and greatneſs of ſoul.   He
held, that luſts and paſſions, being implanted in our
nature by GOD himſelf, were conſequently void of
guilt, and had nothing in them criminal ; and not
only allowed his diſciples full liberty to ſin, but recommended to them a vicious courſe of life, as a
matter both of obligation and neceſſity, aſſerting that
eternal ſalvation was only attainable by thoſe who
had committed all ſorts of crimes, and had daringly
filled up the meaſure of iniquity.   He alſo taught
that all things ſhould be poſſeſſed in common. [See
Gnoſtics]

*Moſheim's ibid, vol 4. p. 184, 185.*

**CATAPHROGGIANS.**   [See Montaniſts]

G    **CATHARISTS,**

**CATHARISTS,** A branch of the Manichæns, in the twelfth century. This fect agreed in the following points of doctrine, viz. That Matter was the fource of all evil; that the Creator of this world was a Being diftinct from the fupreme Deity; that Chrift was not cloathed with a real body, neither could be properly faid to have been born, or to have feen death; that human bodies were the production of the evil principle; that baptifm and the Lord's fupper were ufelefs inftitutions; and that human fouls endued with reafon, were fhut up by an unhappy fate in the dungeons of mortal bodies, from whence only they could be delivered by fafting, mortification, and continence of every kind. Hence they exhorted all who embraced their doctrine to a rigorous abftinence from animal food, wine, and wedlock, and recommended to them, in the moft pathetic terms, the moft fevere acts of aufterity and mortification.

This denomination treated all the books of the Old Teftament with the utmoft contempt, but expreffed a high veneration for the New, particularly for the four Evangelifts.

*Mofheim's Ecclef. Hift. vol. 2. p. 444.*

**CERDONIANS,** A branch of the Gnoftics in the fecond century, which derive their name from Cerdo; they are alfo called Marcionites, from Marcion, who propagated his doctrines with aftonifhing fuccefs throughout the world.

The fentiments taught by this denomination were as follow:

That there are two principles, the one perfectly good, and the other perfectly evil; and between
these

thefe there is an intermediate kind of Deity, neither perfectly good nor perfectly evil, but of a *mixed nature* ;
and fo far juft and powerful, as to adminifter rewards
and inflict punifhments. This *middle Deity* is the
creator of this inferior world, and the God and le-
giflator of the Jewifh nation ; he wages perpetual
war with the *evil Principle* ; and both the one and
the other afpire to the place of the *fupreme Being,*
and ambitioufly attempt fubjecting to their authority
all the inhabitants of the world.

The Jews are the fubjects of that powerful *genius*
who formed the globe : the other nations, who
worfhip a variety of Gods, are under the empire of
the *evil Principle.* Both thefe conflicting powers
exercife oppreffions upon rational and immortal
fouls, and keep them in a tedious and miferable captivity. Therefore, the *fupreme God,* in order to terminate this war, and to deliver from their bondage
thofe fouls, whofe origin is celeftial and divine, fent
to the Jews a Being moft like to himfelf, even his
fon JESUS CHRIST, cloathed with a certain
fhadowy refemblance of a body, that thus he might
be vifible to mortal eyes. The commiffion of this
celeftial meffenger was to deftroy the empire both
of the *evil Principle,* and of the *Author of this world,*
and to bring back wandering fouls to God. On
this account he was attacked with inexpreffible fury
by the *Prince of Darknefs,* and by *the God of the
Jews,* but without effect, fince having a body only
in appearance, he was thereby rendered incapable
of fuffering. Thofe who follow the facred directi-
ons of the celeftial conductor, mortify the body by
fafting, and aufterities, call off their minds from the
allurements of fenfe, and renouncing the precepts of



the

the *God of the Jews*, and of the *Prince of Darkness*, turn their eyes towards the *Supreme Being*, shall after death afcend to the manfions of felicity and perfection.

This denomination rejected all the Old Teftament, and received only part of St. Luke's gofpel, and ten of St. Paul's epiftles in the New. [See Gnoftics]

*Mofheim's Ecclef Hift. vol.* 1, *p* 178.
*Broughton's Hiftorical Library, vol.* 2. *p.* 48.

CERINTHIANS, A fect which arofe in the firft century; fo called from Cerinthius, who taught, That the creator of the world, whom he confidered alfo as the fovereign and law-giver of the Jewifh people, was a Being endowed with the greateft virtues, and derived his birth from the fupreme God; that this Being fell by degrees from his native virtue and his primitive dignity; that the fupreme God, in confequence of this, determined to deftroy his empire, and fent upon earth, for this purpofe, one of the ever-happy and glorious *Æons*, whofe name was CHRIST; that this CHRIST chofe for his habitation the perfon of JESUS, a man of the moft illuftrious fanctity and juftice, the fon of Jofeph and Mary, and defcending in the form of a dove, entered into him, while he was receiving the baptifm of John in the waters of Jordan: that JESUS, after his union with CHRIST, oppofed himfelf with vigor to the God of the Jews, and was, by his inftigation, feized and crucified by the Hebrew chiefs: that when JESUS was taken captive, CHRIST afcended up on high, fo that the man JESUS alone was fubjected to the pains of an ignominious death.

Cerinthius

Cerinthius required of his followers that they
should worship the Father of CHRIST, even the
supreme GOD, in conjunction with the Son ; that
they should abandon the law-giver of the Jews,
whom he looked upon as the creator of the world ;
that they should retain a part of the law given by
Moses, but should, neverthelefs, employ their principal attention and care to regulate their lives by the
precepts of CHRIST. To encourage them to this,
he promifed them the refurrection of this mortal body, after which was to commence a fcene of the moft
exquifite delights, during CHRIST's earthly reign
of a thoufand years, which was to be fucceeded by
a happy and never-ending life in the celeftial world.
[See Gnoftics.]

*Mofheim's Ecclef. Hift. vol.* 1. *p.* 117, 118.

**CHAZINZARIANS,** A fect which arofe in Armenia, in the feventh century. They are fo called
from the Armenian word chazus, which fignifies
a *crofs*, becaufe they were charged with adoring the
cro s.

*Hiftory of Religion,* vol. 4. [*See Chazinzarians*]

**CHILIASTS.** [See Millenarians]

**CHRISTIANS OF St. JOHN,** So called be-
caufe they fay they received their faith, books, and traditions from *John the Baptift.* They always inhabit
near a river in which they baptize, for they never baptize but in rivers, and only on Sundays. Before they go
to the river, they carry the infant to church, where
there is a Bifhop who reads certain prayers over the
head of the child ; from thence they carry the child
to the river, with a train of men and women, who,
together

together with the Bifhop, go up to the knees in water: then the Bifhop reads again certain prayers out
of a book, which d.ne, he fprinkles the infant three
times, faying, *In the name of the Lord, firft and laft
of the world and parudife, the high creator of all
things.* After that the Bifhop reads again in his
book, while the god-father plunges the child all
over in the water ; after which they all go to the parents houfe to feaft. They have no knowledge of
the myftery of the holy Trinity, only they fay that
Chrift is the *fpirit* and *word* of the *eternal Father.*
They confefs he became *man* to free u; from the
punifhment of *fin* : but when the Jews came to take
him, he deluded their cruelty with a fhadow.

'They believe the angel Gabriel is the Son of
GOD, begotten upon light; and that he undertook
to create the world, according to the command
which GOD' gave him, * and took along with him
three hundred and thirty-fix thoufand demons, and
made the earth fo fertile that it was but to fow in
the morning and reap at night ; and that the fame
angel taught Adam all the neceffary fciences.

In

------

* They fay, that after the angel Gabriel had formed the world
by the command of GOD, he thus difcou fed,—Lord GOD, I
have built the world as thou didft command me. It has put me
and my brethren to a vaft deal of trouble to raife fuch high mountains, which feem to fuftain Heaven : but, inftead of that fatisfac-
tion I ought to feel, for having accomplifhed fo great a work, I
find reafon to be altogether grieved. When GOD demanded
the caufe, the angel Gabriel anfwer'd, My GOD and Father, I
will tell you what afflicts me : after the making of the world, I
forefee that there will come into it a prodigious number of Jews,
Turks and Infidels, enemies to your name, who will be unworthy
to enjoy the fruits of our labour. To whom GOD thus replied ;
Never grieve, my fon, there fhall live in this world, which thou
haft built, certain chriftians of St. John, who fhall be my friends,
and fhall all be faved.

In reference to the life to come, it is said they believe that when any one lies at the point of death, three hundred and sixty demons come and carry his soul to a place full of serpents, dogs, lions, tygers, and devils ; who, if it be the soul of a wicked man, tear it in pieces ; but being the soul of a just man, it creeps under the bellies of those creatures into the presence of GOD, who fits in his seat of majesty to judge the world ; and that there are angels also, who weigh the souls of men in a balance, who being thought worthy, are admitted immediately into glory.

They have no canonical books, but a number full of charms, &c.  Their chief festivals are three ; one in the winter, which lasts three days, in memory of our first parents and the creation of the world ; the other in the month of August, which is called the feast of *St. John ;* the third, which lasts five days, in June, during which time they are all re-baptized.

In the Eucharist, they make use of meal or flour kneaded, with wine and oil ; they add oil to signify the benefit we receive by the sacrament, and put us in mind of our love to GOD and our neighbour. The words of their consecration are certain long prayers, which they make to praise and thank GOD, at the same time blessing the bread and wine. After all the ceremonies are ended, the Priest takes the bread, and having eaten some of it, distributes the rest to the people.

These Christians reside in Persia and Barsora.

Tavinier's Travels. p. 90 91. 92, 93.

**CHRISTIANS OF St. THOMAS,** A sect in the peninsula of India, on this side the gulph.  They
are

are called Chriſtians of St. Thomas, becauſe that apoſtle preached the goſpel, and ſuffered martyrdom in that peninſula ; and for whom thoſe Chriſtians have a peculiar veneration.

They admit of no images, and receive only the croſs, to which they pay a great veneration. They affirm, that the ſouls of the ſaints do not ſee GOD, till after the day of judgment. They acknowledge but three ſacraments, viz. *Baptiſm, Ordrs*, and the *Eucbariſt*. They make no uſe of holy oils in the adminiſtration of baptiſm ; but after the ceremony, anoint the infant with an unction, compoſed of oil and walnuts, without any benediction. They have no knowledge of confirmation, or *extreme unction* ; and abhor *auricular confeſſion*. In the *Eucbariſt*, they conſecrate with little cakes, made of oil and ſalt ; and, inſtead of wine, make uſe of water in which raiſins have been infuſed.

*Broughton's Hiſtorical Library, vol.* 1. *p.* 236.

**CIRCUMCELLIANS**, in Latin *Circumcelliones*, A branch of the ſect of the Donatiſts. They abounded chiefly in Africa. They had no fixed abode, but rambled up and down, begging, or rather exacting, a maintenance from the country people. It was from this wandering courſe of life they had their name.

*Broughton, ibid. p.* 249.

**COCCEIANS**, A ſect which aroſe in the ſeventeenth century, ſo called from John Cocceius, Profeſſor of Divinity, in the Univerſity of Leyden. He repreſented the whole hiſtory of the *Old Teſtament* as a *mirror*, which held forth an accurate view of the tranſactions and events that were to happen in

the

the church under the difpenfation of the *New Tefta-ment*, and unto the end of the world. He main-tained that by far the greateft part of the ancient prophecies foretold CHRIST's miniftry and media-tion, and the rife, progrefs, and revolutions of the church, not only under the figure of perfons and *tranfactions*, but in a literal manner, and by the very fenfe of the *words* ufed in thefe predictions ; and laid it down as a fundamental rule of interpretation, that the *words* and *phrafes* of fcripture are to be un-derftood *in every fenfe* of which they are fufceptible; or, in other words, that they fignify *in effect*, every thing that they can poffibly fignify.

Cocceius alfo taught that the covenant made be-tween GOD and the Jewifh nation, by the miniftry of Mofes, was of the fame nature of the new cove-nant obtained by the mediation of JESUS CHRIST.

In confequence of this general principle, he main-tained, That the *ten commandments* were promulga-ted by *Mofes*, not as a *rule of obedience*, but as a *re-prefentation of the covenant of grace* :—That when the Jews had provoked the Deity by their va-rious tranfgreffions, particularly by the worfhip of the golden calf, the fevere and fervile yoke of the ceremonial law was added to the decalogue, as a punifhment inflicted on them by the fupreme Being in his righteous difpleafure,—that this yoke which was painful in itfelf, became doubly fo on account of its typical fignification, fince it admonifh-ed the Ifraelites, from day to day, of the imperfec-tion and uncertainty of their ftate, filled them with anxiety, and was a perpetual proof that they had merited the righteous difpleafure of God, and could not expect before the coming of the Meffiah the

H

entire

entire remiſſion of their iniquities,—that indeed good men, even under the Moſaic diſpenſation, were immediately after death made partakers of everlaſting glory ; but that they were neverthelefs, during the whole courſe of their lives, far removed from that firm hope and aſſurance of ſalvation, which rejoices the faithful under the diſpenſation of the *goſpel*,—and that their anxiety flowed naturally from this conſideration, that their ſins, though they remained unpuniſhed, were not pardoned, becauſe Chriſt had not, as yet, offered himſelf up a ſacrifice to the father to make an entire atonement for them.

*Moſheim's Eccleſiaſtical Hiſtory, vol.* 4 *p.* 545, 546 547. 548.

## COLARBARSIONS.   [See Marcoſians]

## COLLEGIATES,

A name given to a ſociety of Mennonites at Holland, becauſe they called their religious aſſemblies colleges.   They are alſo called Rhinſtergers.   [See Mennonites]

*Moſheim's ibid vol.* 5 *p.* 59.
*Collier's Hiſt. Dictionary.   [See Mennonites]*

## COLLUTHIANS,

A ſect which aroſe in the fourth century ;  ſo called from Colluthus, a Prieſt of Alexandria, who taught that GOD was not the author of the evils and afflictions of this life.

*Broughton's Hiſt. Library, vol.* 1. *p.* 264.

## COLLYLYRIDIANS.

An Arabian ſect, in the fourth century ; ſo denominated from their idolizing the virgin Mary, worſhiping her as a goddeſs, and offering to her little cakes.

*Hiſt. of Religion, vol.* 4.   *[See Collylyridians]*

## CONGREGATIONALISTS,

A denomination of *Proteſtants*, who maintain, that each particular
church

church has authority from Chriſt for exerciſing go-vernment, and enjoying all the ordinances of wor-ſhip within itſelf.

This denomination differ from the Independents in this reſpect, viz. They invite councils which are adviſary only ; but the Independents formerly deci-ded all difficulties within themſelves.*

Neal's Hiſt. of New-England. vol. 2. p. 314.

CONONITES, A ſect which appeared in the ſixth century ; they derive their name from Conon, Biſhop of Tarſus, he taught, that the body never loſt its form,—that its matter alone was ſubject to corruption and decay, and was to be reſtored when this mortal ſhall put on immortality.

In other points they agree with the Philoponiſts. [See Philoponiſts and Tritheiſts]

Moſheim's Eccleſ. Hiſt. vol. 1 p. 473.

COPHTES, Chriſtians of Egypt, Nubia, and the adjacent countries ; their ſentiments are ſimilar with the Jacobites. [See Jacobites. See alſo the Appendix]

Father Simons' Religion of the Eaſtern Nations, p. 110.

CORRUPTICOLA, A ſect which aroſe in the ſixth century ; they derived their name from their maintaining that the body of Chriſt was corruptible, that the fathers had owned it, and that to deny it was to deny the truth of our Saviour's paſſion.

Dictionary of Arts and Sciences, vol. 1. p. 492.

H 2        DAMIANISTS,

* Thoſe who are deſirous of ſeeing a particular account of Congregational principles, may conſult their platform of church diſcipline, which the brevity of this work does not admit of in-ſerting.

## D

**D**AMIANISTS, A sect in the sixth centu-ry ; so called from Damian, Bishop of Alex-andria. The opinions maintained by this denomi-nation were similer to those of the Angelites. [See Angelites]

*Mosheim's Ecclesiastical Hist vol.* 1 *p.* 473.

**DANCERS,** A sect which arose at *Aix-la-Cha-pelle,* in the year 1373, from whence they spread through the district of *Liege,* *Hainault,* and other parts of *Flanders.* It was customary among them for persons of both sexes, publicly, as well as in pri-vate, to fall a dancing all of a sudden, and holding each others hands, to continue their motions with extraordinary violence, till, being almost suffocated, they fell down breathless together ; and they affirm-ed that, during these intervals of vehement agitation, they were favoured with wonderful visions. Like the Flagelants, they wandered about from place to place, had recourse to begging for their sustenance, treated with the utmost contempt, both the priest-hood, the public rites and worship of the church, and held secret assemblies.

*Mosheim ibid, vol.* 3 *p.* 206 207.

**DAVIDISTS,** A sect in the sixteenth century ; so called from David George, a native of *Delft,* who acquired great reputation by his prudent conversati-on.

He deplored the decline of vital and practical re-ligion, and endeavoured to restore it among his fol-lowers ; but rejected, as mean and useless, the ex-ternal services of *piety.*

He

He was charged with afferting, that he was the third David, fon of GOD ; and that he ought to fave men by grace and not by death : and with denying the exiftence of angels and demons, the authority of the fcriptures, and the refurrection of the body.

Mofheim's Ecclefiaftical Hiftory, vol. 4 p. 164, 165.<br>Crofby's Hiftory of the Englifh Baptifts, vol. 1 p. 64.<br>Dufrefnoy's Chronological Tables, vol. 2. p. 249.

**DIGGERS,** A fect which fprung up in Germany in the fifteenth century ; fo called, becaufe they dug their affemblies under ground, in caves and forefts.— They derided the church, its minifters and facraments.

Broughton's Hiftorical Library, vol. 1. p. 328.

**DIMOERITES.**   [See Appollinarians]

**DOCETOE,** A fect in the firft and fecond centuries ; fo called from the Greek of [apò toù dòkèè in] to appear, becaufe they held that Jefus Chrift was born, lived in the world, died, and rofe again, not in reality, but in *appearance* only.  It was the common opinion of the Gnoftics.  [See Gnoftics]

Broughton, ibid. p. 339.

**DONATISTS,** A fect which arofe in the fourth century.  They derived their name from Donatus, Bifhop of Numedia.

They maintained, that their community was *alone* to be confidered as  the true church, and avoided all communication with other churches, from an apprehenfion of contracting their impurity and corruption. Hence they pronounced the facred rites and inftitutions void of all virtue and efficacy among thofe chriftians, who were not precifely of their fentiments ;

and

and not only re-baptized thofe who came over to their party from other churches, but with refpect to thofe who had been ordained minifters of the gofpel, they either deprived them of their office or obliged them to be ordained the fecond time.

*Mofheim's Ecclef. Hift. vol. 1. p. 333.*

**DULCINISTS**, The followers of Dulcinus, a layman, of Novara, in Lombardy, about the beginning of the fourteenth century. He taught that the law of the father, which had continued till Mofes, was a law of grace and wifdom, but that the law of the Holy Ghoft, which began with himfelf in the year 1307, was a law entirely of love, which would laft to the end of the world.

*Broughton's Hiftorical Library, vol. 1. p. 344.*

**DUNKERS**, A denomination which took its rife in the year 1724, and was formed into a fort of commonwealth, moftly in a fmall town called Ephrata, in or near Pennfylvania. They feem to have obtained their name from their manner of baptizing their new converts, which is by plunging. Their habit feems to be peculiar to themfelves, confifting of a long tunic or coat, reaching down to their heels, with a fafh or girdle round the waift, and a cap or hood hanging from the fhoulders, like the drefs of the Dominican Friars.—The men do not fhave the head or beard.

The men and women have feparate habitations, and diftinct governments. For thefe purpofes, they have erected two large wooden buildings ; one of which is occupied by the brethren, the other by the fifters of the fociety ; and in each of them
there

there is a banqueting-room, and an apartment for public worſhip ; for the brethren and ſiſters do not meet together even at their devotions.

They live chiefly upon roots and other vegetables ; the rules of their ſociety not allowing them fleſh, except upon particular occaſions, when they hold what they call a *Love-feaſt* ; at which time the brethren and ſiſters dine together in a large apartment, and eat *mutton*, but no other meat. No member of the ſociety is allowed a bed, but in caſe of ſickneſs. In each of their little cells they have a bench fixed to ſerve the purpoſe of a bed, and a ſmall block of wood for a pillow. The *Dunkers* allow of no intercourſe betwixt the brethren and ſiſters, not even by marriage.

The principal tenet of the *Dunkers* appears to be this : That future happineſs is only to be obtained by penance and outward mortifications in this life ; and that as Jeſus Chriſt, by his meritorious ſufferings, became the Redeemer of mankind in general, ſo each individual of the human race, by a life of abſtinence and reſtraint, may work out his own ſalvation. Nay, they go ſo far as to admit of works of ſupererogation ; and declare, that a man may do much more than he is in juſtice or equity obliged to do ; and that his ſuperabundant works may therefore be applied to the ſalvation of others.

This denomination deny the eternity of future puniſhments ; and believe that the dead have the goſpel preached to them by our Saviour, and that the ſouls of the juſt are employed to preach the goſpel to thoſe who have had no revelation in this life.— They ſuppoſe the *Jewiſh Sabbath, ſabbatical year,*

and

and *year of jubilee*, are typical of certain periods after the general judgment, in which the fouls of thofe, who are not then admitted into happinefs, are purified from their corruption. If any within thefe fmaller periods are fo far humbled as to acknowledge GOD to be holy, juft and good, and CHRIST their only Saviour, they are received into felicity : while thofe who continue obftinate, are referved in torment until the grand period, typified by the jubilee, arrives, when all fhall be made happy in the endlefs fruition of the Diety.

*Cafpipini's Letters, p.* 70, 71, 72, &c.
*Ann. Reg p.* 343.

## E

EBIONITES, A fect in the firft and fecond century ; fo called from their leader Ebion, or from their poverty, which Ebionites fignifies in Hebrew.

They believed the celeftial miffion of CHRIST, and his participation of a Divine nature, yet they regarded him as a man born of *Jofeph* and *Mary*, according to the ordinary courfe of nature : they moreover afferted, that the ceremonial law, inftituted by *Mofes*, was not only obligatory upon the Jews, but alfo upon all others ; and that the obfervance of it was very effential to falvation. They obferved both the Jewifh Sabbath and the Chriftian Sunday ; and in celebrating the Eucharift, made ufe of unleavened bread. They abftained from the flefh of animals, and even from milk.

They rejected the Old Teftament ; and in the New Teftament received only the gofpel of St. Matthew,

and

and made ufe of a book which they ftiled, *The gofpel according to the Hebrews.*

*Mofheim's Ecclef. Hift vol. 1. p. 173. 174.*
*Hearnes Ductor Hiftoricus, vol. 2, p. 74.*

**EICETÆ**, A fect in the year 680, who affirmed, that in order to make prayer acceptable to God, it fhould be performed dancing.

*Dufrefnoy's Chronolog.cal Tables. vol 1. p. 213.*

**EFFRONTES**, So called from their fhaving their foreheads till they bleed, and then anointing them with oil, ufing no other baptifm but this.

They fay, the Holy Ghoft is nothing but a bare motion infpired by God in the mind ; and he is not to be adored.

*R.fs's View of all Re igions, p. 233.*

**ELCESAITES**, A fect in the fecond century ; fo denominated from their prophet Elcefai. His fundamental doctrine was, that Jefus Chrift, who was born from the beginning of the world, had appeared from time to time under divers bodies.

*Hiftory of Religion, vol. 4.* [*See Elcefaites*]

**ENCRATITES**, or **CONTINENTS**, A name given to a fect in the fecond century, becaufe they condemned marriage, forbid the eating of flefh, or drinking of wine, and rejected, with a fort of horror, all the comforts and conveniencies of life. Tatian, an Affyrian, was the leader of this denomination. He regarded Matter as the fountain of all evil ; and therefore recommended, in a peculiar manner, the mortification of the body. He diftinguifhed the creator of the world from the Supreme

I                                    Being

Being ; denied the reality of CHRIST's body ; and blended the Chriſtian religion with ſeveral other tenets of the Oriental philoſophy.

*Moſheim's Eccleſ. Hiſt. vol.* 1, *p* 180.

ENERGIA, A ſect in the ſixteenth century ; ſo called becauſe they held, the Euchariſt was the *energy* and *virtue* of Jeſus Chriſt ; not his body, nor a repreſentation thereof.

*Hiſt. of Religion, vol.* 4. [*See Energici*]

EONITES, A ſect in the twelfth century, followers of *Eon de Etoile*, a gentleman of *Bretagne*. Having heard it ſung in the church, *per eum, qui venturus eſt judicare vivos æt mortuos*, he concluded that he was the perſon who was to judge both quick and dead, from the reſemblance between the word Eum and his name. He was followed as a great prophet ; ſometimes he walked with a great number of people ; ſometimes he lived in ſolitude, and appeared afterwards in greater ſplendor than before. He ended his days in a miſerable priſon, and left a conſiderable number of followers, whom perſecution and death in the moſt dreadful forms could not perſuade to abandon his cauſe.

*Moſheim's Eccleſ. Hiſt. vol.* 2. *p.* 457, 458.
*Broughton's Hiſtorical Library, vol.* 1. *p.* 361.

EOQUINIANS, A ſect in the ſixteenth century ; ſo called from one Eoquinus, their maſter, who taught that Chriſt did not die for the wicked, but only for the faithful.

*Roſs's View of all Religions. p.* 234.

EPISCOPALIANS, So called from [*èpi*] and [*ſkòpèō*] They maintain, that Biſhops, Preſbyters, and

and Deacons, are three diftinct fubordinate callings in God's church. That the Bifhops have a fuperiority over the Priefts *jure divino*, and directly from God. To prove this point they alledge, that Bifhops were inftituted by the *apoftles* themfelves to fucceed them in great cities, as Timothy, at Ephefus; Titus, at Crete, &c. It is faid in 1ft of Timothy, v. 19 : *Againft an Elder receive not an accufation, but before, one or two witneffes.* Therefore, fay they, Timothy was a judge : Prefbyters were brought before him, and he was fuperior to them. And they affert that *epifcopacy* was the conftitution of the primitive church. [See Appendix]

*Neal's Hift. of the Puritants, vol.* 1. *p* 494.
*Dr. Edwards's Remains, p.* 229.

**ERASTIANS**, So called from *Eraftus*, a *German* divine of the fixteenth century. The paftoral office according to him was only perfuafive, like a profeffor of fciences over his ftudents, without any power of the keys annexed. The Lord's fupper, and other ordinances of the gofpel, were to be free and open to all. The minifter might diffuade the vicious and unqualified from the communion, but might not refufe it, or inflict any kind of cenfure ; the punifhment of all offences, either of a civil or religious nature, being refered to the civil magiftrate.

*Neal's Hift. of the Puritans. vol.* 3. *p.* 140.

**ETHNOPHRONES**, [Greek] In Englifh Paganizers. So they called a fect in the eighth century, who profeffing Chriftianity, joined thereto all the ceremonies of Paganifm, fuch as judicial aftrology, divinations of all kinds, &c. and who obferved all feafts, times, and feafons of the Gentiles.—



The

The word is compounded of the Greek [èthnòs] nation, and [phrēn] thought or fentiment.

*Broughton's Hiftorical Library, vol. 1 p. 378.*

**EUCHITES.**   [See Maffalians]

**EUDOXIANS,** A branch of the Arians in the fourth century ; fo called, from Eudoxis,  who after the death of Arius,  became head of the party. [See Arians]

*Hift. of Religion, vol 4 [See Eudoxians]*

**EUNOMIANS.**   [See Arians]

**EUSEBIANS,** So called from Eufebius, Bifhop of *Cæfarea,* in *Paleftine,* in the fourth century.  He maintained that there was a certain difparity and fubordination between the perfons of theGod-Head. [See Arians]

*Mofheim's Ecclef Hift. vol. 1. p. 291.*

**EUSTATHIANS, A** feĉt in the fourth century ; fo called from Euftathius, a Monk ; he prohibited marriage, the ufe of wine and flefh, feafts of charity, and other things of that nature.  To thofe who were joined in wedlock, he prefcribed immediate divcrfe ; and obliged his followers to quit all they had, as incompatible with the hopes of heaven.

*Mofheim's ibid. p. 313*
*Bayley's Dĉtionary, vol. 2. [See Euftathians]*

**FUTUCHITES, A** feĉt in the third century ; fo called from the Greek [èutuchèin,] which fignifies, *to live without pain,*  or *in pleafure.*

They held that our fouls are placed in our bodies only to honour the angels who created them ; that

we

we ought to rejoice equally in all events, becaufe to grieve would be to difhonour the angels, their creators. They alfo held that Jefus Chrift was not the Son of God, but of an unknown God.

*Broughton's Hiftorical Library, vol. 2 p. 532.*

EUTYCHIANS, A fect in the fifth century; fo called from Eutyches, a Monk and Abbot, of Conftantinople.

They maintained, that there was only one nature in Jefus Chrift. The divine nature, according to them, had fo entirely fwallowed up the human, that the latter could not be diftinguifhed; infomuch that JESUS CHRIST was merely GOD, and had nothing of humanity but the appearance.

*Barclay's Dictionary.* [*See Eutychians*]

## F

FAMILISTS, A fect which appeared in Holland, about the year 1555; * they derive their origin from *Henry Nicholas*, a *Weftphalian*, who ftiled his followers the *Family of Love.* He pretended he had a commiffion to teach mankind; and that there was no knowledge of Chrift, nor of the fcriptures, but in his *family.*

To prove this point, he argued from 1ft of Cor. xiii. 5, 9, 10. *For we know but in part, and we prophefy in part: but when that which is perfect is come, then that which is imperfect fhall be done away.* Hence he inferred that the doctrine of Chrift is imperfect, and a more perfect doctrine fhould be revealed

* This fect appeared in England about the year 1580, where, when their founder was difcovered, their books were ordered to be publicly burnt.

vealed to the *Family of Love*. This denomination also taught the following doctrines.

I. That the essence of religion consisted in the feelings of *Divine love*; and that it was a matter of the most perfect indifference, what opinions christians entertained concerning the Divine nature, provided their hearts burned with the pure and sacred flame of piety and love.

II. That the union of the soul with CHRIST transforms it into the essence of the Deity.

III. That the letter of the scripture is useless, and those sacred books ought to be interpreted in an allegorical manner.

IV. That it was lawful for them (if for their convenience) to swear to an untruth, either before a magistrate, or any other person who was not of their society.

*Mosheim's Ecclesiastical History, vol. 4. p. 166.*
*Broughton's Hist. Library, vol. 2 p. 30.*
*More's Mystery of Godliness, p. 256.*
*Leigh's Critica Sacra, p. 253.*
*Fulfilling of the Scriptures, vol. 1. p. 166.*

**FARVONIANS,** A branch of the Socinians; so called from Stanislaus Farvonius, who flourished in the sixteenth century. He asserted that CHRIST had been engendered, or produced, out of nothing, by the Supreme Being, before the creation of this terrestial globe; and warned his disciples against paying religious worship to the *Divine Spirit*. [See Socinians]

*Mosheim's Ecclesiastical History, vol. 4 p. 201 202.*

**FIFTH MONARCHY-MEN,** A sect which arose in the seventeenth century. They derived their name from their maintaining, that there will be a *fifth univerſal monarchy* under the perſonal reign of *King Jeſus* upon earth. In conſequence of this tenet, they aimed at the ſubverſion of all human government.

*Moſheim ibid,* p. 533.

FLACIANS, The followers of Matthias Flacius Illyricus, who flouriſhed in the ſixteenth century. He taught that *original ſin is the very ſubſtance of human nature,* and that the fall of man was an event which extinguiſhed in the human mind, every virtuous tendency, every noble faculty, and left nothing behind it but univerſal darkneſs and corruption.

*Moſheim's ibid,* p 43.

FLAGELLANTS, A ſect which ſprung up in Italy in the year 1260, and was propagated from thence through almoſt all the countries of Europe. They derive their name from the Latin *flagello*, to *whip*. The ſociety that embraced this new diſcipline ran in multitudes, compoſed of perſons of both ſexes, and all ranks and ages, through the public ſtreets, with whips in their hands, laſhing their naked bodies with the moſt aſtoniſhing ſeverity, with a view to obtain the Divine mercy for themſelves and others by their voluntary mortification and penance. This ſect made their appearance anew in the fourteenth century, and taught, among other things, that flagellation was of equal virtue with baptiſm and the other ſacraments : that the forgiveneſs of all ſins was to be obtained by it from GOD, without the merit of JESUS CHRIST : that the old law of CHRIST was ſoon to be aboliſhed, and that a new law, enjoining the baptiſm of blood to be adminiſtred by whipping, was to be ſubſtituted in its place,

A

A new sect of Whippers arose in the fifteenth century, who rejected the sacraments and every branch of external worship, and placed their only hopes of salvation in *faith* and *flagellation*.

*Mosheim's Eccles. Hist. vol. 3. p. 94, 206. 277.*

**FLANDRIANS.** [See Mennonites]

**FLORINIANS,** A branch of the Valentinians, in the second century; so called from Florinus, their leader. [See Valentinians.]

*Mosheim. ibid, vol. 1. p. 189.*

**FRATES ALBATI,** A name which distinguished a sect in the fifteenth century; they owed their origin to a certain Priest, who descended from the Alps, arrayed in a white garment, and accompanied with a prodigious number of both sexes, who, after the example of their chief, were also cloathed in white linen; hence they acquired the name *Frates Albati*, i. e. *White Brethren.* They went in a kind of procession through several provinces, following a cross, which their leader held erected like a standard, and by the striking appearance of their sanctity and devotion, captivated to such a degree the minds of the people, that persons of all ranks and orders, flocked in crouds to augment their number. The new chief exhorted his followers to oppease the anger of an incensed Deity; emaciated his body by voluntary acts of mortification and penance, endeavoured to persuade the European nations to renew the war against the Turks in *Palestine,* and pretended, that he was favoured with divine visions, which instructed him in the will and in the secrets of Heaven.

*Mosheim, ibid, vol. 3. p. 275.*

**FRATRICELLI,**

FRATRICELLI, In Englifh *Little Brothers*, a fect which appeared in Italy about the year 1298, and fpread all over Europe. Their origin is attributed by fome, to one Herman Pongilup, who pretended that Ecclefiaftics ought to have no poffeffion of their own.

*Broughton's Hiftorical Library, vol.* 1. *p.* 427.

FRENCH-PROPHETS, They firft appeared in Dauphiny and Vivarais. In the year 1688 five or fix hundred Proteftants of both fexes gave themfelves out to be Prophets, and infpired of the Holy Ghoft. They foon became fo numerous that there were many thoufands of them infpired.* They had ftrange fits, which came upon them with tremblings and faintings as in a fwoon, which made them ftretch out their arms and legs, and ftagger feveral times before they dropt down : they ftruck themfelves with their hands ; they fell on their backs ; fhut their eyes, and heaved with their breafts ; they remained awhile in trances, and coming out of them with twitchings, uttered all which came into their mouths : they faid they faw the *heavens* open, the *angels, paradife* and *hell.* Thofe who were juft on the point of receiving the fpirit of prophefy, dropt down, not only in the affemblies, crying out *mercy*, but in the fields, and in their own houfes. The leaft of their affemblies made up four or five hundred, and fome of them amounted to even three or four thoufand perfons. When the *Prophets* had for a while been under agitations of body, they began to prophefy : the burden of their prophefies was, *amend your lives ; repent ye ;*

K *the*

---

* They were people of all ages and fexes, without diftinction, though the greateft part of them were boys and girls from fix or feven to twenty-five years of age.

*the end of all things draws nigh.* The hills rebound-
ed with their loud cries for *mercy*; and with impre-
cations againſt the *Prieſts,* the *Church,* the *Pope,*
and againſt the *Antichriſtian dominion*; with predictions of the approaching fall of Popery.—All they
ſaid at theſe times was heard and received with reverence and awe.

In the year 1706, three or four of theſe *Prophets*
came over into England, and brought their *prophetic ſpirit* along with them; which diſcovered itſelf
in the ſame ways and manners, by extaſies and agitations, and inſpirations under them, as it had done in
France; and they propagated the like ſpirit to others,
ſo that before the year was out, there were two or
three hundred of theſe *Prophets* in and about London, of both ſexes, of all ages, men, women and
children; and they had delivered under inſpiration,
four or five hundred *prophetic* warnings.

The great thing *they* pretended by their ſpirit was,
to give warning of the *near approach of the kingdom
of God, the happy times of the church, the millennium
ſtate.* Their meſſage was, (and they were to proclaim it as heralds to the Jews, and every nation under heaven, beginning firſt at England) that the
grand *jubilee*; the acceptable year of the Lord; the
accompliſhment of thoſe numerous ſcriptures concerning the *new heavens* and the *new earth*; the
*kingdom of the Meſſiah*; the *marriage of the Lamb*;
the *firſt reſurrection,* or the *new Jeruſalem deſcending from above,* was *now* even at the door; that
this great operation was to be wrought, on the part
of man, by ſpiritual arms only, proceeding from the
mouths of thoſe, who ſhould, by inſpiration, or
the mighty gift of the ſpirit, be ſent forth in
                                                   great

great numbers to labour in the vineyard; that this mission of his servants should be witnessed to, by signs and wonders from heaven, by a deluge of judgments on the wicked universally throughout the world, as *famine, pestilence, earthquakes,* &c. That the exterminating angels, shall root out the tares, and there shall remain upon earth only good corn; and the works of men being thrown down, there shall be but one *Lord,* one *faith,* one *heart,* and one *voice,* among mankind. They declared that all the great things they spoke of, *would be manifest over the whole earth, within the term of three years.*

These *Prophets* also pretended to the gift of languages; of discerning the secrets of the heart; the gift of ministration of the same spirit to others by laying on of hands, and the gift of healing.

To prove they were really inspired by the Holy Ghost, they alledged the compleat joy and satisfaction they experienced; the spirit of prayer which was poured forth upon them; and the answer of their prayers by God.

*Chauncy's Works, vol.* 3. *p.* 2, 3, 4. 10, 11, 25, 28, 31, 37. 38. 39.

## G

GACIANITÆ, A sect sprung from the Eutychians; they derive their name from Gaian, a bishop of Alexandria, in the sixth century, who denied that Jesus Christ, after the hypostatical union, was subject to any of the infirmites of human nature.

*History of Religion vol* 4. [*See Gainanitæ*]

GAZARES, A sect which appeared about the year 1197, at Gazare, a town of Dalmatia. They



held

held almoſt the ſame opinions with the *Albigenſes* ; but their diſtinguiſhing tenet was, that no human power had a right to ſentence men to death for any crime whatever.

— *Broughton's Hiſtorical Library, vol.* 1. *p.* 598.

GEORGIANS. [See Iberians]

GNOSIMACHI, A name which diſtinguiſhed thoſe in the ſeventh century, who were profeſſed enemies to the *Gnoſis* i. e. the ſtudied knowledge, or *ſcience* of chriſtianity ; which they reſted wholly on good works, calling it an uſeleſs labour to ſeek for knowledge in the ſcripture. In ſhort, they contended for the practice of morality in all ſimplicity, and blamed thoſe who aimed at improving and perfecting it by a deeper knowledge and inſight into the doctrines and myſteries of religion. The *Gnoſimachi* were the very reverſe of the *Gnoſtics*. [See Gnoſtics]

— *Broughton, ibid, p* 599.

GNOSTICS, So called from their boaſting of being able to reſtore mankind to the knowledge, [Gnoſis] of the ſupreme Being which had been loſt in the world. This denomination ſprung up in the firſt century, but was not conſpicuous for its numbers, or reputation, before the time of Adrian.* It derives its origin from the Oriental philoſophy. It was one of the chief tenets of this philoſophy, that rational ſouls were impriſoned in corrupt matter, contrary to the will of the ſupreme Deity. They looked upon Matter as the ſource of all evil, and argued

---

* Under the general appellation of Gnoſtics, are comprehended all thoſe, who in the firſt ages of chriſtianity, blended the Oriental philoſophy with the doctrines of the goſpel.

gued in this manner :—There are many evils in this
world, and men seem impelled by a natural instinct,
to the practice of those things which reason condemns ; but that eternal Mind, from which all spirits
derive their existence, must be inaccessible to all
kinds of evil, and also of a most perfect and benificent
nature ; therefore, the origin of those evils, with
which the universe abounds, must be sought some-
where else than in the Deity. It cannot reside in
Him who is all perfection ; therefore, it must be
*without* him. Now, there is nothing *without* or
*beyond* the *Deity* but *Matter* ; therefore, *Matter* is
the centre and source of all evil, and of all vice.
Having taken for granted these principles, they proceeded further, and affirmed, That Matter was e-
ternal, and derived its present form, not from the
will of the supreme God, but from the creating
power of some inferior intelligence, to whom the
world and its inhabitants owed their existence. As
a proof of this assertion they alledged, that it was
incredible that the supreme Deity, perfectly good,
and infinitely removed from all evil, should either
create or modify Matter, which is essentially malignant and corrupt ; or bestow upon it, in any degree,
the riches of his wisdom and liberality. The Gnostic doctrine, concerning the creation of the world
by one or more inferior Beings of an evil, or, at
least, of an imperfect nature, led them to deny the
Divine authority of the books of the Old Testament.* Such was their aversion to these sacred
                                             books,

* When the Gnostics were challenged to produce authorities
for their doctrines, some referred to writings of Abraham, Zoro-
after, Christ, and his apostles : others boasted of their having
drawn these opinions from secret doctrines of Christ : others, that
                                                    they

books, that they lavifhed their encomiums upon the *Serpent*, the firſt author of fin, and he'd in veneration fome of the moſt inpious and profligate perſons, of whom mention is made in the ſacred hiſtory.

The Oriental fages expeċted the arrival of an extraordinary meſſenger of the moſt high upon earth ; a meſſenger inveſted with a divine authority, endowed with the moſt eminent ſanċtity and wiſdom, and peculiarly appointed to enlighten, with the knowledge of the fupreme being, the darkened minds of miferable mortals, and to deliver them from the chains of the tyrants and uſurpers of this world. When therefore fome of theſe philoſophers perceived that Chriſt and his followers wrought miracles of the moſt amazing kind, and alſo of the moſt ſalutary nature to mankind, they were eaſily induced to believe that he was the great meſſenger expeċted from above, to deliver men from the power of the malignant *genii*, or fpirits, to which, according to their doċtrine, the world was fubjeċted, and to free their fouls from the dominion of corrupt matter. But though they confidered him as the Son of the fupreme God, ſent from the pleroma, or, habitation of the everlaſting Father, they denied his divinity, looking upon him as the Son of God, and confequently inferior to the Father ; they rejeċted his humanity, upon the fuppoſition that every thing concrete and corporeal is in itſelf eſſentially and intrinſically evil. From hence the greateſt part of the Gnoſtics denied that Chriſt was cloathed with a *real* body, or that he fuffered *really* for the ſake of
mankind,

<hr>

they h.d arrived at theſe degrees of wiſdom by an innate vigour of mind : others, that they were inſtruċted by Theudas, a diſciple of St. Paul, and by Matthias, one of the friends of our Lord.

mankind, the pains and forrows which he is faid to have fuftained, in the facred hiftory. They maintained that he came to mortals with no other view than to deprive the tyrants of this world of their influence upon virtuous and heaven-born fouls, and deftroying the empire of thefe wicked fpirits, to teach mankind how they might feparate the divine mind from the impure body, and render the former worthy of being united to the Father of Spirits.

Their perfuafion, that *evil* refided in *Matter*, rendered them unfavourable to wedlock ; and led them to reject the doctrine of the refurrection of the body, and its future re-union with the immortal fpirit. Their notion that the malevolent *genii* prefided in nature, and that from them proceed all difeafes and calamities, wars, and defolations, induced them to apply themfelves to the ftudy of magic, to weaken the powers, or fufpend the influences of thefe malignant agents.

Their doctrine relating to morals and practice was of two kinds, and thofe extremely different from each other. The greateft part of this fect adopted rules of life that were full of aufterity, recommended a ftrict and rigorous abftinence, and prefcribed the moft fevere bodily mortifications, from a notion that they had a happy influence in purifying and enlarging the mind, and in difpofing it for the contemplation of celeftial things. Others maintained that there was no moral difference in human actions ; and afferted the innocence of following blindly all the motions of the paffions, and of living by their tumultuous dictates.

The Egyptian Gnoftics are diftinguifhed from the Afiatic, by the following difference in their religious fyftem :— 1, That,

I. That, besides the existence of a *Deity*, they maintained *that* also of an *eternal Matter*, endued with life and motion, yet they did not acknowledge an *eternal Principle of Darkness*, or the evil principle of the Persians.

II. They supposed that our blessed Saviour was a compound of two persons, of the man Jesus, and of Christ the Son of God ; that the divine nature entered into the man Jesus, when he was baptized by John in the river *Jordan*, and departed from him when he was seized by the Jews.

III. They attributed to Christ a real, not an imaginary body.

IV. Their discipline, with respect to life and manners, was much less severe than that of the Asiatic sect.

Both these branches of the Gnostics were subdivided into various denominations. [See Antitactes, Ascodrutes, Bardesanistes, Basilidians, Bogomiles, Carpocratians, Cerdonians, Cerinthians, Marcosians, Ophites, Saturnians, Simonians and Valentinians]
*Mosheim's Eccles. Hist. vol.* 1. *p.* 69. 70, 107, 108, 109, 110, 111, 181.

GREEK-CHURCH, In the eighth century there arose a difference between the eastern and western churches, which in the ninth century terminated in a separation which continues to this day. [For an account of the extent of the Greek or eastern church, see Appendix]

The principal tenets which distinguish the Greek-church from the Latin, are as follow.

I. They disown the authority of the Pope, and deny that the church of Rome is the true *Catholic church.*　　　　　　　　　　　　　　II. They

II. They do not baptize * their children, till they are three, four, five, six, ten, nay sometimes eighteen years of age.

III. They insist, that the sacrament of the Lord's supper ought to be administered in both kinds: and they give the sacrament to children immediately, after baptism.

IV. They deny that there is any such place as purgatory, † notwithstanding they pray for the dead, that GOD would have mercy on them at the general Judgment.

V. They exclude *confirmation, extreme unction,* and matrimony out of the seven sacraments.

VI. They deny *auricular confession* to be a divine precept, and say, it is only a positive injunction of the church.

VII. They pay no religious homage to the Eucharist.

VIII. They administer the communion in both kinds to the laity, both in sickness and in health, though they have never applied themselves to their confessors ; because they are persuaded, that a lively faith is all which is requisite for the worthy receiving the Lord's supper.

IX. They maintain, that the Holy-Ghost proceeds only from the Father, and not from the Son.

L  X. They

* They perform baptism by dipping the person three times under water distinctly, in the name of the *Father, Son,* and *Holy Ghost.*

† Yet the Greeks, and all the Eastern nations in general, are of opinion, that departed souls will not be immediately and perfectly happy ; that the first Paradise will be a state of the next of eternal felicity.

X. They admit of no images in *bafs-relief*, or *embossed work* ; but use paintings and sculptures in copper or silver.

XI. They approve of the marriage of Priests; provided they enter into that state before their admission into Holy Orders.

XII. They condemn all fourth marriages.

They observe a number of holy days ; and keep four Fasts in the year more solemn than the rest; of which the Fast in Lent, before Easter, is the chief.

*Father Simons' Religions of the Eastern Nations, p 5 6, 7, 8.*
*Thevenot's Travels, p. 412.*
*Broughton's Hist. Library, vol. 1. p. 145 246. 247.*
*Bayley's Dictionary, vol 2. [See Greeks]*
*Hist. of Religion, number vi p. 251, 253.*

H

HATTEMISTS, A Dutch sect which arose in the seventeenth century : they derive their name from Pontium Van Hattem, a minister in the province of Zealand. He interpreted the Calvinistical doctrine concerning *absolute decrees*, so as to deduce from it the system of a *fatal* and *uncontroulable necessity*. Having laid down this principle to account for the origin of all events, he denied the difference between *moral good* and *evil*, and the corruption of human nature.

From hence he concluded, That mankind were under no sort of obligation to correct their manners, to improve their minds or to endeavour after a regular obedience to the divine laws—that the whole of religion consisted not in *acting* but in *suffering*—and that all the precepts of Jesus Christ are reducible to this single one, that we bear with chearful-
nefs

ness and patince the events that happen to us through the divine will, and make it our conſtant and only ſtudy to maintain a permanent tranquility of mind.

This denomination alſo affirmed, that CHRIST had not ſatisfied the divine juſtice, nor made an ex-expiation for the ſins of men by his death and ſufferings, but had only ſignified to us, by his mediation, that there was nothing in us that could offend the Deity. They maintained that this was Chriſt's manner of juſtifying his ſervants, and preſenting them blameleſs before the tribunal of GOD. *

They alſo taught, *That God does not puniſh men for their ſins, but by their ſins.*
*Moſheim's Eccleſ. Hiſt. vol. iv. p. 553, 554.*

HELSAITES, A ſect which aroſe in the ſecond century; they denied ſome parts of the old and new Teſtament, and did not own St. Paul to be an apoſtle, and thought it an indifferent thing if in *perſecution, they denied the faith in words :* they received a certain book which they ſaid came down from Heaven, and contained their doctrine.
*Athenian Oracle, vol. ii. p. 128.*

HENRICIANS, A ſect in the twelfth century, founded by Henry, a Monk, he rejected the baptiſm of infants, cenſured with ſeverity the licentious manners of the clergy, and treated the feſtivals and ceremonies of the church with the utmoſt contempt.
*Moſheim's Eccleſ Hiſt. vol. ii. p. 448.*

HERACLEONITES, A branch of the Valentinians, in the ſecond century; they derived their
L 2                    name

* This opinion was peculiar to the Hattemiſts, and diſtinguiſhed them from the Verſchoriſts.

name from Heracleon, who maintained that the world was not the immediate production of the Son of God; but that he was only the occasional cause of its being created by the *Demiurgus*. The Heracleonites denied the authority of the prophecies of the *old Teftament*, maintaining that they were meer random founds in the air, and that St. John the Baptift was the only true voice which directed to the Meffiah.

*Broughton's Hiftorical Library, vol. i. p. 484.*

HERMOGENIANS, A fect which arofe towards the clofe of the fecond century; fo denominated from Hermogenes, a Painter by profeffion.— He regarded *Matter* as the fountain of all evil, and could not perfuade himfelf that GOD had created it from nothing by an almighty act of his will; and therefore he maintained, that the world, with whatever it contains, as alfo the fouls of men, and other fpirits, were formed by the Deity from an uncreated and eternal mafs of corrupt *Matter*.

*Mofheim's Ecclef. Hift. vol. 1, p 190.*

HERRENHUTTERS.   [See Moravians]

HETEROUSIANS, A name given to one of the Arian divifions.   [See Arians]

HIERACITES, A fect in the third century; fo called from their leader Hierax, a philofopher and magician of Egypt. Hierax maintained, that the principal object of CHRIST's office and miniftry was the promulgation of a *new law*, more fevere and perfect than that of *Mofes*; and from hence he concluded, that the ufe of flefh, wine, wedlock,
and

and of other things agreeable to the outward fenfes,
which had been permitted under the Mofaic difpenfation, was abfolutely prohibited and abrogated by
CHRIST. He excluded, from the kingdom of
Heaven children who died before they had arrived
to the ufe of reafon ; and that, upon the fuppofition
that GOD was bound to adminifter the rewards of
futurity to thofe only who had fairly finifhed their
victorious conflict with the body and its lufts. He
maintained alfo, that Melchifedic was the Holy
Ghoft. His difciples taught, that the *Word*, or Son
of God, was contained in the *Father*, as a little veffel in a great one ; whence they had the name of
*Metangimonifts*, from the Greek word [mètangimò-
nòs] which fignifies *contained* in a veffel.

Hierax alfo denied the doctrine of the refurrection
of the body.

*Mofheim's ibid.* p. 246.
*Broughton's Hiftorical Library,* vol 1. p. 493.

HOMOUSIANS, A name given to a branch of
the Arians. [See Arians]

HOPKINTONIANS, or HOPKINSIANS, So
called from the Rev. Mr. Samuel Hopkins, paftor of
the firft congregational church at Newport ; who
in his fermons and tracts has made feveral additions
to the fentiments firft advanced by the celebrated
Mr. Jonathan Edwards, late Prefident of New-Jer-
fey College.

The following is a fummary of the diftinguifhing
tenets of this denomination, together with a few of
the reafons of which they make ufe to fupport their
fentiments :

1. That all true *virtue*, or real *holinefs*, confifts
in *difinterefted benevolence*. -The

The object of benevolence is univerſal Being, including GOD, and all intelligent creatures ; it wiſhes
and ſeeks the good of every individual ſo far as con-
ſiſtent with the greateſt good of the whole, which is
compriſed in the glory of GOD, and the perfection
and happineſs of his kingdom.

The law of GOD is the ſtandard of all moral rectitude, or holineſs.*   This is reduced into love to
GOD, and our neighbour as ourſelves ; and univerſal good-will comprehends all the love to GOD, our
neighbour and ourſelves required in the  divine law ;
and therefore muſt be the whole of holy obedience.
Let any ſerious perſon think what are the particular branches of true piety ; when he has viewed
each one by itſelf, he will find, that diſintereſted,
friendly affection is its diſtinguiſhing characteriſtic.
For inſtance, all the holineſs in pious fear, which
diſtinguiſhes it from the fear of the wicked, conſiſts
in love.   Again, holy gratitude is nothing but good-
will to GOD and our neighbour, in which we ourſelves are included ; and correſpondent affection excited by a view of the good-will and kindneſs of
GOD.

Univerſal good-will alſo, implies the whole of the
duty we owe to our neighbour.   For juſtice, truth,
and faithfulneſs, are compriſed in univerſal benevolence ; ſo are temperance and chaſtity : for, an undue indulgence of our appetites and paſſions is contrary to benevolence,  as  tending  to hurt ourſelves or
                                               others ;

_________________________

* The law requires us to love GOD with all our hearts, becauſe
he is the LORD, b cauſe he is juſt ſuch a Being as he is.  On this
account, primarily and antecedently to all other conſiderations, he
is infinitely amiable ; and therefore, on this account, primarily
and antecedently to all other conſiderations, ought he to appear
infinitely amiable in our eyes.

others; and so opposite to the general good, and the Divine command, in which all the crime of such indulgence consists. In short, all *virtue* is nothing but *benevolence* acted out in its proper nature and perfection, or love to GOD and our neighbour made perfect in all its genuine exercises and expressions.

II. That all *sin* consists in *selfishness*.

By this is meant an interested, selfish affection, by which a person sets himself up as supreme, and the only object of regard; and nothing is good or lovely, in his view, unless suited to promote his own private interest. This self-love is in its whole nature and every degree of it, enmity against God. *It is not subject to the law of God*; and is the only affection that can oppose it. It is the foundation of all spiritual blindness; and therefore the source of all the open idolatry in the heathen world; and false religion under the light of the gospel. All this is agreeable to that self-love which opposes God's true character: under the influence of this principle men depart from the truth, it being itself the greatest practical lie in nature, as it sets up that which is comparatively nothing, above Universal Existence. Self-love is the source of all the profaneness and impiety in the world; and of all pride and ambition among men, which is nothing but selfishness acted out in this particular way. This is the foundation of all covetousness and sensuality; as it blinds peoples eyes, contracts their hearts, and sinks them down, so that they they look upon earthly enjoyments as the greatest good. This is the source of all falsehood, injustice, and oppression, as it excites mankind by undue methods to invade the property of others.—

Self-love

Self-love produces all the violent paſſions, envy, wrath, clamour and evil ſpeaking, and every thing contrary to the divine law, is briefly comprehended in this fruitful ſource of all iniquity, ſelf-love.

III. That there are no promiſes of *regenerating-grace* made to the *doings of the unregenerate.*

For as far as men act from ſelf-love, they act from a bad end. For thoſe who have no true love to God really do no duty, when they attend on the externals of religion : and as the Unregenerate act from a ſelfiſh principle, they do nothing which is commanded. Their impenitent doings are wholly oppoſed to repentance and converſion, therefore not implied in the command, To repent, &c. So far from this, they are altogether diſobedience to the command. Hence it appears, that there are no promiſes of ſalvation to the doings of the Unregenerate.

IV. That the impotency of ſinners, with reſpect to believing in Chriſt, is not natural but *moral.*

For it is a plain dictate of common ſenſe, that natural impoſſibility excludes all blame. But an unwilling mind is univerſally conſidered as a crime, and not as an excuſe, and is the very thing wherein our wickedneſs conſiſts. That the impotence of the ſinner is owing to a diſaffection of heart, is evident from the promiſes of the goſpel. When any object of good is propoſed and promiſed to us upon aſking, it clearly evinces that there can be no impotency in us with reſpect to obtaining it, beſides the diſapprobation of the *will,* and that inability which conſiſts in diſinclination, never renders any thing improperly the ſubject of precept or command.

V. That

V. That in order to faith in Chrift, a finner muft approve in his heart of the divine conduct, even though God fhould caft him off forever ; which, however, neither implies *love to mifery* nor *hatred of happinefs.**

For, if the law is good, death is due to thofe who have broken it. The Judge of all the earth cannot but do right. It would bring everlafting reproach upon his government to fpare us, confidered merely as in ourfelves. When this is felt in our hearts, and not till then, we fhall be prepared to look to the free grace of God through the redemption which is in Chrift, and to exercife faith in his blood, *who is fet forth to be a propitiation to declare God's righteoufnefs, that he might be juft, and yet the juftifier of him who believeth in Jefus.*

VI. That the infinitely wife and holy GOD has exerted his omnipotent power in fuch a manner, as he purpofed fhould be followed with the exiftence and entrance of *moral evil* in the fyftem.

M

For,

---

* As a particle of water is fmall in comparifon of a generous ftream, fo the man of humility feels fmall before the great family of his fellow creatures He values his foul, but when he compares it to the great foul of mankind he almoft forgets and lofes fight of it : for the governing principle of his heart is to eftimate things according to their worth When, therefore, he indu'ges a humble comparifon with his Maker, he feels loft in the infinite fullnefs and brightnefs of divine love, as a ray of light is loft in the Sun, and a particle of water in the ocean. It infpires him with the moft grateful feelings of heart, that he has opportunity to be in the hand of GOD as clay in the hand of the Potter : and as he confiders himfelf in this humble light, he fubmits the nature and fize of his future veffel intirely to God. - As his pride is loft in the duft, he looks up with pleafure toward the throne of God, and rejoices with all his heart in the rectitude of the divine adminiftration.

For, it muſt be admitted on all hands, that God has a perfect knowledge, foreſight and view of all poſſible exiſtences and events ; if 'that ſyſtem and ſcene of operation in which moral evil ſhould never have exiſtence was actually *preferred* in the divine mind, certainly the Deity is infinitely diſappointed in the iſſue of his own operations. Nothing can be more diſhonourable to God than to imagine that the ſyſtem, which is actually formed by the divine hand, and which was made for his pleaſure and glory, is, yet, not the fruit of wiſe contrivance and deſign.

VII. That the introduction of *ſin*, is, upon the whole, for the *general good*.

For, the wiſdom and power of the Deity are diſplayed in carrying on deſigns of the *greateſt good :* and the exiſtence of *moral evil* has undoubtedly occaſioned a more full, perfect and glorious diſcovery of the infinite perfections of the divine nature, than could otherwiſe have been made to the view of creatures. If the extenſive manifeſtations of the pure and holy nature of God, and his infinite averſion to ſin, and all his inherent perfections, in their genuine fruits and effects, is either itſelf the greateſt good, or neceſſarily contains it ; it muſt neceſſarily follow, that the introduction of *ſin* is for the *greateſt good*.

VIII. That repentance is before faith in Chriſt.

By this is not intended, that repentance is before a ſpeculative belief of the *being* and *perfections* of God, and of the *perſon* and *character* of Chriſt ; but only, that true repentance is previous to a ſaving faith in Chriſt, in which the believer is united to

Chriſt,

Chrift, and entitled to the benefits of his mediation and atonement. That repentance is before faith in this fenfe, appears from feveral confiderations.

1ft. As repentance and faith refpect different objects, fo they are diftinct exercifes of the heart, and therefore not only may, but muft be prior to the other.

2d. There may be genuine repentance of fin without faith in Chrift ; but there cannot be true faith in Chrift without repentance of fin : and fince repentance is neceffary in order to faith in Chrift, it muft neceffarily be prior to faith in Chrift.

3d. John the Baptift, Chrift and his apoftles taught, that repentance is before faith. John cried, *Repent, for the kingdom of Heaven is at hand*; intending, that true repentance was neceffary in order to embrace the gofpel of the kingdom. Chrift commanded, *Repent ye, and believe the gofpel.* And Paul preached *repentance toward God, and faith toward our Lord Jefus Chrift.*

IX. That though men became finners by Adam according to a Divine conftitution, yet they have, and are accountable for no fins but perfonal. For,

1ft. Adam's act in eating the forbidden fruit was not the act of his pofterity, therefore, they did not fin at the fame time he did.

2d. The finfulnefs of that act could not be transferred to them afterwards, becaufe the finfulnefs of an act can no more be transferred from one perfon to another than an act itfelf. Therefore,

3d. Adam's act in eating the forbidden fruit was not the caufe, but only the occafion of his pofterity's being finners. God was pleafed to make a conftitution, that, if Adam remained holy through his ftate of trial, his pofterity fhould, in confequence of it, be holy too ; but if he finned, his pofterity, in confequenec of it, fhould be finners too. Adam finned, and now God brings his pofterity into the world finners. *By* Adam's fin we are become finners, not *for* it ; his fin being only the *occafion*, not the *caufe* of our committing fins.

X. That though believers are juftified through Chrift's righteoufnefs, yet his righteoufnefs is not transferred to them. For,

1ft. Perfonal righteoufnefs can no more be tranfferred from one perfon to another than perfonal fin.

2d. If Chrift's perfonal *righteoufnefs* were tranfferred to *believers*, they would be as perfeдly holy as Chrift, and fo ftand in no need of forgivenefs. But,

3d. Believers are not confcious of having Chrift's perfonal righteoufnefs, but feel and bewail much indwelling fin and corruption. And,

4th. The fcripture reprefents believers as receiving only the *benefits* of Chrift's righteoufnefs in juftification, or their being pardoned and accepted for Chrift's righteoufnefs fake. And this is the proper fcripture notion of imputation. Jonathan's righteoufnefs was imputed to Mephibofheth when David fhewed kindnefs to him for his father Jonathan's fake.

*Hopkins on Holinefs, p.* 7, 8, 11, 12, 19, 26 27, 28, 29, 34, 171, 197, 202.
*Edwards on the Will, p.* 234, 289.
*Bellamy's True Religion Delineated. p* 16.
———— *Dialogues between Theron and Paulinus, p.* 185.
*Smalley's Impotency of Sinners, p.* 16.
*Weft's Effay on Moral Agency, p.* 170, 177, 181.
*Spring's Nature of Duty, p* 23.
*Manufcript, by the Rev. Mr. Emmons.*

HUSSITES,

HUSSITES, A fect in Bohemia ; fo called from John Huts, one of their principal teachers, who about the year 1414 embraced and defended the opinions of Wickliff.  [See Wickliffites]

*Brandt's Hift of the Reform  vol ii. p 18.*

## I & J

JACOBITES, A fect of *Eaftern* chriftians, in the fixth and the beginning of the feventh century ; fo denominated from *Jacob Bardeus,* or *Zanzalus,* a *Syrian,* and a difciple of *Eutyches* and *Dyofcorus.*

His doctrines fpread in *Afia* and *Africa* to that degree, that the fect of the Eutychians were fwallowed up by that of the *Jacobites,* which alfo comprehended all the *Monophyfites* of the *Eaft,* i. e. Such as acknowledged but one nature, and that human in *Jefus Chrift,* by that taking in the *Armenians* and *Abyfines* : They denied the three perfons in the Trinity, and made the fign of the crofs with one finger, to intimate the one-nefs of the Godhead. Before baptifm they applied a hot iron to the foreheads of children after they had circumcifed them, founding that practice upon the words of *John* the *Baptift.* Mat. iii. 11. *He will baptize you with the Holy Ghoft and with fire.*

*Bayley's Dictionary, vol. ii,*   [*See Jacobites*]

JANSENISTS, A denomination of Roman Catholics in France, which was formed in the year 1640. . They follow the opinions of Janfenius, Bifhop of Yp-efs, from whofe writings the following propofitions are faid to have been extracted :

1. That there are divine precepts, which good men, notwithftanding their defire to obferve them,
are

are, neverthelefs, abfolutely unable to obey ; nor has God given them that meafure of grace which is ef-fentially neceffary to render them capable of fuch obedience.

II.  That no perfon, in this corrupt ftate of na-ture, can refift the influence of divine grace, when it operates upon the mind.

III.  That, in order to render human actions me-ritorious, it is not requifite that they be exempt from *neceffity*, but that they be free from *conftraint*.*

IV.  That the Semi-pelagians err greatly in maintaining that the human will is endowed with the power of either receiving, or refifting the aids and influences of preventing grace.

V.  That whofoever affirms, that *Jefus Chrift* made expiation, by his fufferings and death, for the fins of all mankind, is a Semi-pelagian.

This denomination are alfo diftinguifhed from the generality of the Roman Catholics, by their maintaining that the people ought to be carefully inftructed in all the doctrines and precepts of chri-ftianity ; and that, for this purpofe the holy fcrip-tures and public liturgies fhould be offered to their perufal in their mother tongue ; and finally, they look upon it as a matter of the higheft moment to perfuade all chriftians that true piety does not confift in the performance of external acts of devo-tion, but in inward holinefs and divine love.

*Mofheim's Ecclef. Hift. vol. iv p 373 379.*

IBERIANS,

IBERIANS, A fect of Eaftern chriftians, which derive their name from Iberia, a province of Afia, now called Georgia : hence they are alfo called Georgians.

Their tenets are faid to be the fame with thofe of the Greek Church. [See Greek Church]

*Father Simons' Hiftory of the Eaftern Chriftians, p 64, 65.*

JESUITS, A famous religious order in the Romifh church, eftablifhed in the year 1540, under the name of the company of JESUS.

Ignio, or, Ignatius Loyola, a Spanifh gentleman of illuftrious rank, was the founder of this order, which has made a moft rapid and aftonifhing progrefs through the world.

The doctrinal points which diftinguifh the Jefuits from many others of the Roman communion, are as follow :

I. This order all maintain, that the Pope is *infallible* ;—that he is the only vifible fource of that univerfal and unlimited power which CHRIST has granted to the church ;—that all Bifhops and fubordinate rulers derive from him alone the authority and jurifdiction with which they are invefted ; and that he alone is the fupreme law-giver of that facred community ; a law-giver whofe edicts and commands it is in the higheft degree criminal to oppofe or difobey.

II. They comprehend within the limits of the church, not only many who live feparate from the communion of Rome, but even extend the inheritance of eternal falvation to nations that have not the leaft knowledge of the Chriftian religion, or of

its

its divine author ; and confider as true members of the church open tranfgreffors, who profefs its doctrines.

III. The Jefuits maintain that *human nature* is far from being deprived of *all power* of doing good ; —that the *fuccours of grace* are adminiftered to *all mankind* in a meafure *fufficient* to lead them to eternal life and falvation ;—that the *operations* of grace offer no violence to the faculties and powers of nature, and therefore may be *refifted* ;—and that God from all eternity has appointed everlafting rewards and punifhments, as the portion of men in a future world; not by an *abfolute, arbitrary,* and *unconditional* decree, but in confequence of that divine and unlimited *prefcience* by which he forefaw the *actions, merits* and *characters* of every individual.

IV. They reprefent it as a matter of perfect indifference, from what motives men obey the laws of God, provided thefe laws are really obeyed : and maintain that the fervice of thofe who obey from the fear of punifhment, is as agreeable to the Deity, as thofe actions which proceed from a principle of love to him and his laws.

V. They maintain, that the facraments have in themfelves an *inftrumental* and efficient power, by virtue of which they work in the foul (independently on its previous preparation or propenfities) a difpofition to receive the divine grace.

VI. The Jefuits recommend a devout ignorance to fuch as fubmit to their direction, and think a Chriftian fufficiently inftructed when he has learned to yield a blind and unlimited obedience to the orders of the church.          The

The following maxims are said to be extracted from the moral writings of this order :

I. That persons *truly wicked*, and *void of the love of God*, may expect to obtain *eternal life* in Heaven, provided that they be impressed with a fear of the divine anger, and avoid all heinous and enormous crimes *through the dread of future punishment.*

II. That those persons may transgress *with safety*, who have a *probable reason* for transgressing, i. e. any plausible argument or authority in favour of the sin they are inclined to commit.

III. That actions *intrinsically evil*, and directly *contrary to the divine law*, may be *innocently* performed by those who have so much power over their own minds as to join, even ideally, a *good end* to this *wicked action*.

IV. That *philosophical sin* * is of a very light and trivial nature, and does not deserve the pains of Hell.

V. That the transgressions committed by a person blinded by the seductions of tumultuous passions, and destitute of all sense and impression of religion, however detestible and heinous they may be in themselves, are not imputable to the transgressor before the tribunal of God ; and that such transgressions may be often as involuntary as the actions of a madman.

VI. That the person who takes an oath, or enters into a contract, may, to elude the force of the

N one

---

* By philosophical sin, the Jesuits mean, *an action contrary to the dictates of nature and right reason, which is done by a person who is either absolutely ignorant of GOD, or does not think of him during the time this action is committed.*

one and obligation of the other, add to the form of
the words that exprefs them certain mental additions and tacit refervations.

This entire fociety is compofed of four forts of
members, viz. Novices, Scholars, fpiritual and
temporal Coadjutors, and profeffed Members. Befides the three ordinary vows of poverty, chaftity,
and obedience, which are common to all the monaftic tribes, the profeffed Members are obliged to
take a fourth, by which they folemnly bind themfelves to go, without deliberation or delay, wherever the Pope fhall think fit to fend them. They
are governed by a General, who has four Affiftants;
and the inferiors of this order are required to confider their Chief as infallible, and entirely to renounce their own will in all things, and abandon
themfelves blindly to his conduct.

*Mofheim's Ecclefiaftical Hiftory, vol.* iii. *p.* 465—470.
*vol* iv *p.* 354, 355 *&c.*
*Hift. of Don Ignatius. vol. p* 2—190.
*Broughton's Hiftorical Library, vol.* i. *p.* 512.

**ILLUMINATI,** i. e. the *Enlightened,* A denomination which appeared in Spain about the year
1575. They were charged with maintaining, that
mental prayer and contemplation had fo intimately
united them to God, they were arrived to fuch a
ftate of perfection, as to ftand in no need of good
works, or the facraments of the church ; and that
they might commit the groffeft crimes without fin.

After the fuppreffion of the Illuminati in Spain,
there appeared a fect in France which took the fame
name. They maintained, that one Anthony Buck-
uet, a Friar, had a fyftem of belief and practice revealed to him, which exceeded every thing Chriftianity

anity had yet been acquainted with ; that by this method, perſons might in a ſhort time arrive at the ſame degrees of perfection and glory which the Saints and the ' leſſed Virgin have attained to ; and this improvement might be carried on till our actions became divine, and our minds wholly given up to the influence of the Almighty. They ſaid further, that none of the Doctors of the church knew any thing of religion ; that St. Peter and St. Paul were well-meaning men, but knew nothing of devotion ; that the whole church lay in darkneſs and unbelief ; that every one was at liberty to follow the ſuggeſti- ons of his conſcience ; that God regarded nothing but himſelf ; and that within ten years their doctrine would be received all over the world, and then there would be no more occaſion for Prieſts, Monks, and other ſuch religious diſtinctions.

*Broughton's Hiſtorical Library, vol* i. *p.* 523 524.

**INDEPENDENTS,** A denomination of Pro- teſtants, in England and Holland : they appeared in England in the year 1616. John Robinſon, a Nor- folk Divine, was the leader of this party. They derive their name from their maintaining, that every particular congregation of Chriſtians has an entire and compleat power of juriſdiction over its members, to be exerciſed by the Elders of each church within itſelf, without being ſubject to the authority of *Bi- ſhops, Synods, Preſbyteries,* or any eccleſiaſtical aſ- ſembly compoſed of the deputies from different churches.

The Independents alledge, that the *church* of Corinth had an entire judicature within itſelf : for St. Paul thus addreſſes them, *Do not ye judge them which are within?* 1ſt of Cor. v. 12. So they



were

were not dependent upon the apoftle to come to him for a fentence.

*Mofheim's Ecclefiaftical Hiftory. vol. iv p 526.*
*Neal's Hift. of the Puritants, vol. iii. p. 142.*
*Goodwin's Works, vol. iv. p. 71.*

INVISIBLES, A name of diftinction given to the difciples of Ofiander, Flacius, Illyricus, Swenk-feld, &c. becaufe they denied the perpetual vifibility of the church.

*Collier's Hiftorical Dictionary.*   [*See Invifibles*]

JOACHIMITES, A fect which appeared about the commencement of the thirteenth century ; fo called from Joachim, Abbot of Sora, in Calabria.

He foretold the deftruction of the church of Rome, and the promulgation of *a new and more perfect gofpel in the age of the Holy Ghoft*, by a fett of poor and auftere minifters, whom God was to raife up, and employ for that purpofe. For he divided the world into three ages, relative to the three difpenfations of *religion* which were to fucceed each other in it. The two imperfect ages, viz. the age of the Old Teftament, which was that of the *Father*, and the age of the New which was under the adminiftration of the *Son*, were according to his predictions now paft, and the third age, even that of the Holy Ghoft, was at hand.

*Mofheim's Ecclef. Hift vol. iii, p. 66.*

ISBRANIKI, A fect which appeared in Ruffia, about the year 1666, and affumed this name, which fignifies *the multitude of the elect*, but they were called by their adverfaries, Rolfkolfnika, or *the feditious faction*. They profeffed a rigorous zeal for the letter of the holy fcriptures,

They

They maintained, that there is no subordination of rank among the faithful; and that a Christian may kill himself for the love of Christ.

*Mosheim's ibid, vol. iv. p. 406.*

## K

KEITHIANS, A party which separated from the Quakers, in Pennsylvania, in the year 1691. They were headed by the famous George Keith, from whom they derived their name.

Those who persisted in their separation, after their leader deserted them, practised *baptism* and received the *Lord's supper.*

This party were also called *Quaker-Baptists,* because they retained the language, dress and manners of the Quakers.

*Edwards' Hist. of the American Baptists, p 55, 56, 57, 60.*

KTISTOLATRÆ, A branch of the Monophysites, which maintained, that the body of Christ before his resurrection, was corruptible.

*Mosheim's Ecclef. Hist. vol. i. p. 471, 472.*

## L

LABBADISTS, A sect which arose in the seventeenth century; so called from their founder John Labbadie, a native of France, a man of no mean genius, and remarkable for a natural and masculine eloquence. He maintained among other things,

I. That God might, and did, on certain occasions, deceive men.

II. That the holy scripture was not sufficient to lead men to salvation, without certain particular *illuminations* and *revelations* from the Holy Ghost.

III. That

III. That in reading the fcripture we ought to give lefs attention to the literal fenfe of the words than to the inward fuggeftions of the fpirit, and that the efficacy of the word depended upon him that preached it.

IV. That the faithful ought to have all things in common.

V. That there is no fubordination or diftinction in the true church of CHRIST.

VI. That CHRIST was to reign a thoufand years upon earth.

VII. That the *contemplative life* is a ftate of grace and union with God, and the very height of perfection.

VIII. That the Chriftian, whofe mind is contented and calm, fees all things in God, enjoys the Deity, and is perfectly indifferent about every thing that paffes in the world.

IX. That the Chriftian arrives at that happy ftate by the exercife of a perfect felf-denial ; by mortifying the flefh and all fenfual affections, and by mental prayer.

*Mofheim's Ecclef. Hift. vol.* 5. *p.* 63.

LAMPETIANS, A fect in the feventeenth century, the followers of Lampetious, a Syrian Monk.

He pretended that as man is born free, a Chriftian, in order to pleafe God, ought to do nothing by neceffity ; and it is therefore unlawful to make vows, even thofe of obedience.

To this fyftem he added the doctrines of the Arians, Carpocrations, and other fects. [See Arians and Carpocrations]

*Broughton's Hiftorical Library, vol.* ii *p* 3.

LIBERTINES,

LIBERTINES, A sect which arose in Flanders about the year 1525; the heads of this party were one Copin and one Quintin of Picardy.

The doctrines they taught are comprised in the following propositions.

I. That the Deity was the sole *operating cause* in the mind of man, and the immediate *author* of all human actions.

II. That, consequently, the distinctions of *good* and *evil*, that had been established with respect to those actions, were false and groundless, and that men could not, properly speaking, commit sin.

III. That religion consisted in the union of the spirit or rational soul with the supreme Being.

IV. That all those who had attained this happy union, by sublime contemplation and elevation of mind, were then allowed to indulge, without exception or restraint, their appetites and passions, as all their actions were then perfectly innocent.

V. That after the death of the body, they were to be united to the Deity.

This sect permitted their followers to call themselves either Catholics or Lutherans.

*Broughton, ibid, p. 543.*
*Mosheim's Eccles. Hist. vol. iv. p. 122, 123.*

LOLLARDS.   [See Wickliffites]

LUCIANISTS, So called from Lucianus, a disciple of Marcion.   [See Marcionites and Cerdonians]

LUCIFERIANS, A sect in the fourth century; so called from Lucifer, Bishop of Cagliari ; they are

are said to have maintained, that the soul was trans-
fused from the parents to the children.

Mosheim's ibid, vol. i. p 314.

LUTHERANS, Those who follow the opinions of Martin Luther, an Augustine Friar, who was
born at Isleben, in the country of Mansfield, in the
circle of Upper Saxony, in the year 1483. He possessed an invincible magnanimity, and an uncommon
vigour, and acuteness of genius.

This denomination took its rise from the distaste
taken at the indulgences which were granted in
1517, by Pope Leo X, to those who contributed
towards finishing St. Peter's church at Rome.———
Those famous indulgences administered remission of
all sins, past, present and to come, however enormous their nature, to those who were rich enough
to purchase them. At this, Luther raised his warning voice; and in ninety-five propositions maintained
publicly, at Wittenberg, on the 30th of September,
in the year 1517, exposed the doctrine of indulgences, which led him to attack the authority of the
Pope; and was the commencement of that memo-
rable revolution in the church which is stiled the
*Reformation.*

The capital articles which Luther maintained are
as follow; to which are added, a few of the arguments which are made use of in their defence.

I. That the *holy scriptures* are the only source
from whence we are to draw our religious sentiments,
whether they relate to faith or practice.

For, the apostle declares, 2 Tim. iii. 15, 16, 17,
that, *The scriptures are able to make us wise unto
salvation; and are profitable for doctrine, for re-*
*proof,*

*proof, for correction, and for instruction in righte-
ousness.* To which may be added a cloud of divine
witnesses to the same effect.—Prov. i. 9.   Isa. viii.
20.   Luke i. 4.   John v. 39; xx. 31.   1 Cor.
iv. 6, &c.

Reason also confirms the sufficiency of the scriptures ; for if the written word is allowed to be a
rule in one case, how can it be denied to be a rule in
another ? for the rule is but one in all, and is perfect in its nature.

II.    That *justification* is the effect of *faith*, ex-
clusive of *good works*, and that faith ought to produce good works, purely in obedience to God, and
not in order to our  justification. *

For the doctrine of the gospel attributeth all
things to God, and nothing to man.   St. Paul in his
epistle to the  Galatians, strenuously opposed those
who ascribed our justification partly to  our  works.
He asserts, that *if righteousness come by the law, then
Christ is dead in vain.* Gal. ii. 21.   Therefore it is
evident we are not justified  by the law,  or  by our
works;  but to him  who believeth,  sin is pardoned
and righteousness imputed.

III.   That no man is able to make satisfaction for
his sins.

For our Lord expressly tells his disciples, *when ye
have done all, ye are unprofitable servants.* Luke xvii.
10. Christ's sacrifice is alone sufficient to satisfy for sin :

O                                            and

* Luther constantly opposed this doctrine to the Romish tenet—
That man, by works of his own, prayer, fasting and corporal
afflictions, might merit and claim pardon. He used to call the
doctrine of justification by *faith alone*, the article of a standing
or falling church.

and nothing need be added to the infinite value of his merit and sufferings.

. In consequence of these leading articles, Luther rejected *tradition, purgatory, penance, auricular confession, masses, invocation of saints, monastic vows,* and other doctrines of the church of Rome.

The Lutherans differ from the Calvinists in the following points:

I. The Lutherans have Bishops, and superintendants for the government of the church, but the Ecclesiastical government which Calvin introduced was called *Presbyterian,* and does not admit of the institution of Bishops, or of any subordination among the Clergy.

II. They differ in their notions of the sacrament of the Lord's supper.

The Lutherans reject *transubstantiation,* but affirm that the body and blood of Christ are *materially present* in the *sacrament,* though in an incomprehensible manner; and that they are really exhibited both to the worthy and unworthy receiver.

This union of the body and blood of Christ with the bread after consecration, is, by the *Lutherans,* called *consubstantiation.*

The *Calvinists* hold on the contrary, that the man Christ, is only present in this ordinance, by the external signs of bread and wine.

III. They differ in their doctrine of the *eternal decrees of God respecting man's salvation.* The *Lutherans* maintain, that the *Divine decrees* respecting the salvation and misery of men, are founded upon a previous knowledge of their sentiments and characters.

racters.  The *Calvinists* on the contrary, confider the *Divine decrees* as *free* and *unconditional*. [See Calvinists]

[For an account of the particulars in which Luther differed from Zuingle, fee Zuinglians]

The *Lutherans* are generally divided into the moderate and the rigid.  The *moderate Lutherans* are those who fubmitted to the *Interim*, * published by the Emperor Charles V.  Melanchthon was the head of this party.  They were called *Adiaphorists*.

The *rigid Lutherans* are those who would not endure any change in their mafter's fentiments. Matthias Flacius was the head of this party.

To thefe are added another divifion called Luthero-Zuinglians, becaufe they held fome of Luther's tenets, and fome of Zuinglius's.

The Lutherans are alfo fubdivided into a variety of denominations.  [See Ainfdorfians, Calixtins, Flacians, Ofiandrians, Synergifts, and Ubiquitarians]

[For an account of the extent of the *Lutherans,* fee Appendix]

*Luther on Galatians,* p 142. 144.
*Hiftory of Popery,* vol. i. p. 226.
*Mofheim's Ecclef. Hift.* vol. iii. p. 331. vol. iv. p. 108, 109.
*Robertfon's Hiftory of Charles V.* vol. ii. p. 42.
*Broughton's Hiftorical Library,* vol. ii. p. 33, 36.
*Hiftory of Religion,* Number xii. p. 121, 128.
*Chriftian Magazine,* vol. i. p. 4, 6.

O 2          MACEDONIANS,

* This was a name given to a confeffion of faith enjoin'd upon the *Proteftants* after the death of *Luther,* by the Emperor *Charles* the Vth.  It was fo called, becaufe it was only to take place in the *Interim,* till a general council fhould decide all the points in queftion between the Catholics and Proteftants.

## M.

MACEDONIANS, A sect which arose in the fourth century; so called from Macedonius, Bishop of Constantinople. He considered the Holy Ghost as a Divine energy diffused throughout the universe, and not as a distinct person proceeding from the Father and the Son.

*Mosheim's Ecclef. Hist. vol. i. p. 346.*

MANICHEANS, A sect founded by one Manes or Manicheus, in the third century, and settled in many provinces. He was a Persian by birth, educated among the Magi, and himself one of the number before he embraced Christianity. His genius was vigorous and sublime, but redundant and ungoverned. He attempted a coalition of the doctrine of the Magi with the Christian system, or rather the explication of the one by the other: and in order to succeed in the enterprize, affirmed that Christ had left the doctrine of salvation imperfect and unfinished; and that he was the comforter whom the departing Saviour had promised to his diciples to lead them into all truth—The principles of Manes are comprehended in the following summary.

That there are two principles from which all things proceed: the one, a most *pure and subtle matter* called *Light*; and the other *a grofs and corrupt fubftance* called *Darkness:* Each of these are subject to the dominion of a superintending *Being*, whose existence is from all eternity: the *Being* who presides over the *Light* is called GOD; he that rules the *land of Darkness* bears the title of *Hyle*, or *Demon*. The *Ruler of the Light* is supremely happy, and in consequence thereof benevolent and good: the Prince

of

of Darkneſs is unhappy in himſelf, and deſiring to render others partakers of his miſery, is evil and malignant. Theſe two beings have produced an immenſe multitude of creatures, reſembling themſelves, and diſtributed them through their reſpective provinces.

The *Prince* of *Darkneſs* knew not for a long ſeries of ages, that *light* exiſted in the univerſe; and no ſooner perceived it by means of a war kindled in his dominions, than he bent his endeavours towards the ſubjecting it to his empire. *The Ruler of the Light* oppoſed to his efforts an army commanded by the *firſt man*, but not with the higheſt ſucceſs; for the Generals of the *Prince of Darkneſs*, ſeized upon a conſiderable portion of the celeſtial elements, and of the *light* itſelf, and mingled them in the maſs of corrupt matter. The ſecond General of *the Ruler of the Light*, whoſe name was the *Living Spirit*, made war with more ſucceſs againſt the *Prince of Darkneſs*, but could not entirely diſengage the pure particles of the celeſtial matters, from the corrupt maſs through which they had been diſperſed. The *Prince of Darkneſs* after his defeat, produced the firſt parents of the human race: the beings engendered from this original ſtock, conſiſt of a body formed out of the corrupt matter of the kingdom of *Darkneſs* and of two ſouls, one of which is *ſenſitive and luſtful*, and owes its exiſtence to the *evil principle*; the other *rational* and *immortal*, a particle of that Divine *light* which was carried away by the army of *Darkneſs*, and immerſed into the maſs of malignant matter.

Mankind being thus formed by the *Prince of Darkneſs*, and thoſe minds that were the productions of the eternal *Light*, being united to their mortal bodies,

bodies, God created the earth out of the corrupt mass of matter, by that *living Spirit* who had vanquished the *Prince of Darkness.* The design of this creation was to furnish a dwelling for the human race, to deliver by degrees the captive souls from their corporeal prisons, and to extract the celestial elements from the gross substance in which they were involved. In order to carry this design into execution, God produced *two Beings* of eminent dignity from his own substance, which were to lend their auspicious succours to imprisoned souls ; one of these sublime entities was *Christ*, and the other the *Holy-Ghost.* Christ is that glorious intelligence which the Persians called *Mythras* ; he is a most splendid substance, consisting of the brightness of the eternal *Light* : subsisting in and by himself : endowed with life ; enriched with infinite wisdom ; and his residence is in the Sun : *The Holy-Ghost* is also a luminous animated body, diffused through every part of the atmosphere, which surrounds this terrestrial globe　This *genial principal* warms and illuminates the minds of men, renders also the earth fruitful, and draws forth gradually from its bosom the latent particles of celestial fire, which it wafts upon high to their primitive station.

After that, the *Supreme Being* had, for a long time, admonished and exhorted the captive souls, by the ministry of the angels and holy men raised up and appointed for that purpose, he ordered Christ to leave the solar regions and to descend upon earth, in order to accelerate the return of those imprisoned spirits to their celestial country. In obedience to this Divine command, Christ appeared among the

Jews

Jews cloathed with the shadowy form of a human body, and not with the real substance. During his ministry, he taught mortals how to disengage the rational souls from the corrupt body, to conquer the violence of malignant matter, and he demonstrated his divine mission by stupendous miracles : on the other hand the *Prince of Darkness* used every method to inflame the Jews against this Divine messenger, and incited them at length to put him to death upon an ignominious cross; which punishment, however, he suffered not in reality, but only in appearance, and in the opinion of men. When Christ had fulfilled the purposes of his mission, he returned to his throne in the Sun, and appointed a certain number of chosen apostles to propagate through the world, the religion he had taught during the course of his ministry.

But before his departure he promised, that at a certain period of time, he would send an apostle superior to all others in eminence and dignity, whom he called the *Paraclete*, or *Comforter*, who should add many things to the precepts he had delivered, and dispel all the errors under which his servants laboured with respect to Divine things.——— This *Comforter* th s expresly promised by *Christ* is *Manes* the Persian, who by the order of the *Most High* declared to mortals the whole doctrine of salvation without exception, and without concealing any of its truths under the veil of metaphor, or any other covering.

Those souls who believe *Jesus Christ* to be the Son of GOD, renounce the worship of the God of the Jews, who is the Prince of *Darkness*, obey the laws delivered by Christ as they are enlarged and
illustrated

illuftrated by the Comforter, *Manes*, and combat with perfevering fortitude, the lufts and appetites of a corrupt nature, derive from this faith and obedience the ineftimable advantage of being gradually purified from the contagion of matter. The total purification of fouls cannot indeed be accomplifhed during this mortal life. Hence it is, that the fouls of men, after death, muft pafs through two ftates more of probation and trial, by *water* and *fire*, before they can afcend to the regions of *light*. They mount therefore firft into the Moon, which confifts of benign and *falutary water*; from whence, after a luftration of fifteen days, they proceed to the Sun, whofe purifying *fire* removes entirely all their corruption, and effaces all their ftains. The bodies, compofed of malignant matter which they have left behind them, return to their firft ftate, and enter into their original mafs.

On the other hand, thofe fouls who have neglected the falutary work of their purification, pafs, after death, into the bodies of animals or other natures, where they remain until they have expiated their guilt and accomplifhed their falvation.

Some, on account of their peculiar obftinacy and perverfenefs, pafs through a feverer courfe of trial, being delivered over, for a certain time, to the power of malignant ærial fpirits, who torment them in various ways. When the greateft part of the captive fouls are reftored to liberty and to the regions of light, then a devouring fire fhall break forth at the Divine command from the caverns in which it is at prefent confined, and fhall deftroy the frame of the world. After this tremendous event, the *Prince* and *Powers of Darknefs* fhall be forced to return to their primitive

mitive feats of anguish and misery, in which they shall dwell forever. For to prevent their ever renewing this war in the regions of *light*, GOD shall surround the mansions of *darkness* with an invincible guard, composed of those souls who have fallen irrecoverably from the hopes of salvation, and who set in array like a military band, shall surround those gloomy seats of woe, and hinder any of their wretched inhabitants from coming forth again to the *light*. *

To support their fundamental doctrine of two Principles, the Manicheans argue in this manner: If we depend only on one Almighty cause, *infinitely good* and *infinitely free*, who disposes universally of all beings, according to the pleasure of his will, we cannot account for the existence of *natural* and *moral evil*. If the author of our Being is supremely good, he will take continual pleasure in promoting the happiness of his creatures, and preventing every thing which can diminish or disturb their felicity. We cannot therefore explain the evils we experience but by the hypothesis of two Principles, for it is impossible to conceive that the first man could derive the faculty of doing ill from a good principle; since this faculty, and every thing which can produce evil is vicious, for evil cannot proceed but from a bad cause; and therefore the free-will of Adam was derived from *two opposite Principles*. He depended upon the *good Principle* for his power to

P

persevere

---

* To remove the strongest obstacles to this system Manes rejected the old Testament, the four Gospels, and the Acts of the Apostles, and said the Epistles of St. Paul were falsified in a variety of places. He wrote a Gospel which he pretended was dictated to him by God himself, and distinguished it by the title of Erteng.

perſevere in innocence ; but his power to deviate from virtue owed its riſe to an *evil Principle*. Hence it is evident there are *two* contrary Principles, the one the ſource of good, the other the fountain of all miſery and vice.

Manes commanded his followers to mortify and macerate the body, which he looked upon as *eſſentially corrupt* ; to deprive it of all thoſe objects which could contribute either to its conveniency or delight ; to extirpate all thoſe deſires which lead to the purſuit of external objects ; and to diveſt themſelves of all the paſſions and inſtincts of nature. But he did not impoſe this ſevere manner of living, without diſtinction upon his adherents, he divided his diſciples into two claſſes ; the one of which comprehended the perfect Chriſtians under the name of the Elect ; and the other the imperfect and feeble, under the title of Hearers. The Elect were obliged to an entire abſtinence from fleſh, eggs, milk, fiſh, wine, all intoxicating drink, wedlock, and all amorous gratifications ; and to live in a ſtate of the ſharpeſt penury, nouriſhing their ematiated bodies with bread, herbs, pulſe, and melons. The diſcipline appointed for the Hearers, was of a milder nature : They were allowed to poſſeſs houſes, lands and wealth, to feed upon fleſh, to enter into the bonds of conjugal tenderneſs ; but this liberty was granted them with many limitations, and under the ſtricteſt conditions of moderation and temperance.

The General Aſſembly of the Manicheans was headed by a Preſident, who repreſented JESUS CHRIST. There were joined to him *twelve rulers,* or *maſters,* who were deſigned to repreſent the *twelve apoſtles ;*

*apoſtles*; and theſe were followed by *ſeventy-two Bi-ſhops*, the images of the *ſeventy-two diſciples* of our Lord. Theſe Biſhops had *Preſbyters* and *Deacons* under them ; and all the members of theſe religious orders were choſen out of the claſs of the *Elect*.

*Moſheim's Ecclef. Hiſt vol. i. p 239—245.*
*Bayle's Hiſtorical Dictionary vol. iv p 2487. 2489.*

**MARCELLIANS,** A ſect in the fourth century; ſo called from Marcellus, who held the ſentiments of the Sabellians. [See Sabellians]

*Bayley's Dictionary. [See Marcellaniſm]*

**MARCIONITES,** So called from Marcion, a diſciple of Cerdo. [For an account of their ſentiments, ſee Cerdonians]

**MARCOSIANS,** A branch of Gnoſtics in the ſecond century ; their leaders were Marc and Colobarſus.

They taught, that the ſupreme God did not conſiſt of a Trinity but a Quaternity, to wit, the Ineffable, Silence, the Father, and Truth. They held two Principles, denied the reality of Chriſt's ſufferings, and the reſurrection of the body : Their doctrine concerning the Æons was the ſame with the Valentinians. [See Valentinians]

Marc maintained that the *plenitude* and *perfection* of Truth reſided in the Greek *Alphabet* ; and alledged *that* as the reaſon why JESUS CHRIST was called the *Alpha* and *Omega*.

*Moſheim's Eccleſiaſtical Hiſtory, vol. i p. 188.*
*Broughton's Hiſtorical Library, vol. ii. p. 48.*

**MARONITES,** Certain Eaſtern Chriſtians, who inhabit near MountLibanus, in Syria. The name is



derived

derived either from a town in the country called Maronia, or from St. Maron, who built a monaſtry there in the fifth century.

This ſect retained the opinions of the Monothelites until the twelfth century, when abandoning and renouncing the doctrine of *one will* in CHRIST, they were re-admited in the year 1182, to the communion of the Roman church.

As to the particular tenets of the Maronites, before their reconciliation to the church of Rome, they obſerved Saturday as well as the Sabbath ; and held, that all ſouls were created together, and that thoſe of good men do not enter into Heaven till after the reſurrection ; they added other opinions which were ſimilar to the Greek Church. [See Greek Church]

*Broughton's Hiſtorical Library, vol.* ii. *p.* 51.<br>*Moſheim's Eccleſiaſtical Hiſtory, vol.* ii *p* 37.

MASSALIANS, A ſect which aroſe in the fourth century. They derived their name from a Hebrew word ſignifying *prayer,* it being their diſtinguiſhing tenet, that a man is to *pray without ceaſing,* in the literal ſenſe of the words.

Hereupon they ſhunned not only the ſociety of other men, but renounced all the exterior part of religion, the uſage of the ſacraments and the faſts ; dwelt with their wives and children in the woods, and foreſts, that they might wait ſolely and continually on prayer. They imagined, that two ſouls reſided in man, the one *good* the other *evil* ; and taught, that it was impoſſible to expel the *evil dæmon* by any other means than by conſtant prayer and ſinging of hymns : and that, when this malignant
ſpirit

spirit was caft out the *pure mind* returned to GOD, and was again united to the *Divine effence* from whence it had been feparated. They boafted of having perpetual revelations and vifions, and thefe they expected particularly in the night. They added many opinions which bear a manifeft refemblance to the Manichean fyftem, and are derived from the fame fource, even from the tenets of the *Oriental philofophy.* The authors of this denomination were certain Monks of Mefopotamia.

*Mofheim's Ecclefiaftical Hift. vol.* i *p.* 350, 351,
*Formey's Ecclef. Hift. vol.* i *p.* 82.
*Hift of Religion. vol.* iv [*See Maffalians*]
*Bayley's Dictionary vol.* ii [*See Maffalians*]

**MELCHITES,** The Syrian, Egyptian, and other Eaftern Chriftians in the Levant; who, tho' they are not Greeks, follow the doctrines of the Greek Church, except in fome few points which relate only to ceremonies and ecclefiaftical difcipline. They were called Melchites, i. e. Royalifts, by their adverfaries by way of reproach, on account of their implicit fubmiffion to the edict of the Emperor Marcion, in favour of the council of Chalcedon.

*Mofheim's Ecclef. Hift. vol.* ii *p* 31.
*Collier's Hiftorical Dictionary, vol.* ii. [*See Melchite*]

**MELECIANS,** A fect in the fourth century, fo called from their leader Melecias, Bifhop of Lycopolis in Egypt.

This Prelate declared with great zeal againft thofe *Chriftians,* who, having apoftatized, defired to be reconciled to the *Church*; and would not have thofe admitted to repentance who fell into *fin,* though their contrition was ever fo great.

The

The Melecians faftened little bells to the bottom of their garments, and fung their prayers, dancing all the time; and this they thought a fure means to appeafe the wrath of God.

Broughton's Hiftorical Library, vol. ii. p. 547.<br>Chevreau's, Hift. vol. iii p 98.

**MELCHIZEDICHIANS,** A feƈt which arofe about the beginning of the third century; and affirmed, that Melchizedek was not a man, but a heavenly power fuperior to Jefus Chrift : for Melchizedek, they faid, was the interceffor and mediator of the angels, and Jefus Chrift was only fo for men, and his priefthood only a copy of that of Melchizedek.

This denomination was revived in Egypt by one Hierax. [See Hieracites]

Dictionary of Art: and Sciences, vol. iii. p. 2049.

**MELATONI,** So called from one Mileto; who taught, that not the foul, but the body of man, was made after GOD's image.

Rofs's View of all Religions, p. 211.

**MENANDERIANS,** A feƈt in the firft century; fo called from Menander, a difciple of Simon Magus.

He pretended to be one of the *Æons* fent from the *Pleroma,* or celeftial regions, to fuccour the fouls that lay groaning under bodily oppreffion and fervitude, and to maintain them againft the violence and ftratagems of the *dæmons* that hold the reins of empire in this fublunary world. He baptized his difciples in his own name; and promifed them after this baptifm a more eafy viƈtory over the evil fpirits; and that, after this life, they fhould become partakers of the refurreƈtion of the dead, and of immortality.

Mofheim's Ecclef Hift. vol. i. p. 116.<br>Formy's Ecclef. Hift vol. i. p. 21.

**MENNONITES,**

MENNONITES, A fociety of *Baptifts*, in Holland ; fo called from Mennon Simonis, of Friezland, who lived in the fixteenth century.

It is a univerfal maxim of this denomination, that practical piety is the effence of religion, and that the fureft mark of the *true church* is the fanctity of its members : they all unite in pleading for toleration in religion, and debar none from their affemblies who lead pious lives and own the fcriptures for the word of GOD. They teach, that infants are not the proper fubjects of baptifm, and that minifters of the gofpel ought to receive no falary, and that it is not lawful to fwear or wage war upon any occafion. They alfo maintain, that the terms Perfon and Trinity are not to be ufed in fpeaking of the Father, Son, and Holy Ghoft.

The Mennonites meet privately, and every one in the affembly has the liberty to fpeak, to expound the fcriptures, to pray and fing. They affemble twice every year from all parts of Holland, at Rynfbourg, a village about two leagues from Leyden, at which time they receive the communion fitting at a table, where the firft diftributes to the reft ; and all fects are admitted, even the *Roman Catholics* if they pleafe to come.

The ancient Mennonites profeffed a contempt of erudition and fcience : and excluded all from their communion who deviated, in the leaft, from the moft rigorous rules of fimplicity and gravity in their looks, their geftures, their cloathing, or their table. But this primitive aufterity is greatly diminifhed in the moft confiderable fects of the Mennonites. Thofe who adhere to their ancient difcipline are called Flemings or Flandrians.

The

The Mennonites in Pennsylvania do not bap*ize by immersion, though they administer the ordinance to none but adult persons. Their common method is this—the person to be baptized kneels; the minister holds his hands over him, into which the deacon pours water and through which it runs on the crown of the kneeling person's head; after which follow imposition of hands and prayer.

*Mosheim's Ecclef. Hist vol. iv. p. 151. 155. 162.*
*Dictionary of Arts and Sciences. vol. iii p. 3037.*
*Edwards' Hist. of the American Baptists, vol. i. p 94.*

**MEN OF UNDERSTANDING,** This title distinguished a sect which appeared in Flanders and Brussels in the year 1511. They owed their origin to an illiterate man whose name was Egidius Cantor, and to William of Hildenison, a Carmelite Monk. They pretended to be honoured with celestial visions, denied that any could arrive at perfect knowledge of the holy scriptures without the extraordinary succours of a Divine illumination; and declared the approach of a new revelation from Heaven, more perfect than the gospel of Christ: they said that the resurrection was accomplished in the person of Jesus, and no other was to be expected,—that the inward man was not defiled by the outward actions whatever they were,—that the pains of *Hell* were to have an end, and not only all mankind, but even the Devils themselves, were to return to GOD and be made partakers of eternal felicity.

They also taught among other things,

I. That CHRIST alone had merited eternal life and felicity for the human race, and that therefore men could not acquire this inestimable privilege by their own actions alone.

II. That

II. That the priefts to whom the people confeffed their tranfgreffions, had not the power of abfolving them, but this authority was vefted in CHRIST, alone.

III. That voluntary penance and mortification was not neceffary to falvation.

This denomination appear to have been a branch of the Brethren and Sifters of the Free Spirit.

*Mofheim's Ecclef. Hift. vol. iii. p. 276.*

## METANGONISTS. [See Hieracites]

METHODISTS, This name firft diftinguifhed a number of ftudents in Oxford College; who, in the year 1729, joined in a religious fociety, and agreed upon certain methods and rules for fpending their time in fafting, praying, communicating, vifiting the fick and the prifoners, inftructing the ignorant, &c. and hence they were called Methodifts.

The Rev. Mr. George Whitefield, a celebrated itinerant preacher, became the leader of this denomination: he was a profeffed member of the Church of England, and maintained the Calviniftical doctrines as expreffed in the articles of that church. In all his public difcourfes, he infifted largely on the neceffity of regeneration. He maintained that the form of ecclefiaftical worfhip and prayers, whether taken from the common prayer-book, or poured forth extempore, was a matter of indifference, and accordingly made ufe of both forms.

Another party of Methodifts embraced the opinions of the Rev. Mr. John Wefley, who warmly oppofed the Calviniftical doctrines of *election* and *final perfeverance.* He maintained that finlefs per-



fection

fection was attainable in this life : and to prove this point, afferted that Mat. v. 28. ought to be tranflated thus,—*Therefore ye fhall be perfect as your Father who is in Heaven is perfect.* He a'fo fupported this doctrine from 1ft of John, iii. 9 *Whofoever is born of GOD doth not commit fin ; for his feed abideth in him, and he cannot fin, becaufe he is born of GOD.*

This fociety obferve a love-feaft once a month. They have alfo a cuftom of keeping watch-nights, i. e. finging, and praying, and preaching, from eight o'clock to twelve. They have this fervice alfo once a month.

The Methodifts, in particular Mr. Whitefield's fociety, are at prefent very numerous in England. [See Appendix]

*Formey's Ecclef Hift vol ii. p. 262.*
*Gillie's Succefs of the Gofpel vol ii p. 52.*
*Whitefield's letters, vol. i. p. 211.*
*Wefley's Notes, vol. i. p. 33, vol. iii. p. 196.*

MILLENARIANS, or CHILIASTS, A name given to thofe who, in the primitive ages, believed that the faints will reign on earth with Jefus Chrift a thoufand years.

The former appellation is of Latin original, the latter of Greek, and both of the fame import.

The Millenarians hold, that after the coming of antichrift, and the deftruction of all nations which fhall follow, there fhall be a firft refurrection of the juft alone : that all who fhall be found upon earth, both good and bad, fhall continue alive ; the good to obey the juft who are rifen as their princes ; the bad to be conquered by the juft, and to be fubject to them : that Jefus Chrift will then defcend from Heaven in his glory : that the city of Jerufalem will

be

be rebuilt, enlarged, embelished, and its gates stand open night and day. They applied to this new Jerusalem what is said in the Apocalypse, chap xxi. and to the temple, all that is written in Ezekiel, xxxvi. Here they pretended Jesus Christ will fix the seat of his empire, and reign a thousand years with the saints, patriarchs and prophets, who will enjoy perfect and uninterrupted felicity.

The Millenarians were divided in opinion; some pretended that the saints should pass their time in corporeal delights; others that they should only exercise themselves in spiritual pleasures.

*Broughton's Historical Library, vol.* ii. *p.* 93 94.

MOLINISTS, So called from Lewis Molina, a Spanish Jesuit, Professor of Divinity in the University of Ebora in Portugal; who, in the year 1598, published a book to shew that the operations of *Divine grace* were entirely consistent with the *freedom* of the *human will*, and who introduced an hypothesis to remove the difficulties attending the doctrines of predestination and liberty.

He asserted, that the *decree* of predestination to eternal glory, was founded upon a previous knowledge and consideration of the merits of the elect; that the grace, from whose operations these *merits* are derived, is not efficacious by its own intrinsic power only, but also by the consent of our own will, and because it is administered in those circumstances in which the Deity, by that branch of his knowledge which is called *Scientia Media*, foresees that it will be efficacious. The kind of prescience, denominated in the schools *Scientia Media* is that foreknowledge of future contingents which arises from



an

an acquaintance with the nature and faculties of rational beings, of the circumſtances in which they ſhall be placed, of the objects that ſhall be preſented to them, and of the influence that theſe circumſtances and objects muſt have on their actions.

*Moſheim's Ecclef Hiſt. vol. l. p. 475. 476.*

**MONARCHIANS,** A ſect which aroſe in the ſecond century: they derived their origin from Praxeas, a man of genuis and learning. He denied any real diſtinction between the *Father, Son* and *Hoiy Ghoſt* ; and maintained, that the *Father*, ſole creator of all things, had united to himſelf the *human nature* of CHRIST. Hence his followers were called Monarchians.

This ſect were alſo ſtiled Patropaſſians.

*Moſheim. ibid, vol. 1, p. 190.*

**MONOPHYSITES,** A ſect which aroſe in the fifth century. They maintained that the *divine* and *human nature* of CHRIST were ſo united as to form only *one nature*, yet without any *change, confuſion,* or mixture of the two natures.

*Moſheim's ibid, p 420.*

**MONOTHELITES,** A ſect in the ſeventh century ; ſo called from the Greek words [mònòs] and [thèlòs] Their founder was Theodore, Biſhop of Pharan, in Arabia, who maintained the following doctrines :

I. That in CHRIST there were two diſtinct natures, which were ſo united, though without the leaſt mixture or confuſion, as to form by their union only one perſon.

II. That

II.   That the foul of Chrift was endowed with a will or faculty of volition, which it ftill retained after its union with the divine  nature.

For they taught that CHRIST was not only perfect GOD, but was endowed  with the faculty of volition.

III.   That this faculty of volition in  the foul of CHRIST, was not abfolutely unactive, but that it co-operated with the divine will.

IV.  That,  in  a  certain  fenfe, there  was in CHRIST but one will and one manner of operation.

*Mofheim's Ecclef. Hift. vol. ii. p  36.*
*Broughton's Hiftorical Library, vol. ii. p. 123.*

MONTANISTS, A fect which arofe in the  fecond century ;  fo called  from Montanus, who pretended, that he was  the *Paraclete*, or Comforter,* which the divine Saviour at his departure from earth, promifed to fend to his difciples to  lead them to all truth ;  and declared  that he was fent  with a divine commiffion  to give to the moral precepts delivered by Chrift and his apoftles the finifhing *touch* that was to bring them to perfection.  He was of opinion, that Chrift and his apoftles made, in their precepts, many allowances to the infirmities of thofe among whom they lived, and that this condefcending indulgence rendered their fyftem of moral laws imperfect and incomplete.  He therefore inculcated
the

* Montanus made a diftinction between the *Paraclete* promifed by *Chrift* to his apoftles, and the *Holy Spirit*, which was fhed upon them on the day of Penticoft, and u derftood by the former, a divine teacher pointed out by *Chrift* under the name of *Paraclete*, or Comforter, who was to perfect the gofpel by the addition of fome doctrines omitted by our Saviour.  It was this divine meffenger which Montanus pretended to be, and not the *Holy Ghoft*.

the neceffity of multiplying fafts ; prohibited fecond marriages as unlawful ; maintained that the church fhould refufe abfolution to thofe who had fallen into the commiffion of enormous fins ; and condemned all care of the body, efpecially all nicety of drefs, and all female ornaments. He alfo gave it as his opinion, that philofophy, arts, and whatfoever favoured of polite literature, fhould be banifhed from the Chriftian church.

He looked upon thofe Chriftians as guilty of a moft heinous tranfgreffion, who faved their lives by flight, from the perfecuting fword, or who ranfomed them by money, from the hands of their cruel and mercenary judges.

This fect were firft called Cataphrygoans, from the place where they had their firft principal abode ; they were alfo ftiled Pepuzians, becaufe Montanus lived in a Phrygian village, called Pepuza.

Mofheim's Ecclef Hift. vol. i. p. 192. 193.<br>Formey's Ecclefiaftical Hiftory, vol. i. p. 48.

**MORAVIANS, A** name given to the followers of Nicolas Lewis, Count of Zinzendorf ; who in the year 1721, fettled at Bartholdorf, in Upper Lufatia. There he made profelytes of two or three Moravian families, and having engaged them to leave their country, received them at Bartholdorf. They were directed to build a houfe in a wood, about half a league from that village, where, in 1722, this people held their firft meeting.

This fociety encreafed fo faft, that in a few years they had an orphan houfe and other public buildings. An adjacent hill, called the Huth-Berg, gave the colonifts occafion to call this dwelling place Herenhuth ;

huth ; which may be interpreted, the guard, or protection of the Lord : hence this society are sometimes called Herrenhutters.

The following doctrines are maintained by this denomination, to which is added a short specimen of the arguments they make use of in defence of their sentiments :

I. That creation and sanctification ought not to be ascribed to the Father, Son and Holy Ghost ; but belongs principally to the Saviour : and to avoid idolatry, people ought to be taken from the *Father* and Holy Ghost ; and be first directed singly to Jesus, who is the appointed channel of the Deity.

For the essence of God, both Father, Son and Holy Ghost, is a depth so unfathomable, that in contemplating it we may ruin our intellectual faculties, and yet not be able to form one just expression concerning this mistery, yet we can have all the gifts and effects of their offices, through him who is daily agent between God and man.

II. That Christ has not conquered as God but as man, with precisely the same powers we have to that purpose.

For as his *Father* assisted him he assists us ; the only difference is, it *was his meat and drink to do the will of his Father who is in Heaven.*

III. That the law ought not to be preached under the gospel dispensation.

For Paul is very express, that the messengers of Christ are not appointed for the ministration of the letter, 2d of Cor. iii. 6. Therefore, the method of preaching the gospel is alone to be preferred.

IV. That

IV. That the children of God have not to combat with their own sins, but with the kingdom of corruption in the world.

For the *apostle* declares, that *sin is condemned in the flesh*. Rom. viii. 3 : and our marriage with it dissolved, through the body of Christ, the *Lamb of God*; who has undergone this conflict once for all, and instead of all.

The Moravians assert, that *faith* consists in a joyful persuasion of our interest in Christ, and our title to his purchased salvation.

They deny the *Calvinistical* doctrines of *particular redemption*, and *final perseverance*.

This denomination have established among themselves a sort of *discipline*, which closely unites them to one another, divides them into different *classes*, puts them under an entire dependence of their superiors, and confines them to certain exercises of devotion, and to the observing of different little rules.

The church at Herenhuth is so divided, that first the husbands, then the wives, then the widows, then the maids, then the young men, then the boys, then the girls, and lastly the little children, are in so many distinct classes : each of which is daily visited, the married men by a married man, the wives by a wife, and so of the rest. Each class has its director chosen by its members, and frequent particular assemblies are held in each class, and general ones by the whole society.

The members of each class are subdivided into people, who are *dead, awaked, ignorant, willing disciples, and disciples who have made a progress*. Proper assistance is given to each of these subdivisions ;

fions; but above all, great care is taken of thofe who are fpiritually dead.

The *Elder*, the *Co-elder*, the *Vice-elder*, fuperintend all the claffes. There are likewife Informers by office, fome of them known, fome kept fecret, befides many other employments, and titles too tedious to enumerate.

A great part of their worfhip confifts in finging: and their fongs are always a connected repetition of thofe matters which have been preached juft before.

At all hours, whether day or night, fome perfons of both fexes are appointed by rotation to pray for the fociety.

When the brethren perceive that the zeal of the fociety is declining, their devotion is revived by celebrating *agapes*, or *love-feafts*.

The cafting of lots is much practifed among them. They make ufe of it to learn the mind of the Lord.

TheElders have the fole right of making matches. No promife of marriage is of any validity without their confent.

This denomination affert, that they are defcended from the ancient ftock of the old Bohemian and Moravian brethren, who were a little church fixty years before the reformation, and fo remained without infringement till that time, retaining their particular ecclefiaftical difcipline, and their own Bifhops, Elders and Deacons.

Rimius's *Hiflory of the Moravians*, p. 16, 18, 19.
*Moravian Maxims*, p 18, 20. 44, 45, 67, 86.
*Zinzendorf's Sermons*, p. 200.
*Manual of Doctrine* p 9
*Gillie's Succefs of the Gofpel*, vol. ii. p. 66.
*Dickinfon's Letters*, p 169

R MUGGLETONIANS.

MUGGLETONIANS, A sect which arose in England about the year 1657 ; so denominated from their leader Lodowic Muggleton, a journeyman taylor ; who, with his associate Reeves, set up for great *prophets*, pretending, as it is said, to have an absolute power of saving and damning whom they pleased ; and giving out that they were the two last witnesses of GOD, who should appear before the end of the world.

They denied the doctrine of the *Trinity*, & affirmed, among other things, that GOD the Father, leaving the government of Heaven to Elias, came down and suffered upon earth in an human form.

*Dictionary of Arts and Sciences, vol.* iii. *p.* 2149.
*Collier's Historical Dictionary,* vol. iii. [*See Muggletonian.*]

MYSTICS, A sect which appeared in the third century, distinguished by their professing a *pure, sublime, and perfect devotion*, with an *entire disinterested love of GOD*, and by their aspiring to a state of passive contemplation.

The first promoters of these sentiments proceeded from the known doctrine of the *Platonic* school, that *the Divine nature was diffused through all human souls*, or in other words, that the *faculty of reason*, from which proceeds the health and vigor of the mind, was *an emanation from GOD into the human soul, and comprehended in it the principles and elements of all truth, human and divine.*

They denied that men could, by labour or study, excite this celestial flame in their breasts, and therefore they disapproved highly of the attempts of those who by definitions, abstract theorems, and profound speculations, endeavoured to form distinct notions of
truth,

truth, and to difcover its hidden nature. On the contrary, they maintained that *filence, tranquility, repofe* and *folitude*, accompanied with fuch acts of mortification as might tend to extenuate and exhauft the body, were the means by which the *hidden* and *internal word* was *excited* to produce its *latent virtues*, and to inftruct men in the knowledge of Divine things. For thus they reafoned :

They who behold, with a noble contempt, all human affairs, who turn away their eyes from terreftrial vanities, and fhut all the avenues of the outward fenfes againft the contagious influence of an outward world, muft neceffarily return to GOD, when the fpirit is thus difengaged from the impediments which prevent this happy union : and in this bleffed frame they not only enjoy inexpreffible raptures from their communion with the Supreme Being, but alfo are invefted with the ineftimable privilege of contemplating truth undifguifed in its native purity, while others behold it in a vitiated and delufive form.

The apoftle tells us, that *the fpirit makes interceffion for us,* &c. Now if the fpirit prays in us, we muft refign ourfelves to its motions, and be fwayed and guided by its impulfes by remaining in a ftate of mere inaction.

*Mofheim's Ecclef. Hift. vol.* i. *p.* 222, 223.
*Dictionary of Arts and Sciences, vol.* iii *p.* 2171.
*Hiftory of Religion, vol.* iv. [*See Myftics*]

# N

**N**AZAREANS, A name originally given to all Chriftians in general, on account that Jefus Chrift was of the city of Nazareth ; but afterwards

wards it was reftrained to a fect in the firft and fecond century, which blended Chriftianity and Judaifm together. They held, that CHRIST was born of a virgin, and was alfo in a *certain manner* united to the Divine nature. They refufed to abandon the ceremonies prefcribed by the law of *Mofes*, but were far from attempting to impofe the obfervance of thefe ceremonies upon the Gentile Chriftians.* They rejected alfo all thofe additions that were made to the Mofaic inftitutions by the Pharifees and Doctors of the law.

Like the Ebionites, this denomination made ufe of a gofpel which was called indifcriminately, the gofpel of the Nazarites or Hebrews †

*Mofheim's Ecclef. Hift. vol. i. p. 173.*
*Broughton's Hiftorical Library, vol. ii. p. 155.*

**NEONOMIANS,** So called from the Greek [neòs] *new*, and [nòmòs] *law*, fignifying a *new law*, becaufe this denomination maintain, that the gofpel is a *new law*, the condition whereof is imperfect, though fincere, and perfevering obedience.

*Chauncy's Neonomianifm Unmafked.*

**NESTORIANS,** A fect which arofe in the fifth century; fo called from Neftorius Bifhop of Conftantinople.

This denomination maintain, that the *union of Chrift's divinity* with his *humanity*, is an *union of will, operation* and *benevolence.* For the *Divine word* is

perfect

---

* In this refpect, as well as in fome others, this denomination diff:red from the Ebionites; for they received both the Old and New Teftament. [See Ebionites]

† This is fuppofed by fome to be the gofpel St. Paul refers to in Gal. i. 6.

perfect in his *nature* and *person*. The *human nature* united to him, is likewise a perfect *humanity* in its *nature* and *person :* neither of them is changed, or undergoes any alteration. Therefore there are two *persons* in *Jesus Christ,* and two *natures* united by one *operation* and *will.*

Nestorious asserted, that though the *Virgin Mary* was the mother of *Jesus Christ* as a man, yet she was not the mother of *GOD*, because no human creature could impart that to another which she did not possess herself.

The generality of *Christians* in the *Levant* go under this name.
*Bayley's Dictionary, vol* ii. [*See Nestorians*]<br>*Memoirs of Literature, vol.* v. *p.* 137.

**NICOLAITANS,** A sect in the first century ; so called from Nicolas, one of the first seven Deacons of Jerusalem.

They made no difference between ordinary meats and those offered to idols ; allowed a community of wives, and indulged themselves in all sensual pleasures without restraint.
*Dupin's Church History, vol.* i *. p.* 30.<br>*Broughton's Historical Library, vol.* ii. *p.* 170.

**NOETIANS,** A sect which arose in the third century, followers of Noetus, who pretended that he was another Moses sent by God ; and that his brother was a new Aaron.

He affirmed, that the supreme God, whom he called the *Father*, and considered as absolutely indivisible, united himself to the man CHRIST, whom he called the *Son*, and was born and crucified with him. From this opinion *Noetus* and his followers were

were diftinguifhed by the title of Patripaffions, i. e. perfons who believe that the fupreme Father of the univerfe, and not any other divine perfon had expiated the guilt of the human race.

*Mofheim's Ecclefiaftical Hiftory, vol. i. p. 246 247.*
*Broughton's Hiftorical Library, vol. ii. p. 172.*

**NOVATIONS,** A fect in the third century ; they derive their name from their founders, Novat and Novation ; the firft a Prieft of the church of Carthage, the other of that of Rome.

This denomination laid it down for a fundamental tenet, that the church of Chrift ought to be pure and free from every ftain ; and that the finner who had once fallen into any offence, could not again become a member of it, though they did not refufe him the hopes of eternal life.

Hence they looked upon every fociety which readmitted thofe to their communion, who after baptifm had fallen into heinous crimes, as unworthy the title of a Chriftian church.

They feparated from the Church of Rome, becaufe they admitted to communion thofe who had fallen off in time of perfecution, which opinion they founded on Heb. vi. 6. They obliged fuch as came over to them from the general body of Chriftians, to fubmit to baptifm a fecond time, as a neceffary preparation for entering into their fociety.

This denomination alfo condemned fecond marriages, and denied communion forever to fuch as after baptifm married a fecond time.

They

They affumed to themfelves the title of *Cathari*,
i. e: *the pure.*

*Formey's Ecclefiaftical Hiftory, vol.* i *p.* 64.
*Mofheim's ibid, vol.* i. *p* 250, 251.
*Hift. of Religion, vol.* iv. [*See Novatians*]
*Broughton's Hiftorical Library, vol.* ii. *p.* 173.

## O.

OPHITES, A fect which appeared in the
fecond century; whofe leader was called Euphrates.   They derive their name from their maintaining the following tenet, viz. That the ferpent
by which our firft parents were deceived, was either
Chrift himfelf, or Sophia, concealed under the form
of that animal : and in confequence of this opinion,
they offered a fubordinate kind of Divine worfhip to
a certain number of ferpents, which they nourifhed
and efteemed facred.

It is faid they kept a live ferpent in a kind of cage.
At certain times they opened the door, and called
the ferpent.   The animal came out, and mounting
upon the table, twined itfelf about fome loaves of
bread.   This bread they broke, and diftributed
among the company, who all kiffed the ferpent.
This they called their *Eucharift.*

Their other opinions were fimilar with the reft of
the Egyptian Gnoftics.      [See Gnoftics]

*Broughton, ibid. p.* 191.
*Mofheim's Ecclef. Hift. vol.* i. *p.* 189, 190.

ORIGINISTS, A denomination which appeared
in the third century, and derived their opinions from
the writings of Origen, a Prefbyter of Alexandria,
and a man of vaft and uncommon abilities, who
interpreted the Divine truths of religion according to
                                        the

the tenour of the Platonic philofophy : He alledged, that the fource of many evils lies in adhering to the literal and external part of fcripture ; and that the true meaning of the facred writers was to be fought in a myfterious and hidden fenfe, arifing from the nature of things themfelves.

The principal tenets afcribed to Origin, together with a few of the reafons made ufe of in their defence, are comprehended in the following fummary.

I. That there is a pre-exiftent ftate of human fouls.

For the nature of the foul is fuch as makes her capable of exifting eternally backward as well as forward : for her fpiritual effence, as fuch, makes it impoffible that fhe fhould either through age or violence be diffolved, fo that nothing is wanting to her exiftence but his good pleafure from whom all things proceed ; and if according to the Platonic fcheme, we affign the production of all things to the exuberant fullnefs of life in the Deity, which thro' the bleffed neceffity of his communicative nature empties itfelf into all poffibilities of being, as into fo many capable receptacles, we muft fuppofe her exiftence in a fenfe neceffary, and in a *degree* co-eternal with God.

II. That fouls were condemned to animate mortal bodies, in order to expiate faults they had committed in a pre-exiftent ftate.

For we may be affured from the infinite goodnefs of their Creator, that they were at firft joined to to the pureft matter,* and placed in thofe regions of
the

---

* Origin fuppofed that our fouls being incorporeal and invifible, always ftand in need of bodies fuitable to the nature of the places where they exift.

the universe which were most suitable to the purity of essence they then possessed : for that the souls of men are an order of essentially incorporate spirits, their deep immersioninto *terrestial matter*, the modification of all their operations by it, and the *heavenly body* promised in the gospel, as the highest perfection of our renewed nature, clearly evinces. Therefore, if our souls existed before they appeared inhabitants of the earth, they were placed in a purer element, and enjoyed far greater degrees of happiness, and certainly he, whose overflowing goodness brought them into existence, would not deprive them of their felicity, until, by their mutability, they rendered themselves less pure in the whole extent of their powers, and became disposed for the susception of such a degree of corporeal life as was exactly answerable to their present disposition of spirit : hence it was necessary that they should become terrestrial men.

III. That the *soul* of CHRIST was united to the *word* before the incarnation.*

For the scriptures teach us, that the *soul* of the Messiah was created before the beginning of the world : see Phillipians ii. 5, 6, 7. This text must be understood of Christ's human soul, because it is unusual to propound the Deity as an example of humility in scripture. Though the humanity of *Christ* was so God-like, he emptied himself of this fulness of life and glory *to take upon him the form of a servant*. It was this Messiah who conversed with the Patriarchs under a human form : it was he who appeared to Moses upon the holy Mount : it was he who spoke to the prophets under a visible appearance :

S                              ance :

* See this subject more fully illustrated in Dr. Watt's Glory of Christ.

ance : and it is he who will at laſt come in triumph upon the clouds, to reſtore, the univerſe to its primitive ſplendor and felicity.

IV. That at the reſurrection we ſhall be cloathed with etherial bodies.

For the elements of our terreſtrial compoſitions are ſuch as almoſt fatally entangle us in vice, paſſion and miſery : the purer the vehicle the ſoul is united with, the more perfect is her life and operations ; beſides, the Supreme Goodneſs, which made all things, aſſures us, he made all things beſt at firſt ; and therefore his recovery of us to our loſt happineſs, (which is the deſign of the goſpel) muſt reſtore us to our better bodies and happier habitations ; which is evident from 1ſt of Cor. xv. 49.—2d of Cor. v. 1. and other texts of ſcripture.

V. That after long periods of time, the damned ſhall be releaſed from their torments, and reſtored to a new ſtate of probation.

For the Deity has ſuch reſerves in his gracious providence, as will vindicate his ſovereign goodneſs and wiſdom from all diſparagement. Expiatory pains are a part of his adorable plan ; for this ſharper kind of favour has a righteous place in ſuch creatures as are by nature mutable. Though ſin has extinguiſhed or ſilenced the Divine life, it has not deſtroyed the faculties of reaſon and underſtanding, conſideration and memory, which will ſerve the life which is moſt powerful. If therefore the vigorous attraction of the ſenſual nature be abated by a ceaſeleſs pain, theſe powers may reſume the ſeeds of a better life and nature.

As

As in the material fyftem there is a gravitation of the lefs bodies towards the greater, there muft of neceffity be fomething analogous to this in the intellectual fyftem : and fince the fpirits created by GOD are *emanations and ftreams* from his own *abyfs of being* ; and as *felf-exiftent power* muft needs fubject all *beings to itfelf*, the Deity could not but imprefs upon their intimate natures and fubftances, a *central tendency* towards himfelf, an *effential principle* of *re-union* to their *great original.*

VI. That the earth, after her conflagration, fhall become habitable again, and be the manfion of men, and other animals, and that in eternal viciffitudes.

For it is thus exprefled in Ifaiah, *Behold I make new heavens and a new earth*, &c. and in Heb. i. 10, 11, 12, *Thou Lord in the beginning haft laid the foundations of the earth ; as a vefture fhalt thou change them and they fhalt be changed*, &c. Where there is only a change the fubftance is not deftroyed ; this change, being only as that of a garment worn out and decaying : *the fafhion of the world paffes away* like a turning fcene, to exhibit a frefh and new reprefentation of things ; and if only the prefent drefs and appearance of things goes off, the fubftance is fuppofed to remain entire.

*Mofheim's Ecclefiaftical Hift. vol.* i. *p.* 219, 225.
*Cudworth's Intellectual Syftem, vol* ii. *p.* 818.
*The Phœnix. vol.* i. *p.* 16, 17, 18, 28, 29, 31, 32,
46 47 49 50, 56 57.
*Cheyne's PhilofophicalPrinciples of Religion, p.* 47,84.
*Travels of Cyrus. p.* 235, 238.

OSIANDRIANS, A fect among the Lutherans, which was founded in the year 1550, by Andrew Ofiander, a celebratedGerman divine, whofe doctrine amounted to the following propofitions.

S 2                    I. That

I. That Chrift, confidered in his *human nature only*, could not by his obedience to the divine law obtain *juftification* and pardon for finners, neither can we be *juftified* before God by embracing and applying to ourfelves, through faith, the *righteoufnefs* and obedience of the *man* CHRIST. It is only through that eternal and *effential righteoufnefs* which dwells in Chrift *confidered as God*, and which refides in his divine nature, that is united to the human, that mankind can obtain compleat juftification.

II. That man becomes a partaker of this *divine righteoufnefs* by faith ; fince it is in confequence of this uniting principle that Chrift dwells in the heart of man, with his divine righteoufnefs ; now wherever this divine righteoufnefs dwells, *there* God can behold no fin, and therefore, when it is prefent with Chrift in the hearts of the regenerate, they are, on its account, confidered by the Deity as *righteous*, although they be finners. Moreover, this *divine* and *juftifying righteoufnefs* of Chrift, excites the faithful to the purfuit of holinefs, and to the practice of virtue.

Mofheim's Ecclefiaftical Hiftory, vol. iv p. 46.

OSSENIANS, A feɛt in the firft century, which taught, that faith may and ought to be diffembled.

Dufrefnoy's Chronological Tables, vol. ii. p. 195.

P.

PAPISTS, So called from their adhering to the Pope, whofe fupremacy is faid to have been eftablifhed in the eleventh century.

The word Pope is derived from the Greek of [papa] which fignifies a father ; hence he is ftiled the Father of the Church.        The

The principal points which distinguish the Papists from the Protestants, together with a few of the reasons they bring to support their sentiments, are comprised in the following summary:

I. That St. Peter was designed by Christ to be the head of the church; and the Bishops of Rome being his lineal successors, have the same apostolic authority; and that the *Roman church* is the *mother* and *mistress* of all *churches.*

For our Saviour declares, in Mat. xi. 18, *Thou art Peter, and upon this rock will I build my church:* Therefore the church is built upon Peter. *

A succession in the church is now necessary in the New Testament, as *Aaron* had his succession in the Old; but there can be no certain succession now shewed, but in the chair of St. *Peter*, at Rome: Therefore the Bishops of Rome are the true successors of *Peter*.

The church of the Old Testament was a figure of the church under the New; but they had a *High Priest* above the rest; therefore the *Pope* is superior to other Bishops.

II. That the *scriptures* are not sufficient without *traditions:* and that their approved *traditions* are of equal authority with the *scriptures*.

For there are divers books of canonical scripture lost; for mention is made of the books of Nathan and Gad, 1st of Chron. xxix, 29. And in 2d of
Chron.

* The general doctrine of the Church of *Rome*, is that Peter was not only appointed by our Saviour, the chief of the Apostles, and head of the Universal Church, but that after having been seven years Bishop at *Antioch* he came to *Rome*, where he was Bishop twenty-five years, and suffered martyrdom under the Emperor *Nero*.

Chron. ix. 29, of the books of Abijah and Iddo ;
and in the New Teftament Col. iv. 16, of the epiftle of Paul to the Laodiceans : all thofe books are
loft : therefore that part of fcripture which remain-
eth is not fufficient.

We are directed in 2d. of Theff. ii. 15, to
*keep the traditions which we have been taught, whe-
ther by word or by epiftle* ; therefore there are traditions of equal authority with the fcripture.

III. That the *Catholic Church* cannot poffibly
*err* : but is not only *infallible* in all things neceffary
to falvation, but alfo in any thing it impofeth and
commandeth, even if it is not contained in the word
of God.

For the *Church* has the fpirit of God to lead it
into all truth : *the gates of Hell fhall not prevail
againft it,* Mat. xi, 18. Chrift hath prayed for
the Church, that it might be *fanctified in the truth.*
The *Church is without fpot or wrinkle.* Eph. v. 27.
Therefore the *Church* cannot *err.*

IV. That there are feven facraments inftituted
by Jefus Chrift, viz. Baptifm, Eucharift, Confirmation, Penance, Extreme Unction, Orders, and
Marriage ; and that the facraments have power to
confer grace.

I. To prove that Confirmation, or impofition of
hands is a facrament, the Papifts argue from Acts
viii, 17. *They did lay their hands* upon *them, and
they received the Holy Ghoft.* This impofition of
hands, together with the prayers here fpecified, was,
no doubt, the facrament of Confirmation : for here

is an outward sign, and a spiritual grace ; therefore Confirmation is a sacrament.*

II. Penance includes in it, contrition and painful sorrow of heart, confession to the Priest, and satisfaction to GOD for our sins : and Christ instituted this sacrament when he breathed upon his apostles after his resurrection, and said unto them, *receive ye the Holy Ghost ; whose sins ye remit, are remitted ; whose sins ye retain, are retained* : John xx. 22. The faculty of the priesthood consisting in remitting of sins, is here bestowed upon the apostles and their successors ; therefore Penance is truly and properly a sacrament.

III. That Extreme Unction, or anointing the sick with oil is truly a sacrament, is evident from James v. 13. *Is any sick among you, let him call for the Elders of the church ; and let them pray over him, anointing him with oil in the name of the Lord.* Here is a remission of sins promised upon anointing the sick with oil ; therefore it is a sacrament.

IV. That Holy Orders is a sacrament appears from 1st of Tim. iv. 14. *Despise not the gift which was given thee, through prophecy, with the laying on of hands.* Holy Orders give grace by an external ceremony and work ; therefore Holy Orders is a sacrament.

V. That Marriage is a sacrament is evident from Eph. v. 32. *This is a great mystery.* Matrimony is
here

* The Church of Rome maintain, that Confirmation is that which makes us perfect Christians : the Priest administers this ceremony after Baptism, by striking consecrated oil and balm, in the manner of a cross upon the forehead of him who is to be confirmed ; and pronounces these words, I *sign thee with the sign of the cross,* and confirm the chrism of salvation in the name of the Father, Son and Holy Ghost.

here a fign of an holy thing reprefenting the conjunction of Chrift, and his church ; therefore it is a facrament.✝

VI. That in the mafs there is offered unto GOD
a true and propitiatory facrifice for the quick and
dead, and that in the facrament of the Eucharift,
under the forms of *bread* and *wine*, is *really* and *fub-
ftantially prefent* the *body and blood*, together with
the *foul and divinity* of our Lord Jefus Chrift : and
that there is a *converfion* made of the *whole fubftance*
of the *bread* into his *body*, and of the *wine* into his
*blood*, which is called *tranfubftantiation*.

For, fay they, Chrift, in the inftitution of this facrament, faid to his apoftles, *This is my body*: that
is, that which is contained under the form of this
*bread* is my very body, 1ft of Cor. x. 16. Chrift
transfigured his body marvelloufly on the Mount,
Mat. ix. therefore, he is able to exhibit his *body* under the forms of *bread* and *wine*.

VII. That the laymen and clergy not faying mafs,
fhall receive the Eucharift in one kind, that is, in
bread only ; and that it is not lawful for them to
communicate in both.

For it is faid, John vi. 57. *He that eateth me fhall
live by me.* But Chrift is eaten only under the form
of *bread* ; therefore under the form of *bread whole
Chrift is prefent.*

VIII. That there is a Purgatory, in which fouls
are cleanfed by *fire* before they can be received into
Heaven,

---

✝ Notwithftanding this, they enjoin the celebacy of the clergy,
and pretend it was enjoined upon them as the condition of their
ordination, even from the apoftolic age.

Heaven, and that souls kept prisoners there, do receive help by the suffrages of the faithful.*

For it is said in 1st. of Cor. iii. 15. *If any man's work shall be burned, he shall suffer loss ; but he himself shall be saved ; yet so as by fire :* which, say they, may be understood of the flames of *Purgatory.*

IX. That the saints reigning together with Christ are to be worshipped and prayed unto ; and that they do offer prayers unto GOD for us, and their relics are to be had in veneration.

For there are certain examples in the scriptures of the adoration of *angels,* as Abraham, Lot, and Joshua adored the *angels* that appeared unto them : therefore *angels,* and consequently *saints,* are to be worshipped and prayed unto.

Rev. v. 8. *The Elders are said to have golden vials full of odour, which are the prayers of the saints ;* therefore the *saints* in Heaven do pray for us.

X. That the *images* of Christ, of the blessed Virgin the mother of GOD, and of other saints, ought to be retained in churches, and honor and veneration ought to be given unto them.†

For, the *images* of *cherubims* were allowed in the temple ; therefore *images* should be placed in churches, and had in veneration.

XI. That the *Pastors* of the *church* have power to dispense the virtues and sufferings of the *saints,*

T                    and

---

* The Papists suppose that souls are released from Purgatory by the masses and prayers of the clergy, who are liberally rewarded for those performances.

† Not, say they, because there is any virtue in images, but because Christ and his saints are worshipped by them, whose similitude they bear.

and thereby to abfolve from all *fins*, and the punifhment of *fins*; to grant indulgencies, difpenfe with
oaths, vows, laws, &c.

This opinion the Papifts found on a notion, that
our Saviour has left an infinite treafure of merits, and
fupererogatory fatisfactions arifing from his own fufferings, and thofe of the blefled Virgin, and the reft
of the faints, and that the *guides of the church*, and
more efpecially the *Popes*, have power to apply this
treafure to the living by virtue of the *keys*, and to
the dead by way of fuffrage, to difcharge them from
their portion of punifhment, by taking as much merit out of this general treafure as they conceive the
debt requires, and offering it to the Deity. Mat. xiii.
18. *Whatfoever you loofe on earth, fhall be loofed in
Heaven*. Confequently the indulgence of the church
fets free from the punifhment of fin.

The following ceremonies, and many others too
tedious to enumerate, are practifed by the Church of
Rome in their religious worfhip.

I. They make ufe of the fign of the crofs in all
their facraments, to give us to underftand, that
they have their whole force, and efficacy from the
crofs.

II. Sprinkling holy water by the Prieft on folemn
days, is ufed likewife, by every one going in, or
coming out of a church.

III. The ceremony of blefling bells, is by the
Catholics called chriftening of them; becaufe the
name of fome faint is afcribed to them, by virtue
of whofe invocation they are prefented, in order that
they may obtain his favour and protection.

IV. They

IV. They keep a number of lamps and wax candles continually burning before the shrines and images of the saints.

V. They have a custom of bowing at the name of Jesus.

The Church of Rome observe a variety of holy days, as the festivals of Christ and his apostles, the festivals of the saints, &c.

For an account of the divisions among the Papists see Borignonists, Yansenists, Jesuits, Molinists, and Quietists.

For an account of the extent and present state of the *Roman Catholic* religion, see *Appendix*.

> *Willett's View of Popery p 51, 57, 70, 152, 165, 406 427, 439 465.*
> *Bingham's Works, vol. i. p. 153.*
> *Brent's Council of Trent, p. 806.*
> *Walch's History of the Popes, p 24.*
> *Hist. of Religion. Number vi p. 233, 238, 242.*
> *Pope Pius's Creed.*

PARMENIANITES. [See Donatists]

PASAGINIANS, A sect which arose in the twelfth century, known also by the name of the *Circumcised.* Their distinguishing tenets were as follow :

I. That the observation of the law of *Moses*, in every thing except the offering of sacrifices, was obligatory upon Christians ; in consequence of which, they circumcised their followers, abstained from those meats, the use of which was prohibited under the Mosaic œconomy, and celebrated the Jewish Sabbath.

II. That Christ was no more than the *first and purest creature of God.*

T 2

This

This denomination had the utmost aversion to the doctrine and discipline of the Church of Rome.

*Mosheim's Ecclef Hift. vol. ii. p. 456.*

PASSALORYNCHITES, A branch of the *Montanifts*. They held, that in order to be faved, it was neceffary to obferve a perpetual filence; wherefore they kept their finger conftantly upon their mouth, and dared not open it even to fay their prayers.

Their name is derived from the Greek [paffalòs] a *nail*, and [rin] a *noftril*; becaufe, when they carried their finger to their mouth, they touched their nofe.

*Broughton's Hiftorical Library, vol. ii. p. 224.*

PATRICIANS, A fect which arofe in the fecond century; fo called from *Patricius* their leader.

Their diftinguifhing tenet was, that the fubftance of the flefh is not the work of GOD but of the Devil: on which account they bore fuch hatred to their own bodies, as fometimes to kill themfelves.

*Bay's Dictionary, vol ii [fee Patricians]*

PATRIPASSIANS, [See Noetians and Monarchians]

PAULIANS, or PAULIANISTS, A fect which appeared in the third century; fo called from *Paul* of *Samofata*, Bifhop of Antioch.

He taught, that the *Son* and the *Holy Ghoft* exift in GOD in the fame manner, as the faculties of *reafon* and *activity* do in man: that CHRIST was born of a mere man; but that the *reafon* or *wifdom* of the Father defcended into him, and by him wrought

wrought miracles upon earth, and inſtructed the nations; and finally, that on account of this union of
the *Divine word* with the *man* JESUS, CHRIST
might, though improperly, be called GOD.

*Moſheim's Eccleſ. Hiſt. vol i. p. 248.*

PAULICIANS, A ſect formed in the ſeventh
century, by two brothers, Paul and John, inhabitants of Jeruſalem; from the former of whom they
derive their name. The tenets attributed to this
ſect are as follow :

I. That the inferior and viſible world is not the
production of the *Supreme Being.*

II. That the *evil principle* was engendered by
*darkneſs* and *fire*; not ſelf-originated and eternal.*

III. That though Chriſt was the Son of *Mary*,
he brought from Heaven his human nature.

IV. That Chriſt was cloathed with an etherial,
celeſtial and impaſſible body, and did not *really* expire
on the croſs; hence they refuſed to pay religious
homage to the croſs.

V. That the bread and wine which Chriſt is
ſaid to have adminiſterèd to his diſciples at his laſt
ſupper, only ſignifies the divine diſcourſes and exhortations of the Saviour, which are a ſpiritual food
and nouriſhment to the ſoul, and fill it with repoſe,
ſatisfaction and delight. Hence they refuſed to celebrate the inſtitution of the Lord's ſupper.

VI. They rejected the books of the old Teſtament, and looked upon its writers as inſpired by
the

* They conſidered eternal matter as the ſource of all evil; and
believed that this matter, endued from all eternity with life and
motion, had produced an active principle; which is the fountain
of vice, miſery and diſorder; and is the author of all material
ſubſtances, while GOD is the Creator and Father of Spirits.

the *Creator of the world,* and not by the *supreme God* : They received all the books of the new Testament, except the epistles of St. *Peter,* which they rejected for reasons unknown to us.

This denomination had not, like the Manichæans, an ecclesiastical government administered by Bishops, Priests and Deacons : they had no sacred order of men distinguished by their manner of life, their habit, or any other circumstance from the rest of the assembly : nor had Councils, Synods, or such like institutions, any place in their religious policy. They had certain Doctors whom they called *Sunecdemi,* i. e. companions in the journey of life ; and also *Notarii.* Among these there reigned a perfect equality, and they had no peculiar rights, privileges, nor any external mark of dignity to distinguish them from the people. The only singularity which attended their promotion to the rank of Doctors was, that they changed their lay-names for scripture ones, as if there had been something peculiarly venerable in the names of holy men, whose lives and actions are recorded in the sacred writings.

For the arguments this sect make use of to support their doctrine of *two principles,*—see Manicheans.

Mosheim's Ecclesiastical History, vol. ii p. 175, 176.

**PELAGIANS,** A sect which arose in the fifth century ; so called from Pelagius, a Monk, who looked upon the doctrines which were commonly received concerning the *original corruption of human nature,* and the necessity of *divine grace to enlighten the understanding and purify the heart,* as prejudicial to the progress of holiness and virtue, and tending to establish mankind in a presumptuous and fatal security. He maintained the following doctrines :

1. That

I.   That the fins of our *firft parents* were imputed to them alone, and not to their pofterity ; and
that we derive no corruption from their fall, but are
born as pure and unfpotted as Adam came out of
the forming hand of his Creator.

II.   That mankind therefore are capable of repentance and amendment, and of arriving to the
higheft degrees of piety and virtue by the ufe of their
natural faculties and powers ; that indeed *external
grace* is neceffary to excite their endeavours, but
that they have no need of the internal fuccours of
the divine fpirit.

III.   That Adam was by nature, mortal ; and
whether he had finned or not, would certainly have
died.

IV.   That the grace of God is given in proportion to our merits.

V.   That mankind may arrive at a ftate of perfection in this life.

VI.   That the law qualified men for the kingdom of Heaven, and was founded upon equal promifes with the gofpel.

*Mofheim's Ecclef. Hift. vol.* i. *p* 412.
*Dictionary of Arts and Sciences, vol.* iii. *p.* 2378.

PEPUZIANS,   [See Montanifts]

PETROBRUSSIANS,  A fect which was formed
about the year 1110 in Languedoc and Provence,
by Peter de Bruys, who taught the following doctrines :

I.   That no perfons whatever were to be baptized before they came to the full ufe of their reafon.

II. That

II. That it was an idle fuperftition to build churches for the fervice of God, who will accept of a fincere worfhip, wherever it is offered ; and that therefore fuch churches as had already been erected, were to be pulled down and deftroyed.

III. That the crucifixes deferved the fame fate.

IV. That the real body and blood of Chrift were not exhibited in the Euchariſt, but were only reprefented in that holy ordinance, by their figures and fymbols.

V. That the oblations, prayers, and good works of the living, could be in no refpect advantageous to the dead.

*Moſheim's Ecclef. Hiſt. vol.* ii *p* 446. 447.

**PHILADELPHIAN-SOCIETY,** The followers of Jane Leadly, who, towards the conclufion of the feventeenth century, by her vifions, predictions and doctrines, gained a confiderable number of difciples ; among whom were fome perfons of learning. This woman was of opinion, that all diffentions among Chriftians would ceafe, and the kingdom of the Redeemer become even here below, a glorious fcene of charity, concord and felicity, if thofe who bear the name of JESUS, without regarding the forms of doctrine and difcipline, which diftinguifh particular communions, would all join in commiting their fouls to the care of this internal guide, to be inftructed, governed and formed by his divine impulfe and fuggeftions. She went ftill further, and declared in the name of the Lord, that this defirable event would happen ; and that fhe had a divine commiffion to proclaim the approach of this glorious communion of faints, who were to be gathered
together

together in one vifible univerfal church, or kingdom, before the diffolution of this earthly globe.
This prediction fhe delivered with a peculiar degree
of confidence, from a notion that her *Philadelphian-
Society* was the true kingdom of CHRIST, in which
alone the Divine fpirit refided and reigned.. She alfo
maintained the final reftoration of *all intelligent beings* to perfection and happinefs.

*Mofheim. ibid, vol.* v. *p.* 66, 67.

PHOTINIANS, A fect in the fourth century ; fo
called from Photinus, Bifhop of Sirmich, in Panno-
nia.

He taught, that JESUS CHRIST was born of the
HOLY GHOST, and the Virgin Mary ; that a
certain *divine emanation*, or ray, (which he called
the word) defcended upon this extraordinary man ;
that on account of the union of the *Divine word*
with his *human nature*, JESUS was called the Son
of GOD, nay, GOD himfelf ; and that the Holy
Ghoft was not a diftinct perfon, but a celeftial *virtue* proceeding from the *Deity*.

*Mofheim's Ecclef. Hift. vol.* i. *p.* 346.
*Broughton's Hiftorical Library, vol.* ii. *p.* 441.

PICARDS. [See Adamites]

PIETISTS, A denomination in the feventeenth
century, which owed its origin to the pious and learned Spenfer, who formed private focieties at Franc-
fort, in order to promote vital religion. His followers laid it down as an effential maxim, that none
fhould be admitted into the miniftry, but fuch as had
received a proper education, were diftinguifhed by
their wifdom and fanctity of manners, and had



hearts

hearts filled with *Divine love*.　Hence they propo-
fed an alteration of the fchools of divinity, which
confifted in the following points.

I. That the fyftematical theology, which reigned
in the academies, and was compofed of intricate and
difputable doctrines, and obfcure and unufual forms
of expreffions, fhould be totally abolifhed.

II. That polemical divinity, which comprehended the controverfies fubfifting between Chriftians of
different communions, fhould be lefs eagerly ftudied,
and lefs frequently treated, though not entirely neglected.

III. That all mixture of philofophy and human
learning with Divine wifdom, was to be moft carefully avoided.

IV. That on the contrary, all thofe who were defigned for the miniftry fhould be accuftomed from
their early youth, to the perufal and ftudy of the
*holy fcriptures*, and be taught a plain fyftem of theology, drawn from thefe unerring fources of truth.

V. That the whole courfe of their education was
to be fo directed as to render them ufeful in life, by
the practical power of their doctrine, and the commanding influence of their example.

*Mofheim's Ecclefiaftical Hiftory, vol. iv. p. 454 460.*

PREDESTINARIANS, A name given to thofe
in the ninth century who followed the doctrines of
Godefcalcus, a German Monk, whofe fentiments
were as follow :

I. That the Deity predeftinated a certain number
to falvation, and others to deftruction, before the
world was formed,

II.　That

II. That GOD predestinated the wicked to eternal punishment, in consequence of their sins, which were freely committed and eternally foreseen.

III. That Christ came not to save all men; and that none shall perish for whom he *shed his blood.*

IV. That since the Fall mankind cannot exercise *free will*, only to do that which is evil.

*Mosheim's Ecclef. Hist vol. ii p 159.*
*Ecclesiastical History of France p. 63.*
*Baxter's Church History. chap. x p. 263.*

PRESBYTERIANS, From the Greek of [présbutéiós] a denomination of *Protestants*; so called from their maintaining that the government of the church, appointed by the New-Testament, was by Presbyteries, that is, by Presbyters and ruling Elders, associated for its government and discipline. The Presbyterians affirm that there is no order in the church, as established by Christ and his apostles, superior to that of Presbyters; that all Ministers, being Ambassadors, are equal by their commission; and the Elder or Presbyter, and Bishop, are the same in name and office; for which they alledge Acts xx. 28. Titus i. 5, 7, &c. Their highest assembly is a Synod, which may be provincial, national, or œcumenical, and they allow of appeals from inferior to superior assemblies, according to Acts xv. 4, 6, &c. The lowest of their Assemblies, or Presbyteries, consists of the Ministers and Elders of a congregation, who have power to cite before them any member, and to admonish, instruct, rebuke, and suspend him from the Lord's table. They have also a Deacon, whose office it is to take care of the poor. Their ordination is by prayer, fasting, and imposition of the hands of the Presbytery.

U 2                    This

This is now the difcipline of the Church of Scotland. [See Appendix]

Collier's Hiftorical Dictionary. vol. ii [See Prefbyterians]
Barclay's Dictionary [See Prefbyterians]

PRIMIANISTS, A party of Donatifts ; fo called from Primianus, who became the head of their fect. [See Donatifts]

PRISCILLIANISTS, A fect which arofe in the fourth century ; fo called from their leader Prifcillian, a Spaniard by birth, and Bifhop of Avila.

He is faid to have practifed magic, and to have maintained the principal tenets of the Manichæans. His followers denied the reality of CHRIST's birth and incarnation : held that the vifible univerfe was not the production of the *Supreme Deity*, but of fome *dæmon* or malignant principle : adopted the doctrine of *Æons*, or emanations from the Divine nature : confidered human bodies as prifons formed by the author of evil to enflave celeftial minds : condemned marriage, and difbelieved the refurrection of the body. [See Manichæans]

Mofheim's Ecclef. Hift vol. i. p 349.

PROCLIANITES, So called from Proculus, a philofopher of Phrygia, who appeared 194, and put himfelf at the head of a band of Montanifts, in order to fpread the fentiments of that fect ; to which he added, that St. Paul was not the author of the epiftle to the Hebrews.

The doctrine which his followers maintained with the greateft warmth was, that Jefus Chrift affumed our nature only in appearance. [See Montanifts and Valentinians]

Broughton's Hiftorical Library. vol. ii. p. 285.

PROTESTANTS,

PROTESTANTS, A name firſt given in Ger+ many to thoſe who adhered to the doctrine of Luther; becauſe in 1529 they proteſted againſt a decree of the Emperor Charles V. and the Diet of Spires;* declaring that they appealed to a General Council. The ſame name has alſo been given to the Calviniſts, and is now become a common denomination for a variety of ſects, which differ from the Church of Rome. [See Lutherans, Calviniſts, Arminians, &c.]

*Dictionary of Arts and Sciences, vol. iii. p 2578 2579.*
*Robertſon's Hiſtory of Charles V. vol. ii. p. 249 250.*

PSATYRIANS, A ſect of the Arians, in the Council of Arians, held in the year 360, maintained that the Son was not like the Father in will; that he was made of nothing, and that in God generation was not to be diſtinguiſh from creation. [See Arians]

*Hiſtory of Religion, vol. iv, See Pſatyrians.*

PTOLEMATTES, A branch of the Valentinians in the ſecond century; ſo called from Ptolemy, their leader; who held, that the law of Moſes came part from GOD, part from Moſes, and part from the traditions of the Doctors.

*Bayley's Dictionary, vol. ii. [See Ptolemattes]*

PURITANS, A name given to a party which appeared in England in the year 1565, and oppoſed the liturgy and ceremonies of the Church of England.

They acquired this denomination from their profeſſed deſign to eſtabliſh a purer form of worſhip and diſcipline.

Thoſe

* This Diet was held at Spires, (March 15, 1529) They decreed to prohibit any farther innovations in religion.

Thofe who were firft ftiled Puritans were Prefbyterians, but the term was afterwards applied to o-
thers who differed from the Church of England.

Thofe who feparated from the Church of England
were alfo ftiled Diffenters.

Neal's Hift. of the Puritans, vol. i. p 138<br>
Dictionary of Arts and Sciences vol iii p 2606.<br>
Bayley's Dictionary. vol. ii.    [See Puritan.]

## Q

QUAKERS, A religious fociety which began
to be diftinguifhed by this name in *England*,
where it firft took its rife about the middle of the
feventeenth century.

*George Fox* was the principal inftrument of
gathering this people into a religious fociety. The
appellation of Quakers, was affixed upon them early
by way of contempt. In their affemblies it fometimes happened that fome were fo ftruck with the
remembrance of their paft follies, and forgetfulnefs
of their condition; others fo deeply affected with
a fenfe of God's mercies to them, that they actually trembled and quaked. This name foon became general. *Friends*, or the *Friends of Truth*,
was the name they were commonly known by to
one another, which they borrow from primitive
example, 3d. of John i. 14, *Our Friends falute
thee*, &c.

The principal points maintained by the Quakers,
together with fome of the moft material reafons
they bring to fupport their fentiments, are comprehended in the following fummary.

I. That God has given to all men fufficient *light*,
which will work their falvation unlefs refifted; that

this

this *light* is not lefs univerfal than the feed of *fin,* and faves thofe who have not the outward means of falvation ; and that this *light* is a *divine principle,* in which God as Father, Son and Holy Spirit, dwells ; which the fcriptures call *Chrift within the hope of glory.*

To prove this point this denomination alledge, that according to this doctrine the mercy of God is excellently well exhibited, in that none are neceffarily excluded from his favour ; that his juftice is demonftrated, in that he condemns none, but fuch to whom he offered the means of falvation.

2d. That it agrees with the nature of the miniftry of *Chrift,* according to which the gofpel is to be preached to every creature.

3d. It magnifies the merits of *Chrift's* death, in that it not only accounts them fufficient to fave all, but declares them brought fo nigh unto all, as to put them in the neareft capacity of falvation.

4th. That it exalts the grace of God to whom it attributeth the fmalleft good actions. This grace faves all who do not refift its divine impulfes ; and whoever will carefully and ferioufly turn into himfelf, with a fincere defire to know and practice his duty, will not fail to find there a fufficient director, a ray from the fountain of light, illuminating his underftanding, and affifting him to diftinguifh good from evil.

II. That the fcriptures are not to be efteemed the principal ground of all truth and knowledge ; nor yet the primary rule of faith and manners ; neverthelefs, becaufe they give a true and faithful teftimony of the firft foundation, they are and may

be

be esteemed a secondary rule subordinate to the spirit, from whom they have all their excellence.

For the principal rule of Christians under the gospel is not an outward letter, but an inward spiritual law, engraven on the heart, *the law of the spirit of life, or the word is that which is nigh in the heart and in the mouth.* But the letter of the scripture is outward, and in itself a dead thing, a mere declaration of good things : therefore, it is not the principal rule of Christians.*

III. That immediate revelation is not ceased, *a measure of the spirit being given to every one.*

For the nature of the new covenant is thus expressed in Jerem. xxxi. 33, *For this is the covenant that I will make with the house of Israel, after those days, saith the Lord, I will put my laws into their minds, and write them in their hearts, and I will be to them a God, and they shall be to me a people.*

Where the law of God is put into the mind, and written in the heart, there the object of faith and revelation of the knowledge of God is *inward,* immediate, and objective.

But the law of God is put into the mind, and written in the heart of every true Christian, under the new covenant ; therefore, the object of faith and revelation of the knowledge of God, to every true Christian, is *inward, immediate, and objective.*

IV. That as by the *light or gift of God* all spiritual knowledge is received, those who have this gift ought to preach, though without human commission

or

---

* Yet this denomination maintain, that divine inward revelations neither do, nor ever can contradict the outward letter of scripture, or right and sound reason.

or literature ; and as they have freely received this holy gift, so ought they freely to give it : and that any one of a sober life, without diftinction of fex, is allowed to preach, when moved by the fpirit.

For it is clear, that women have prophesied and preached in the church, elfe had the faying of Joel been ill applied by Peter, Acts ii. 17. xvii 4. Paul fpeaks of women who laboured with him in the gofpel : and Philip had four daughters who prophefied. Male and female are *one in Chrift Jefus*, and he imparts his fpirit no lefs to one than to the other.

V. That all true and acceptable worfhip to GOD is offered by the *inward and immediate moving of his fpirit.*

For though we are to worfhip GOD always, yet as to the outward fignification thereof in prayer, praifes, or preaching, we ought to do it only when we are moved *by the fecret infpiration of th· fpirit of GOD in our hearts* ; for GOD is never wanting to move us thereunto, when need is, of which he himfelf is the only proper judge.   The duty of filent waiting on the Lord is ftrongly enforced in Rom. viii. 26, 27.[*]

VI. That water baptifm, and the Lord's fupper, were only commanded for a time.

For our Saviour obferved thefe ceremonies only to fhew in a vifible manner the myftical purification of

W

the

[*] This fociety do not plead for entirely filent meetings, but only for a retired waiting for the Divine aid, which alone qualifies to pray or preach.  They apprehend it their duty to be diligent in affembling themfelves together for the worfhip of *Almighty GOD*, when fuch as are duly prepared by being gathered into a compofed awful frame of mind, are enabled, under the influence of Divine grace, to worfhip in folemn filence ; or, if moved thereto, to pray or preach, as the fpirit giveth them utterance.

the foul, under the figure of *baptifm*, and the fpiritual nourifhment of the inward man under that of
the *Lord's fupper.*　　As there is one *faith*, fo there
is one *baptifm*, to wit, the *baptifm* of the *fpirit* and
fire, of which the *baptifm* of *John* was a figure, which
may be proved from the nature of it, as *John's baptifm* was with water ; but *Chrift's* is with the fpirit ;
therefore *John's baptifm* muft be a figure of *Chrift's* ;
and fince it is a figure, it ceafeth and giveth way to
the fubftance.　　The breaking of bread was ufed in
the church for a time for the fake of the weak, even
as the wafhing one another's feet, and anointing the
fick with oil ; all which are commanded with no
lefs authority than the former, yet they are all abolifhed, fince they are but fhadows of better things.

The moral doctrines of the Quakers are chiefly
comprehended in the following precepts :

1. That it is not lawful to give to men fuch flattering titles as, Your Grace, your Lordfhip, your
Honor, &c. nor ufe thofe flattering words commonly called compliments.

II. That it is not lawful for Chriftians to kneel
or proftrate themfelves to any man, or to bow the
body, or to uncover the head to them.

III. That it is not lawful for a Chriftian to ufe
fuch fuperfluities in apparel, as are of no ufe, fave
for ornament and vanity.

IV. That it is not lawful to ufe games, fports or
plays among Chriftians, under the notion of recrea-
tions, which do not agree with Chriftian gravity and
fobriety ; for laughing, fporting, gaming, mocking,
efting, vain talking, &c. are not Chriftian liberty,
nor harmlefs mirth.

V. That

V That it is not lawful for Chriftians to fwear at all under the gofpel, not only vainly, and in their common difcourfe, which was alfo forbidden under the law, but even not in judgment before the Magiſtrate.

VI. That it is not lawful for Chriftians to refift evil, or to war, or to fight in any cafe.

This denomination alledge, that the chief end of religion is to redeem man from the fpirit and vain converfation of the world, and to lead them into inward communion with GOD ; therefore, every thing ought to be rejected which waftes our precious time, and diverts the mind from the witnefs of *GOD* in the heart, and from the living fenfe of his fear, and that evangelical fpirit which is the ornament of Chriftians.

All fwearing, fay they, is forbidden by the words of our *Saviour*, Mat. v. 3?, 34. and the words of the apoftle, James v. 12. *Chriſt* reproved Peter for the ufe of the fword, and commands us to love our enemies ; but war, on the contrary, teacheth us to hate and deftroy them.

With regard to religious liberty, their fentiments are the fame with the *Baptiſts*. [See *Baptiſts*]

Where there are any *Quakers* they meet once a month, to confider of the neceffities of their poor, and provide for their relief ; to hear and determine complaints arifing from among themfelves ; to enquire into the converfation of their refpective members, in regard to morality, and conformity to their religious fentiments ; to allow the paffing of marriages ; and to enjoin a ftrict regard to the peace and good order of fociety ; the proper education of the young people, and a general attention to the principles and practices of their profession. In every country where there are monthly meetings, a meeting for similar purposes is held every quarter, and from these are deputed a number of their members once a year, to attend their annual Assembly at London. In this Assembly accounts are received of the state of the society in every part of the world where it exists; and such advices are sent to the subordinate meetings, as the particular or general state of the society requires.

[Vide Appendix]

*See History of the Quakers. p 6, 672.*
*Barclay's Apology for the Quakers p 5, 10, 11, 12, 31, 35.*
*Henn's Defence of Barclay's Apology p 6, 23, 27.*
*Benezet's Account of the Quakers. p 3, 11, 15.*
*Brief Account of the Quakers. p 3.*

QUARTODECIMANI, A sect in the second century; so called because they maintained, that the festival of Easter was always to be celebrated conformably to the custom of the *Jews*, on the fourteenth day of the moon of March, whatever day of the month that happened to be.

*Broughton's Historical Library, vol. ii   p. 307.*

QUIETISTS, The followers of Michael de Molinos, a Spanish Priest, who flourished in the seventeenth century. They were so called from a kind of absolute *rest* and inaction, which the soul is supposed to be in, when arrived at that state of perfection, which they call *the unitive life.*

The principles maintained by this denomination are as follow: That the whole of religion consists in the present *calm* and *tranquility* of a mind removed from all external and finite things, and centered

in

in God, and in such a *pure love* of the *supreme Being* as is independent on all prospect of interest or reward.

For, say they, the primitive disciples of *Christ* were all of them inward and spiritual ; and when *Jesus Christ* said to them, *It is expedient for you that I go away : for if I go not away the Comforter will not come unto you*, he intended thereby to draw them off from that which was sensible, though very holy ; and to prepare their hearts to receive the fullness of the *Holy Spirit*, which he looked upon as the *one thing necessary*.

To prove that our love to the Deity must be disinterested they alledge, that *the Lord bath made all things for himself*, as saith the scripture, and it is for his glory that he wills our happiness. Our happiness is only a subordinate end, which he has made relative to the last and great end, which is his glory. To conform therefore to the great end of our creation, we must prefer God to ourselves, and not desire our own happiness but for his glory ; otherwise we shall go contrary to his order. As the perfections of the Deity are intrinsically amiable, it is our glory and perfection to go out of ourselves, to be lost and absorbed in the pure love of *infinite beauty*. [See Mystics]

*Mosheim's Ecclef Hist vol.* iv *p* 388
*Broughton's Historical Library. vol* ii *p* 509.
*Cambray, on Pure Love. p* 131—138.
*Lady Guion's Letters. p.* 167.

**QUINTILIANS,** A sect which appeared in Phrygia, about the year 189. They derived their name from their prophetess Quintilia.

Their distinguishing tenet was, that women ought to be admitted to perform the sacerdotal and episcopal

episcopal functions, grounding their practice on that passage of St. Paul. Gal. iii. 28. *There is neither Jew nor Greek, there is neither male nor female.* They added, that Philip the Deacon, had four daughters, who were prophetesses, and were doubtless of their sect.

In their assemblies it was usual to see the virgins enter in white robes, personating prophetesses. This denomination was a branch of the Montanists. [See Montanists]

*Hiftory of Religion. vol* iv [*See Qui*·*tilians* ]
*Broughton's Hiftorical Library, vol* ii *p.* 310.

## R

RANTERS, A sect which arose in the year 1645. They set up the light of nature under the name of Christ in men. With regard to the *church, fcripture, miniftry, &c.* there sentiments were the same with the Seekers. [See Seekers]

*Callamy's Abridgment of Baxter's Hiftory vol.* i. *p.* 1015

REMONSTRANTS. [See Arminians]

ROGEREENS, So called from John Rogers their chief leader. They appeared in New-England, about the year 1677. The principal distinguishing tenet of this denomination was, that worship performed the first day of the week was a species of idolatry which they ought to oppose : in consequence of this, they used a variety of measures to disturb those who were assembled for public worship on the Lord's day.

*Backus's Hiftory, vol* i. *p* 473·.

ROMAN CATHOLICS, A name given to the Papists, because the Bishop of *Rome* is not only stiled

Supreme,

Supreme, but œcumenical or *universal Bishop*. [See Papists]

This Pontiff is likewise ftiled *Holinefs in the abstract, God's Vicegerent, Vicar o. Jefus Chrift, Succeffor of St Peter, Prince of the Apoftles, and Father of all the Kings of the earth.*

He wears three keys; one as an emblem of his power to give ablolution, or of admitting into the kingdom of Heaven; another to denote his power of excommunicating finners; and the third, with much ceremony is delivered unto him, to fignify and imply his univerfal knowledge and infalibility: And he wears a *triple crown*, to inform the Chriftian world that he is *Prieft*, *Emperor* and *King*.

An account of the gradual rife and progrefs of the *Papal authority* cannot be comprifed within the narrow limits of this work, the reader is therefore referred to *Mofheim, Formey*, and other ecclefiaftical hiftorians.

*Hift of Religion, vol. iv p. 130, 131.*

**ROSECRUCIANS,** A name given to thofe in the feventeenth century, who blended the doctrines of *Religion* with the fecrets of *Chymiftry*. Their fentiments were fimilar with thofe of the *Behmenifts*. [See Behmenifts]

*Mofheim's Ecclefiaftical Hiftory, vol. iv. p. 266.*

## S

**SABBATARIANS,** A branch of the Baptifts, who obferve the *Jewifh* or *Saturday Sabbath*, from a perfuafion that it was one of the ten commandments which they plead are all in their nature *moral*, and was never abrogated in the New-Teftament,

*Teflament*, and muft at leaft be deemed of equal validity for public worfhip, as any day never particularly fet apart by *Jefus Chrift* and his *apoftles.* *

*Hiftory of Religion vol iv. [See Sabbatarians]*
*Edwards's Hiftory of the American Baptifts, p. 60.*

SABELLIANS, A fect which arofe in the third century. They derived their name from Sabellius, an African Bifhop or Prefbyter; who taught, that there is but one perfon in the Godhead; and in confirmation of this doctrine, he made ufe of a comparifon. He faid, that, as man, though compofed of body and foul, is but one perfon; fo *God*, though he is *Father, Son* and *Holy Ghoft*, is but one perfon.

The Sabellians, upon their mafter's principles, made the *Word* and the *Holy Spirit* to be only virtues, emanations, or functions of the Deity; and held, that he who in Heaven, is the *Father* of all things, defcended into a Virgin, became a child, and was born of her as a *Son*; and that having accomplifhed the myftery of our falvation, he diffufed himfelf on the the *apoftles* in tongues of fire, and then was denominated the *Holy Ghoft*.

They refembled God to the *Son*, the illuminative virtue or quality whereof was the *Word*, and its warming virtue the *Holy Spirit*. The *Word*, they taught, was darted, like a Divine ray, to accomplifh the work of redemption; and that being reafcended to Heaven, as the ray returns to its fource, the warmth of the *Father* was communicated, after a like manner, to the *apoftles*. They alfo illuftrated this myftery by one light kindled, as it were, from

another;

* The Sabbatarians in Pennfylvania, originated from the Kethian Baptifts, in the year 1700.

another; by the fountain and ſtreams, and by the ſtock and branch.

The *Sabellians* differed from the *Noetians* in this particular: Noetius was of opinion, that the *perſon* of the Father had aſſumed the human nature of Chriſt; but *Sabellius* maintained, that a certain *energy* only, proceeding from the Supreme Parent, or a certain portion of the Divine nature, was united to the Son of GOD, the man *Jeſus*; and he conſidered, in the ſame manner, the *Holy Ghoſt*, as a portion of the everlaſting Father.

*Broughton's Hiſtorical Library, vol. ii p. 348.*
*Moſheim's Eccleſ Hiſt vol i. p 244.*
*Waterland on the Trinity, p 385.*

SACOPHORI, A ſect in the fourth century; ſo called becauſe they always went cloathed in ſack-cloth, and affected a great deal of auſterity and penance.

*Hiſtory of Religion, vol. iv.*   [*See Sacophori*]

SANDEMANIANS, So called from Mr. *Robert Sandeman*, who publiſhed his ſentiments in the year 1757. He was firſt a congregational preacher at Edinburg,* and afterwards came to New-England, and ſettled a ſociety at Boſton, Danbury, and other places. His leading ſentiments appeared to be as follow:

I. That juſtifying *faith* is no more than a ſimple belief of the *truth*, or the Divine teſtimony paſſively received.

II. That this divine teſtimony carries in itſelf ſufficient ground of hope, and occaſion of joy to every one who believes it, without any thing wrought in us, or done by us, to give it a particular direction to ourſelves.          X          To

* He was a diſciple of Mr. *John Glas*, from whom this denomination are called *Glaſites* in *Scotland*.

To support this system the Sandemanians alledge, *that faith is called receiving the love of the truth*, and the apostle often speaks of *faith* and *truth* to the same purpose, as in John xvi. 13, *the spirit of truth*. 2d. of Cor. iv. 13, *the spirit of faith.* Acts vi. 7, *Obedient to the faith.* 1st. Pet. i. 22. *In obeying the truth.* And divers other passages. The scriptures consider *faith* not as a work of *ours*, nor as any action exerted by the *human mind*; but set it in direct opposition to every work, whether of *body* or *mind*. See Rom. iv. 4, 5. This contrast excludes every idea of activity in the *mind*, from the matter of *justification*; so that we cannot speak of preparatory works of any sort, without making the *gospel* a law of works. Rom. iii. 27, *Where is boasting then ? It is excluded*, &c. Now boasting cannot be excluded, if any thing done by us sets us in a more probable way of obtaining the *salvation* which is of *grace*, whether it be called by the names of a *law work, serious exercise of seeking souls*, or labouring to obtain an interest in *Christ*, &c.

Every doctrine then which teaches us to do, or endeavour any thing towards our acceptance with GOD, stands opposed to the doctrine of the apostles, which instead of directing us what to do, sets before us all that the most disquieted conscience can require, in order to acceptance with GOD, as already done and finished by JESUS CHRIST.

The particular practices in the *Sandemanian churches*, are as follow :

I. They constantly communicate together in the Lord's supper every Sabbath : for they look upon the Christian Sabbath as designed for the celebration of divine ordinances, which are summarily comprised, Acts ii. 42.

                                                 II. In

**II.**   In the interval between the morning and the afternoon service, they have their *love-feasts* ; of which every member partakes by dining at the houses of such of the brethren who live sufficiently near, and whose habitations are convenient for that purpose.   Their professed design in these feasts is to cultivate mutual knowledge and friendship, to testify that they are all brethren of one family ;  and that the poor may have  a comfortable meal at the expence of the more wealthy.

This and  other opportunities they take for the *kiss of charity*, or  the saluting each other *with an holy kiss* ; a duty this denomination believe expresly exhorted to in Rom. xvi. 16.   1st. of Cor. xvi. 20. And  other texts of scripture.

They not only use this kiss of  charity at  the *love feasts*, when  each member salutes  the person who sets next him on each side, but at the admission of a new church member ;  to testify  that they heartily welcome  him into their fellowship, and  love  him for  the sake of the *truth* he has professed.   They alledge that these *love-feasts* were not laid aside by St. Paul's writing  to  the  Corinthians, but enjoined to be observed in a  right manner, and  the abuses  of them corrected ;  and  they  continued in practice while the primitive profession of  brotherly love remained among the ancient Christians, and *as charity never faileth*, 1st. of Cor. xiii. 8. so neither should any of the duties, or expressions of it, be  allowed to fail.

Since our Lord  tells  his disciples that they ought *to wash one anothers feet, according  to the example he gave them* :  John xiii. 14, 15.   This denomination enjoin  this  as an incumbent duty.

X 2

They

They are directed to look upon all they possess as open to the calls of the *poor* and *church* ; to contribute according to their ability, as every one has need.

*Sandeman's Letters on Theron and Aspasio, vol.* i. *p.* 16.
     *Vol* ii. *p* 38
*Glass's Works. vol.* iv *p* 9—40.
*Simple Truth vindicated p* 19 - 38
*Practices of the Sandemanian Churches. p.* 5, 6.

**SATANIANS,** So called because they taught, that *Satan*, or the Devil, was extremely powerful ; that he occasioned infinite mischiefs ; and that it was much wiser to respect and adore, than to curse him ; this being a means to render him favourable to men, instead of injuring them.

The *Satanians* were a branch of the *Messalians*, and appeared about the year 390. They pretended, they were the only true observers of the gospel : they possessed no goods, lived by begging, and lay together promiscuously on the pavement of the streets. When any one asked concerning their quality, they would call themselves patriarchs, prophets, angels, and even Jesus Christ.

*Broughton's Historical Library vol.* i. *p* 369.

**SATURNIANS,** A sect which arose about the year 115. They derived their name from Saturnius of Antioch, one of the principal Gnostic chiefs.

He held the doctrine of *two Principles*, from whence proceeded all things ; the *one a wise* and *benevolent Deity* ; and the other, *Matter, a Principle essentially evil*, and which he supposed under the superintendence of a certain intelligence of a malignant nature.

The

The world and its inhabitants were, according to his lyftem, created by feven angels, which prefided over the feven planets. This work was carried on without the knowledge of the *benevolent Deity*, and in oppofition to the will of the *material Principle*. The former, however, beheld it with approbation, and honoured it with feveral marks of his beneficence. He endowed with rational fouls, the Beings who inhabited this new fyftem, to whom their Creators had imparted nothing more that the animal life : and having divided the world into feven parts, he diftributed them among the feven *angelic archi- tects ;* one of whom was the God of the *Jews ;* and referved to himfelf the fupreme empire over all. To thefe creatures, whom the *benevolent Principle* had endowed with reafonable fouls, and with difpo- fitions that led to goodnefs and virtue, the *evil Be- ing,* to maintain his empire, added another kind, whom he formed of a wicked and malignant cha- racter ; and hence the difference we fee among men. When the Creators of the world fell from their al- legiance to the fupreme Deity, God fent from Hea- ven, into our globe, a *reftorer of order*, whofe name was *Chrift.* This Divine conqueror came cloathed with a corporeal appearance, but not with a *real* bo- dy : he came to deftroy the empire of the *material Principle*, and to point out to virtuous fouls the way by which they muft return to *G O D.* This way is befet with difficulties and fufferings ; fince thofe fouls, who propofe returning to the fupreme Being, muft abftain from wine, flefh, wedlock, and, in fhort, from every thing that tends to fenfual gratifi- cation, or even bodily refrefhment. [See Gnoftics]
*Mofheim's Ecclef Hift vol. i. p. 176, 177.*

## SCHEWENKFELDIANS,

**SCHEWENKFELDIANS,** A sect in the sixteenth century; so called from one Gasper Schewenkfeldt, a Silesian Knight. He differed from Luther in the three following points. The *first* of these points related to the doctrine concerning the Eucharist. Schewenkfeldt inverted the following words of Christ, *This is my body*; and insisted on their being thus understood, *My body is this*, i. e. such as this bread, which is broken and consumed: a true and real food, which nourisheth, satisfieth, and delighteth the soul. *My blood is this*, i. e. such its effects as the wine, which strengthens and refresheth the heart.

II. He denied that the *external word* which is committed to writing in the *holy scriptures*, was endowed with the power of *healing, illuminating* and *renewing* the mind; and he ascribed this power to the *internal word*, which according to his notion, was Christ himself.

III. He would not allow Christ's human nature in its exalted state to be called a creature, or a created substance, as such a denomination appeared to him infinitely below its majestic dignity, united as it is in that glorious state with the Divine essence.

*Mosheim's ibid, vol.* iv. *p* 32.


**SECUNDIANS,** A sect in the second century, which derived their name from Secundus, a disciple of Valentine. He maintained the doctrine of two eternal Principles, viz. *Light* and *Darkness*, from whence arose the good and the evil that are observable in the universe. [See Valentinians]

*Mosheim ibid, vol.* i. *p* 188.


**SEEKERS,**

SEEKERS, A sect which arose in the year 1645. They derived their name from their maintaining, that the true *church, ministry, scripture* and *ordinances* were lost, for which they were *seeking*. They taught, *that the scriptures were uncertain ; that present miracles were necessary to faith ; that our ministry is without authority ; and our worship and ordinances unnecessary or vain.*

*Calamy's Abridgment of Baxter's History, vol.* i. *p.* 110.

SELEUCIANS, Disciples of *Seleucus*, a philosopher of Galatia ; who, about the year 380, adopted the sentiments of Hermogenes, and those of Audeus. He taught with the Valentinians, that *Jesus Christ* assumed a body only in appearance. He also maintained, that the soul was only an animated fire, created by the angels, and therefore men should be baptized with fire : and that the pleasures of beatitude consisted in corporeal delights. [See Hermogenians, Audæans, and Valentinians]

*Broughton's Historical Library, vol.* ii. *p* 559.

SEMBIANI, So called from Sembianus their leader ; who condemned all use of wine as evil of itself : he persuaded his followers, that wine was a production of Satan, and the earth : denied the resurrection of the body ; and rejected most of the books of the *Old-Testament.*

*History of Religion, vol.* iv. [*See Sembiani*]

SEMI-ARIANS, So called because they held the opinions of the Arians in part.

For a farther account of their sentiments, see Arians.

*Broughton's Historical Library, vol.* ii. *p.* 382.

SEMI-PELAGIANS,

SEMI-PELAGIANS, A branch of the Pelagians in the fifth century. The Monk Caffian was the leader of this denomination. In order to accommodate the difference between Auguftin and Pelagius, he maintained the following doctrines :

I. That God did not difpenfe his *grace* to one more than another in confequence of *praeflination :* i. e. an *eternal* and *abfolute decree ;* but was willing to fave all men if they complied with the terms of his gofpel.

II. That CHRIST *died for all men.*

III. That the grace purchafed by *Chrift,* and neceffary to falvation, was offered to all men.

IV. That man, before he received grace, was capable of faith and holy defires.

V. That man, born *free,* was confequently capable of refifting the influences of grace, or *complying* with its fuggeftions.

The *Pelagians* and *Semi-Pelagians* differ in this refpect : the Pelagians affert, that there is no neceffity for *inward grace ;* but the Semi-Pelagians maintain, that none can advance in virtue without the affiftance of Divine grace, though they fubject this inward grace to the freedom of the will. [See Pelagians]

*Mofheim's Ecclefiaftical Hiftory, vol i. p. 426.*
*Stackhoufe's Body of Divinity, p. 150.*

SERVERIANS, A fect in the fecond century ; fo called from Serverus ; who taught, that the world was made by Principalities and Powers : that the Devil is the fon of the Great Prince of the Principalities.—They faid, the Serpent that proceeded

from

from him produced the vine, and therefore abstained from wine. They forbid *marriage*, and denied the *resurrection* : they rejected Paul's epistles, and the Acts of the *apostles*.

Broughton's *Historical Library*, vol. ii. p. 540.

Hearne's *Ductor Historicus*, vol. ii. p. 101.

**SERVERITES.** [See Angelites]

SERVETIANS, A name which in the 16th century, distinguished the followers of Michael Servetus, a Spaniard by birth. He taught, that the *Deity*, before the creation of the world, had produced within himself two *personal representations*, or *manners of existence*, which were to be the *medium* of intercourse between him and mortals, and, by whom, consequently, he was to reveal his will, and to display his mercy and beneficence to the children of men :—That these two representatives were the *Word* and the *Holy Ghost* :—That the former was united to the man CHRIST, who was born of the Virgin MARY, by an omnipotent act of the Divine will ; and that, on this account, CHRIST might be properly called *God* :—That the *Holy Spirit* directed the course, and animated the whole system of nature ; and more especially produced in the minds of men, wise counsels, virtuous propensities, and divine feelings : And finally, that these two *representations* were to cease after the destruction of this terrestrial globe, and to be absorbed into the *substance* of the *Deity*, from whence they had been formed.

Y                              *Servetus*

*Servetus* denied *infant baptifm* ; and maintained, that no man ought to be profecuted like a criminal, for any doctrinal point.

*M fhei 's Ecclef. Hift. vol. iv. p 172 173.*
*Memoirs of Literature, vol. iv. p. 199.*

**SETHIANS,** So called becaufe they paid Divine worfhip to *Seth*, whom they looked upon to be Jefus Chrift, the Son of God ; but who was made by a third Divinity, and fubftituted in the room of the two families of Abel and Cain, which had been deftroyed by the deluge.

This denomination appeared in Egypt about the year 190, and continued above two hundred years.

*Broughton's Hiftorical Library, vol. ii. p. 390.*

**SHAKERS,** The firft who acquired this denomination were *Europeans* ; a part of which came from *England* to *New-York* in the year 1774, and being joined by others, they fettled at *Nifqueunia*, above *Albany* ; from whence they have fpread their doctrines, and increafed to a confiderable number.

*Anna Leefe*, whom they ftile the *Elect Lady*, is the head of this party. They affert, that fhe is the woman fpoken of in the twelfth chapter of Revelations ; and that fhe fpeaks feventy-two tongues :—And though thofe tongues are unintelligible to the living, fhe converfes with the dead, who underftand her language. They add further, that fhe is the mother of all the *elect :* that fhe travails for the whole world : and that no bleffing can defcend to any perfon, but only by and through her, and that in the way of her being poffeffed of their fins, by their confeffing and repenting of them, one by one, according to her direction.

The

The principal doctrines which are attributed to the Shakers, by thofe who have had opportunities to be acquainted with their religious tenets, are as follow :

I.  That there is a *new difpenfation* taking place, in which the faints fhall reign a thoufand years with *Chrift*, and attain to perfection ; and that they have entered into this ftate ;  are the only church in the world ; and have all the apoftolic gifts.*

They attempt to prove this doctrine of a new difpenfation by counting the myftical numbers fpecified in the prophefies of Daniel, as well as by their figns and wonders.

II.  That God, thro' Jefus Chrift in the church, is reconciled with man : and that Chrift is come a light into human nature to *enlighten every man who cometh into the world*, without diftinction.

III.  That no man is born of God, until, by faith, he is affimulated to the character of Jefus Chrift in his church.

IV.  That in obedience to that church, a man's faith will encreafe, until he comes to be one with Chrift, in the Millenium church ftate.

V.  That every man is a free agent to walk in the true light, and chufe or reject the truth of God within him ; and, of confequence, it is in every man's power to be obedient to the faith.

VI.  That it is the gofpel of the firft refurrection which is now preached in their church.

Y 2

VII.  That

---

* They affert, that all external ordinances, efpecially *baptifm* and the *Lord's fupper*, ceafed in the *apoftolic age* ; and that *God* had never fent one man to preach fir that time, until they entered into this *new difpenfation*, and were fent to call in the *elect*.

VII.   That all who are born of God, as they explain the new-birth, shall never taste of the *second death.*

VIII.   That those who are said to have been regenerated among Christians, are only regenerated in part ; therefore, not assimulated into the character of Christ in his church, while in the present state, and, of consequence, not tasting the happiness of the first resurrection, cannot escape, in part, the second death.

IX.   That the word everlasting, when applied to the punishment of the wicked, refers only to a limitted space of time—excepting in the case of those who fall from their church :—But for such, there is no forgiveness, neither *in this world, nor that which is to come.*

They quote Matt. xii. 32, to prove this doctrine.

X.   That the second death having power over such as rise not in the character of Christ in the first resurrection, will, in due time, fill up the measure of his sufferings beyond the grave.

XI.   That the righteousness and sufferings of Christ, in his members, are both one : but that every man suffers personally, with inexpressible woe and misery, for sins not repented of, notwithstanding this union, until final redemption.

XII.   That Christ will never make any public appearance, as a single person, but only in his saints :—That the judgment day is now begun in their church ; and the books are opened, the dead now rising and coming to judgment, and they are set to judge the world.  For which they quote 1st of Cor. vi. 2.                              XIII.   That

XIII.    That their church is come out of the order of natural generation, to be as Chriſt was ; and
that thoſe who have wives be as though they had
none ;   that  by theſe means,   Heaven begins upon
earth, and they thereby loſe their ſenſual and earthly relation to Adam the firſt,   and come to be tran-
ſparent in their ideas in the bright and heavenly vi-
ſions of God.

XIV.    That their is no ſalvation out of obedience
to the ſovereignty of their dominion : that all ſin
which is committed againſt God is done againſt them,
and muſt be pardoned for Chriſt's ſake thro' them,
and confeſſion muſt be made to them for that purpoſe.

XV.    They hold  to a  travel and labour for the
redemption of departed ſpirits.

The diſcipline of this denomination is founded on
the ſuppoſed perfection of their leaders :· the mother it is ſaid obeys God through Chriſt ; *European*
elders obey her ; *American* labourers, and the common people obey them, while confeſſion is made of
every ſecret in nature, from the oldeſt to the young-
eſt.   The people are made to believe they are ſeen
through and through in the goſpel glaſs of perfection,
by their teachers, who behold the ſtate of the dead,
and innumerable worlds of ſpirits good and bad.

Theſe  people are generally inſtructed to be  very
induſtrious, and to bring in according to their ability
to keep up the meeting.   They vary in their exerciſes, their heavy dancing, as it is called, is performed
by a perpetual ſpringing from the houſe floor, about
four inches up and down, both in the men's and women's apartment,  moving about with extraordinary
tranſport,  ſinging  ſometimes  one at a time, ſometimes more, making a perfect charm,

This

This elevation affects the nerves, fo that they have intervals of fhuddering as if they were in a ftrong fit of the ague.—They fometimes clap hands, and leap fo as to ftrike the joift above their heads. They throw off their outfide garments in thefe exercifes, and fpend their ftrength very cheerfully this way ; their chief fpeaker often calls for their attention, then they all ftop, and hear fome harrangue, and then fall to dancing again. They affert, that their dancing is the token of the great joy and happinefs of the new *Jerufalem ftate*, and denotes the victory over fin. One of the poftures which increafe among them, is turning round very fwift for an hour or two. This they fay is to fhow the great power of God.

They fometimes fall on their knees and make a found like the roaring of many waters, in groans and cries to God, as they fay, for the wicked world who perfecute them.

*Rathburn's Account of the Shakers, p 4. 5. 6, 14.*
*Taylor's Account of the Shakers, p 4, 7, 8 9 15. 16.*
*Weft's Account of the Shakers, p. 8, 13.*

**SIMONIANS,** A fect in the firft century ; they derived their name from Simon Magos, their leader, who is fo often mentioned in the Acts of the apoftles ; and affumed to himfelf the title of the *Supreme Power of God.*

This denomination maintained the eternity of matter, and alfo the exiftence of an evil Being, who prefided and thus fhared the empire of the univerfe, with the fupreme and beneficent *mind.* They probably embraced the opinion of thofe who held that matter moved from eternity, and by an intrinfic and neceffary activity, had from its innate force, produced, at a certain period of time, from its own

fubftance,

ſubſtance, the *evil Principle* which now exerciſes dominion over it, with all its numerous train of attendants. They are ſaid to have taught, that all human actions were indifferent :—to have attributed a ſurpriſing power to magic :—and to have denied the reſurrection of the dead.

*Simon Magos* taught thoſe who followed him, to fall down before him and his miſtreſs Helena, in his journey from Aſia to Rome, to whom he aſcribed the quality of the firſt intelligence of the ſovereign *virtue* ; to her he attributed the production of angels, and to angels the creation of the world. He pretended that in his perſon reſided the greateſt and moſt perfect of the divine *Æons* ; and another of the female ſex, the mother of all human ſouls, dwelt in the perſon of his miſtreſs Helena, and that he came by the command of God, upon earth, to eſtabliſh the empire of thoſe who had formed the material world, and to deliver Helena from their power and dominion.

*Moſheim's Eccleſiaſtical Hiſtory, vol.* i. *p.* 115.
*Simſon's Hiſtory of the Church, p.* 414.
*Dupin's Church Hiſtory. vol.* ii. *p.* 29.
*Formey's Eccleſiaſtical Hiſtory, vol.* i. *p.* 21.

**SOCINIANS,** A denomination which appeared in the ſixteenth century ; and owed its origin to Lelius Socinus, a man of uncommon genius and learning ; and to Fauſtus Socinus, his nephew ; who propagated his uncle's ſentiments in a public manner after his death.

The principal tenets maintained by this denomination are as follow ; to which are added a few of the arguments they uſe in defence of their ſentiments.

I. That

I. That the holy scriptures were to be understood and explained in such a manner as to render them conformable to the dictates of reason.

In consequence of this leading point in their theology, they maintain, that God, who is infinitely more perfect than man, though of a similar nature in some respects, exerted an act of that power by which he governs all things; in consequence of which, an extraordinary person was born of the Virgin *Mary*. That person was *Jesus Christ*, whom God first translated to Heaven by that portion of his divine power which is called the *Holy Ghost*; and having instructed him fully in the knowledge of his counsels and designs, sent him again into this sublunary world, to promulgate to mankind a new rule of life, more excellent than that under which they had formerly lived—to propagate divine truth by his ministry, and to confirm it by his death.

That those who obey the voice of this *Divine teacher*, (and this obedience is in the power of every one whose will and inclination leads that way) shall, one day, be cloathed with new bodies, and inhabit, eternally, those blessed regions, where God himself immediately resides. Such, on the contrary, as are disobedient and rebellious, shall undergo most terrible and exquisite torments, which shall be succeeded by annihilation, or the total extinction of their being.

Thus the Socinians argue against the *Divinity of Christ*.

1. The scriptures contain the clearest and most express declarations that there is but *one God*, without ever mentioning any exception in favour of a

*Trinity*, or guarding us againſt being led into any miſtake by ſuch geueral and unlimited expreſſions. Ex. xx. 3. *Thou ſhalt have no other GOD but me.* Deut vi. 4. Mark xii. 20. iſt of Cor. viii. 6 Eph. iv. 5.

2. This one GOD is ſaid to have created all things; and no intimation is given of his having employed any *inferior agent* in the work of creation. Gen. i. 1.—" *In the beginning GOD created the heaven and the earth.*" Pſalms xxxiii. 6. v. 9.

3. This one GOD is called the Father, i. e. the Author of all Beings ; and he is called God and Father with reſpect to Chriſt, as well as all other perſons. John vi. 27. xvii. 3. xx. 17. Col. i. 3.

4. Chriſt is ſaid expreſſly to be inferior to the Father ; all his power is ſaid to have been given him by the Father, and he could do nothing without the Father. John xiv. 28.—" *My Father is greater than I.*" iit Cor. iii. 23. John v. 19. Mat. xxviii. 18.

5. Some things were withheld from Chriſt by his Father, Mark xiii. 32.—" *But of that day and that hour knoweth no man, no not the angels which are in Heaven, neither the Son, but the Father.* Mat. xx. 23.

They alledge, that it is impoſſible to reconcile the doctrine of the ſatisfaction for ſin by the death of Chriſt, with the doctrine of free grace ; and if Chriſt paid a full price for our juſtification, there can be no free grace in GOD in pardoning us on that account.

The Socinians reject the doctrines of original ſin, and predeſtination. They maintained that man, before his fall, was naturally mortal, and had no ori-

Z

ginal

ginal righteoufnefs : and that God has no knowledge
of future contingencies but alternately.

This denomination differ from the Arians in the
following particulars :

The Socinians deny that Chrift had exiftence before he was born of the bleffed Virgin.

The Arians fay, that Chrift was generated before
the world ; and in procefs of time became incarnate
in our nature.

The Socinians fay, that the *Holy Ghoft* is the
power and wifdom of God, which is God.

The Arians fay, that the *Holy Spirit* is the creature of the Son, and fubfervient to him in the work
of redemption.

For an account of the Socinian divifions,—fee
Bidelians, Budneians, and Farvonians.

*Mofheim's Ecclef. Hift. vol. iv p. 167. 193. 195.*
*Collier's HiftoricalDictionary, vol. ii. [See Socinians]*
*Lefl·e's Socinian Controverfy, p 36.*
*Prieftley's Appeal. p. 19. 47. 48. 49.*

SOLDINS, So called from their leader one *Soldin*,
a Greek Prieft. They appeared about the middle
of the fifth century, in the kingdoms of Saba and
Godolia. They altered the manner of the facrifice
of the mafs ; their Priefts offered gold ; their Deacons,
incenfe ; and their Sub deacons, myrrh ; and this
in memory of the like offerings made to the infant
JESUS by the wife men. Very few authors mention the *Soldins*, neither do we know whether they
ftill fubfift.

*Broughton's Hiftorical Library, vol. ii. p. 560.*

·STANCARIANS,

STANCARIANS, The disciples of Francis Stancarus, professor of the Hebrew tongue, and a native of Mantua, in Italy.

The tenet which he most eagerly defended was, that Jesus Christ was a Mediator, in quality of a mere man, and not in quality of God and man.

This denomination took its rise in the sixteenth century.

*Broughton's Historical Library vol. ii. p. 561.*

STILITES, So called by the Greeks ; and Sancti Columnaries, or Pillar-Saints, by the Latins. They stood motionless upon the tops of *pillars*, expressly raised for this exercise of their patience, and remained there for several years, amidst the admiration and applause of the populace.

The inventor of this discipline was *Simeon*, a *Syrian*, who, in order to climb as near *Heaven* as possible, * passed thirty-seven years of his life upon five pillars of six, twelve, twenty-two, thirty-six, and forty cubits high ; and thus acquired a most shining reputation, and attracted the veneration of all about him. Many of the inhabitants of *Syria* followed his example, though not with the same degree of austerity : and this practice, which was begun in the fifth, continued in vogue till the twelfth century.

*Mosheim's Ecclesiastical History, vol. i. p. 391.*
*History of Don Ignatius, vol. i. p. 31.*

SUBLAPSARIANS, An appellation given to those *Calvinists* who suppose, that the decree of predestination

Z 2

* It is said that *Simeon* imagined he saw an angel of light coming to him in a fiery chariot to carry him to Heaven, and lifted up his foot, in order to enter the divine vehicle.

deſtination regards man as fallen, by an abuſe of that freedom which *Adam* had, into a ſtate, in which all were to be left to neceſſary and unavoidable ruin, who were not exempted from it by predeſtination.

*Doddridge's Lectures, p 460.*

**SUPRALAPSARIANS,** A title given to thoſe *Calviniſts* who ſuppoſe, that God intended to glorify his juſtice in the condemnation of ſome, as well as his mercy in the ſalvation of others ; and for that purpoſe decreed, that *Adam* ſhould neceſſarily fall, and by that fall bring himſelf and his offspring into a ſtate of everlaſting condemnation.

*Doddridge's Lectures. ibid.*

**SYNCRETISTS,** A name given to the followers of Calixtus.     [See Calixtins]

**SYNERGISTS,** So called from the Greek word [ſunergèia] which ſignifies *co-operation.* Hence this name was given to thoſe in the ſixteenth century, who denied that GOD was the ſole agent in the converſion of ſinful man ; and affirmed, that man co-operated with divine grace in the accompliſhment of this ſalutary purpoſe.

*Moſheim's Eccleſ. Hiſt. vol. iv. p. 40.*

## T

**TABORITES,** A ſect in the fifteenth century ; ſo called from a mountain well known in ſacred hiſtory. They not only inſiſted upon reducing the religion of JESUS to its primitive ſimplicity, but required alſo that the ſyſtem of eccleſiaſtical government ſhould be reformed in the ſame manner ; the authority of the Pope deſtroyed ; the

form

form of divine worſhip changed : they demanded, in a word, the erection of a new church, a new hierarchy, in which CHRIST alone ſhould reign, and all things ſhould be carried on by a Divine direction and impulſe.

The famous *John Ziſca*, a Bohemian Knight, was the leader of this denomination. They maintained, that it was lawful to perſecute and extirpate, with fire and ſword, the enemies of the true religion : and ſome of the principal doctors among the *Taborites*, ſuch as Martin Loquis, and his followers, flattered themſelves that CHRIST would deſcend in perſon upon earth, armed with fire and ſword, to extirpate falſe opinions in religion, and purify the church from its multiplied corruptions. Soon after, however, this denomination abandoned the doctrines which upon ſerious examination, they found to be inconſiſtent with the ſpirit and genius of the goſpel. The *Taborites*, thus new modelled, were the ſame with thoſe *Bohemian brethren*, who joined Luther and his ſucceſſors at theReformation ; and of whom there are at this day many of the deſcendants and followers in Poland, and other countries.

*Moſheim's Eccleſ. Hiſt. vol. iii. p. 260, 262, 263, 264. Gilpin's Life of Ziſca, p. 246.*

**TANQUELINIANS,** So called from Tanquelinus, who formed a numerous ſect in Brabant and Antwerp, in the twelfth century. He treated with contempt the external worſhip of God, the ſacrament of the *Lord's ſupper*, and the rite of *baptiſm* ; and held clandeſtine aſſemblies to propagate his opinions. He declaimed againſt the vices of the clergy with vehemence and intrepidity.

*Moſheim's Eccleſ. Hiſt. vol. ii. p. 448, 449.*

**TATIANITES,**

TATIANITES, A sect in the second century ; so called from their leader Tatian, a disciple of *Justin Martyr*.

They were however more frequently distinguished by the names of Encratites, or Continents ; Hydroparastates, or Drinkers of Water ; Apotactites, or Renouncers.

[For an account of the sentiments of this denomination, see Encratites]

*Mosheim's Ecclesiastical History, vol. i. p. 180.*

THEODOSIANS.　[See Angelites]

THEOPASCHITES, A sect in the fifth century, which derived their name from the Greek of [Theos] God, and [pachö] to suffer.

They were charged with maintaining, that the whole Trinity suffered in the person of *Jesus Christ*.

One Peter, sirnamed Fullo, was the author of this denomination.

*Mosheim's Ibid, p. 417.*
*Bailey's Dictionary, vol. ii. [See Theopaschites]*

TRASKITES, A sect which arose in the year 1634. They derived their name from Mr. John Traske. His opinions were similar to the Sabbatarians. [See Sabbatarians]

*Pagit's Heresiography, p. 135.*

TRISORMIANI, A sect which appeared about the year 408 ; so called from the Latin [tria-forma] They maintained, that the *Divine nature* was one and the same in *three persons* together, but imperfect in the *several persons*.

*Hearne's Ductor Historicus, vol. ii. p. 170.*

TRITHEISTS,

**TRITHEISTS,** A sect in the sixth century, whose chief was John Ascusnage, a Syrian philosopher, and at the same time a Monophysite. This man imagined in the Deity three natures, or substances, absolutely equal in all respects, and joined together by no common *essence :* to which opinion his adversaries gave the name of Tritheism, from the Greek of [*treìs*] three, and [*Theòs*] God. One of the warmest defenders of this doctrine was John Philoponus, an Alexandrian philosopher and grammarian of the highest reputation ; and hence he was considered by many as the author of this sect, whose members have consequently derived from him the title of Philoponists.

This sect was divided into two parties, the Philoponists, and the Cononites ; but they differed only concerning the doctrine of the *resurrection.* Philoponus maintained, that the *form* as well as the *matter* of all bodies was *generated* and *corrupted,* and that both therefore were to be restored in the *resurrection.*

[See Cononites, for an account of the tenets of that denomination]

*Mosheim's Ecclesf. Hist. vol. i. p. 473.*
*Barclay's Dictionary. [See Tritheists]*

**TURLUPINS,** A sect which appeared about the year 1372. Their principal scene was in Savoy and Dauphiny.

They taught, that when a man is arrived at a certain state of perfection, he is freed from all subjection to the divine law. They often went naked : and they allowed of no prayer to God but mental. John Dabantonne was the author of this denomina-

tion.

tion. Some think they were called *Turlupins*, because they usually abode in places exposed to wolves,
[*lupis*] They called themselves the *Fraternity of
the poor.*

*Broughton's Historical Library. vol. ii, p.* 474.
*Dufresnoy's Chronological Tables, vol.* ii *p* 243.

## V

VALENTINIANS, A sect which sprung
up in the second century ; so called from
their leader Valentinus. Their principles were, generally speaking, the same with the Gnostics, whose
name he assumed, yet in many things he entertained
opinions peculiar to himself. He placed, for instance,
in the *Pleroma*, (so the Gnostics called the habitation of the *Deity*) thirty *Æons*, of which the one
half were male, and the other female. To these
he added four others, which were of neither sex, viz.
*Horus*, who guarded the borders of the *Pleroma*,
*Christ*, the *Holy Ghost*, and *Jesus*. The youngest
of the *Æons*, called *Sophia*, (i. e. wisdom) conceived an ardent desire of comprehending the nature of
the *supreme Being*, and by the force of this propen-
sity, brought forth a daughter, named *Achamoth*.
*Achamoth* being exiled from the *Pleroma*, fell
down into the rude and undigested mass of matter,
to which she gave a certain arrangement ; and by
the assistance of *Jesus*, produced the *Demiurge, the
Lord and Creator of all things*. This *Demiurge* separated the subtle or animal matter from that of the
grosser, or more *terrestrial* kind ; out of the former
he created the superior world, or the visible Heavens ; and out of the latter he formed the inferior
world, or this terraqueous globe. He also made
man,

man, in whose composition the subtle, and also the grosser matter were both united, and that in equal portions; but *Achamoth*, the mother of *Demiurge*, added to these two substances, of which the human race was formed a spiritual and celestial substance.

The Creator of this world, according to *Valintine*, arrived, by degrees, to that pitch of arrogance, that he either imagined himself to be God alone, or, at least, was desirous that mankind should consider him as such. For this purpose, he sent forth prophets to the Jewish nation, to declare his claim to the honour that is due to the supreme Being; and in this also the other angels who preside over the different parts of the universe immediately set themselves to imitate his ambition. To chastise this lawless arrogance of *Demiurge*, and to illuminate the minds of rational beings with the knowledge of the true and *supreme Deity*, *Christ* appeared upon earth, composed of an animal and spiritual substance, and cloathed, moreover, with an aerial body. This Redeemer passed through the womb of *Mary*, as the pure water flows through the untainted conduit. *Jesus*, one of the supreme *Æons*, was substantially united to him, when he was baptized by *John* in the waters of *Jordan*. The Creator of the world, when he perceived the foundations of his empire were shaken by this Divine man, caused him to be apprehended and nailed to the cross. But before CHRIST submitted to this punishment, not only *Jesus*, the *Son of God*, but also the rational soul of *Christ* ascended up on high; so that only the animal soul and the etherial body suffered crucifixion. Those who abandoning the service of false Deities, and the worship of the God of the *Jews*, live according to the precepts of

A a

*Christ*

*Chrift*, and fubmit the animal and fenfual foul to the difcpline of reafon, fhall be truly happy : their rational, and alfo their fenfual fouls fhall afcend to thofe glorious feats of blifs which border on the *Pleroma*.—And when all the parts of the Divine nature, or all fouls are purified thoroughly, and feparated from *matter*, then a raging fire, let loofe from its prifon, fhall fpread its flames throughout the univerfe, and diffolve the frame of this corporeal world.

The denomination of the Valentinians was divided into many branches. [See Ptolemates, Secundians, and Heracleonites]

*Mofheim's Ecclef. Hift. vol. i p 185 186 187, 188.*

VANISTS, So called from Sir *Henry Vane*, who was appointed Governor of *New-England* in the year 1636 ; and is faid to have been at the head of that party, in New-England, who were charged with maintaining *Antinomian* tenets. [See *Antinomians*]

*Calamy's Abridgment. vol. i. p 98.*

UBIQUITARIANS, A fect which derived their name from their maintaining, that the body of Jefus Chrift is [ubique] every where, and in every place.

Brentius is faid to have firft advanced this fentiment, about the year 1560. The Ubiquitarians were not quite agreed among themfelves : fome holding, that Jefus Chrift, even during his mortal life, was every where ; and others dating the ubiquity of his body from the time of his afcenfion only.

*Broughton's Hiftorical Dictionary. vol ii. f. 481.*

UCKEWALLISTS, A fect which derives its denomination from Uke-Walles, a native of Friefland, who publifhed his fentiments in the year 1637.

He

He entertained a favourable opinion of the eternal ſtate of Judas, and the reſt of Chriſt's murderers. To give an air of plauſibility to this ſentiment, he invented the following hypotheſis :—That the period of time which extended from the birth of Chriſt to the deſcent of the Holy Ghoſt, was a time of deep ignorance and darkneſs ; during which the Jews were void of light, and entirely deſtitue of Divine ſuccour ; and that of conſequence, the ſins and enormities which were committed during this interval, were in a great meaſure excuſable, and could not merit the ſevereſt diſplays of the Divine juſtice.

This denomination ſtrictly adhere to the doctrine and diſcipline of the primitive *Mennonites.* The ceremony of waſhing the feet of ſtrangers, who come within the reach of their hoſpitality, they eſteem a right of Divine inſtitution.

*Moſheim's Eccleſiaſtical Hiſtory, vol. v. p. 48, 49.*

**VERSCHORISTS,** A Dutch ſect, which derived its denomination from Jacob Verſchoor, a native of Fluſhing, who publiſhed his ſentiments in the year 1680. The religious tenets of this denomination reſemble the Hattemiſts, in moſt points. [See Hattemiſts]

*Moſheim's Eccleſiaſtical Hiſt. vol. iv. p. 552.*

**UNITARIANS,** A name given to the *Antitrinitarians ;* the *Socinians* are alſo ſo called. The term is very comprehenſive, and is applicable to a great variety of perſons, who, notwithſtanding, agree in this common principle, that there is *no diſtinction in the Divine nature.*

*Moſheim's Eccleſiaſtical Hiſtory, vol. v. p. 58.*

                    **UNIVERSALISTS,**

UNIVERSALITS, The sentiment which has acquired its professors this appellation, was embraced by *Origen* in the third century ; and in more modern times by Chevalier *Ramsay*, Dr. *Cheyne*, Mr. *Hartley*, and others. The plan of *universal salvation*, as exhibited by a *learned divine* of the present day, who, in a late performance, entitled, *The salvation of all men*, has made several additions to the sentiments of the above mentioned authors, is as follows.

That the scheme of revelation has the happiness of all mankind lying at bottom, as its great and ultimate end ; that it gradually tends to this end ; and will not fail of its accomplishment, when fully compleated. Some, in consequence of its operation, as conducted by the *Son of God*, will be disposed and enabled, in this present state, to make such improvements in virtue, the only rational preparative for happiness, as that they shall enter upon the enjoyment of it in the next state. " Others, who have proved incurable under the means which have been used with them in this state, instead of being happy in the next, will be awfully miserable ; not to continue so finally, but that they may be convinced of their folly, and recovered to a virtuous frame of mind : and this will be the effect of the future torments upon many ; the consequence whereof will be their salvation—they being thus fitted for it. And there may be yet other states, before the scheme of God may be perfected, and mankind universally cured of their moral disorders, and in this way qualified for, and finally instated in, eternal happiness. But however many states some of the individuals of the human species may pass through, and however

long

long continuance they may be, the whole is intended to fubferve the grand defign of *univerfal happinefs*, and will finally terminate in it ; infomuch, that the *Son of God* and *Saviour of men*, will not deliver up his truft into the hands of the *Father*, who committed it to him, till he has difcharged his obligations in virtue of it ; having finally fixed all men in Heaven, when God will be *All in All.*

A few of the arguments made ufe of in defence of this fyftem, are as follow : *

I. Chrift died not for a felect number of men only, but for mankind *univerfally*, and without *exception* or limitation.

For the facred writers are fingularly emphatical in expreffing this truth. They fpeak not only of CHRIST's " *dying for us,*" " *for our fins,*" " *for finners,*" " *for the ungodly,*" " *for the unjuft* ;" but affirm in yet more extenfive terms, that " *he died for the world,*" for " *the whole world.*" See ift. of Thef. v. 10. ift. of Cor. xv. 3. Rom. v. 6. 8. ift. of Pet. iii. 18. John i. 29. iii. 16, 17. ift. of John. ii. 2. Heb. ii. 9. and a variety of other paffages.

If Chrift died for all, 'tis far more reafonable to believe, that the whole human kind, in confequence of his death, will finally be faved, than that the greateft part of them fhould perifh. More honour is hereby reflected on GOD ; greater virtue is attributed

buted

* The learned author of the performance, from whence thefe arguments are extracted, has illuftrated the paffages of fcripture quoted, by critical notes on the original language ; and by fhewing their analogy to other paffages in the infpired writings. Thofe who would form a juft idea of the arguments muft confult the work itfelf.

buted to the blood of *Chrift* fhed on the crofs ; and inftead of dying in vain, as to any real good which will finally be the event, with refpect to the greateft part of mankind, he will be made to die to the beft and nobleft purpofe, even the eternal happinefs of a whole world of intelligent and moral Beings.

II. It is the purpofe of God, according to his good pleafure, that mankind *univerfally*, in confequence of the death of his Son Jefus Chrift, fhall *certainly* and *finally be faved.*

The texts which afcertain this, are thofe which follow : *Firft.*—Rom. v. 12th to the end. There *Adam* is confidered as the fource of damage to mankind *univerfally :* And *Chrift*, on the other hand, as a like fource of advantage to the fame mankind ; but with this obfervable difference, that the advantage on the fide of CHRIST *exceeds, overflows, abounds,* beyond the damage on the fide of ADAM ; and this to *all mankind.* The 15th, 16th, and 17th verfes are abfolutely unintelligible upon any other interpretation.

Another text to the purpofe of our prefent argument, we meet with in Rom. viii. from the 19th to the 24th verfe. On the one hand it is affirmed of the *creature,* that is, of *mankind in general,* that they are *fubjected to vanity,* that is, the imperfections and infelicities of a vain mortal life here on earth. On the other hand, it is pofitively affirmed of the *creature,* or *mankind in general,* that they were not fubjected to this vanity, *finally* and *forever,* but *in confequence of Hope,* not only that they fhould be delivered from this *unhappy fubjection,* but inftated in *immortal glory,* as *God's fons.*

Another

Another text to this purpose occurs in Col. i. 19, 20. *For it pleased the Father, that in him should all fullness dwell;* " *and (having made peace thro' the blood of the cross) by him to reconcile*" *all things unto himself*, &c.* And in this epistle, ii. chap. 9 verse, the *apostle*, speaking of Christ, says, " *in him dwelleth all the fullness of the Godhead bodily*," that is, he is the glorious *person* in whom God has *really lodged*, and through whom he will actually communicate all that *fullness* wherewith he intends this lapsed *world* shall be *filled*, in order to its *restoration*. And Christ having this *fullness* lodged in him, *ascended up far above all Heavens, that he might fill all things*. Eph. iv. 10. And as the *filling all things in the lapsed world*, that they might be restored, was the *final cause* of the *ascension* of Christ up to Heaven, all things must accordingly be filled in fact by him sooner or later. The apostle, therefore, observes in the following verses, not only that he has imparted gifts, in prosecution of the end of his exaltation, but that, in order to the full accomplishment of it, he would go on to impart them, " *till we all come to the unity of the faith unto a perfect man, unto the measure of the stature of the fullness of Christ*." And it is declared, in Eph. i. 9, 10, that all these things, in *Heaven* and *earth*, shall be reduced from the state they were in by means of the *lapse*, into a well-subjected and subordinate whole, *by* CHRIST.

Another

---

* Our *author* paraphrases these texts in the following manner. " It pleased the Father that all *communicable fullness* should be lodged in his Son *Jesus Christ*, and *by him* as his *great agent*, (having prepared the way for it by his blood shed on the cross) to *change back again all things to himself*; I say, *by him* it pleased the Father to *change the state* of this *lower world*, of *the men*, and the *things of it*, whether they be on *the earth*, or in *the Heaven* that incompasses it.

Another proof of the prefent propofition we find in 1 Tim. ii. 4. If God is able, in confiftency with mens make, as *moral* and *intelligent* agents, to effect their falvation, his defiring they fhould *be faved*, and his *eventually faving them*, are convertible terms.

III. As a means in order to mens being made meet for falvation, God will, fooner or later, *in this ftate or another*, reduce them *all* under a *willing* and *obedient fubjection* to his moral government.

The texts which confirm this propofition are numerous. The apoftle fays, in 1 John iii. 8, *For this purpofe was the Son of God manifefted, that he might deftroy the works of the Devil.* Parallel to this paffage, fee John i. 29, Matt. i. 21, and Pfa. viii. 5, 6, as explained and argued from Heb. ii. 6, 9. Thefe words are applicable to *Chrift* in their ftrict and full fenfe: And if ALL THINGS, without any *limita tion* or *exception*, fhall be brought under fubjection to *Chrift*, then the time muft come, fooner or later, in this ftate or fome other, when there fhall be no rebels among the fons of *Adam*—no enemies againft the moral government of God. For there is no way of reducing rebels, fo as to deftroy their charrcter as fuch, but by making them *willing* and *obedient fubjects*. That this fcripture is thus to be underftood is evident by parallel paffage in Phil. ii. 9, 10, 11.—— The next portion of fcripture in proof of the prefent propofition, we meet with in 1 Cor. xv. chap. from the 24th to the end of the 29th verfe. Though the apoftle, in this paragraph, turns our view to the end of *mediatory fcheme*, it is affirmed, that *univerfal* fubjection to *Chrift* fhall firft be effected, in a variety of as ftrong and *extenfive* terms as could well have been ufed: as by " *putting down all rule, and all authority*

*authority and power :"* by *" putting all enemies un-der his feet,"* &c.   It is worthy of special notice, that before Chrift's delivery of the *mediatorial* king-dom to the Father, the *laſt enemy muſt be deſtroyed, which is Death;* the *SECOND DEATH,* which thoſe who die wicked men muſt ſuffer *BEFORE* they can be *reduced* under willing ſubjection to *Jeſus Chriſt.* For the firſt death cannot be called the *LAST ENEMY* with propriety and truth, becauſe the *ſecond death* is poſterior to it, and has no exiſtence till that has been ſo far deſtroyed as to allow of a reſ-toration to life.

The *two periods,* when the mediatory kingdom is in the hands of *Jeſus Chriſt,* and when *God* as *King,* will be *immediately All in All,* are certainly quite diſtinct from each other.   And the reign of Chriſt in his mediatorial kingdom, may be divided into two general *periods.*—The one takes in this *preſent ſtate* of *exiſtence,* in which *Chriſt* reigns at the head of *God's kingdom of grace,* and that one *effect* whereof will be the *reduction* of a number of the ſons of *Adam* under ſuch an *obedience* to *God,* as that they will be fitted for a *glorious immortality* in the *next ſtate.* The other *period* of *Chriſt's* reign, is *that* which *intervenes* between the general *reſurrection* and *judgment,* and the time when *God* ſhall be *All in All.* This ſtate may contain a duration of ſo long continuance, as to anſwer to the ſcripture phraſe [*èw tòus aiōnas tōn aiōniōn*] for *ever and ever* ; or, as might more properly be rendered, for *ages of ages.* During the whole of this ſtate, the righteous ſhall be happy, and the *wicked,* who are moſt *obdurate,* MISERABLE, till they are *reduced* as *willing* and *obe-dient ſubjects* to *Chriſt ;* which, when accompliſhed,

B b

the

the *grand period* ſhall commence, when *God* ſhall be himſelf *immediately All in All.*

IV. The *ſcripture* language concerning the *reduced* or *reſtored,* in conſequence of the mediatory interpoſition of *Jeſus Chriſt,* is ſuch as to lead us into the thought, that they are comprehenſive of *mankind univerſally.*

There is one text at leaſt ſo fully expreſſive of this idea, as renders it incapable of being underſtood in any other ſenſe ; it is Rev. v. 13 : " *And every creature which is in Heaven, and on the earth, and under the earth, and ſuch as are in the ſea, and all that are in them, heard I ſaying, Bleſſing and honour, and glory, and power, be unto him that ſitteth upon the throne, and unto the Lamb, forever and ever.*

Dr. Chauncy's Saivation of all Men. p 12, 13, 20, 22, 81 9ⁱ 117. 118 123 124, 125, 126 146, 163, 167, 170 171 172, 173, 177, 178, 179, 182 183, 184, 186, 197, 198, 208, 209, 211. 217, 218, 219 222, 237, 238.

UNIVERSALISTS, This title alſo diſtinguiſhes thoſe who embrace the ſentiments of Mr. *Relley,* a modern preacher of *univerſal ſalvation,* in *England,* and Mr. *Murray,* in *America.* This denomination build their ſcheme upon the following foundation, viz.*

That Chriſt as *Mediator* was ſo united to mankind, that his actions were theirs, his obedience and ſufferings theirs, and conſequently he has as fully reſtored the whole human race to the divine favour, as if all had obeyed and ſuffered in their own perſons.

---

* The difference between this party and the *Chaunceean Univerſaliſts,* will appear obvious, by comparing this with the preceding article.

fons.  The divine law now has no demands upon them, nor condemning power over them.  Their falvation folely depends upon their *union to Chrift*, which God conftituted and eftablifhed before the world began.  And by virtue of this *union*, they will all be admitted to Heaven at the *laft day*; not one of *Chrift's* members, not one of *Adam's* race will be finally loft.  Chrift having taken on him the feed of Abraham, he in them, and they in him, fulfilled all righteoufnefs, obeyed the law, and underwent the penalty for the paft tranfgreffion, being all made *perfect in one*.  According to this union, or being in him, *as branches in the vine, as members in the body*, &c. the people are confidered together with him through all the circumftances of his *birth, life, death, refurrection*, and *glory*.  And thus confidering the whole law fulfilled in *Jefus*, and apprehending ourfelves united to him, his condition and ftate is ours.  'And thus ftanding in him we can read the law, or the doctrine of rewards and punifhments without fear; becaufe all the threatenings in the law of God, have been executed upon us (as finners and law-breakers) in him.  And this facrifice of Jefus is *all-fufficient*, without any act of ours, *mental* or *external*.

This denomination alledge, that the *union* of *Chrift* and his *church*, is a neceffary confideration for the right explanation of the following fcriptures; as Pfa. cxxxiv. 16, *In thy book all my members were written* Eph. v. 30, *We are members of his body, of his flefh, and of his bones.*  1ft. of Cor. xii. 26, *Whether one member fuffer, all the members fuffer with it: or one member be honoured, all the members rejoice with it.*  1ft. of Cor. xii. 12, *For as the*



*body*

*body is one, and hath many members, and all the members of that one body, being many, are one body*: So also is Chrift. See Col. i. 18—Eph. i. 22, 23—Col. ii. 10—Rom. xii. 5—Eph. ii. 16—Heb. ii. 11—John xvii. 22, 23, and a variety of other paſſages in the inſpired writings.

The ſcriptures affirm, that "*by the offence of one, judgment came upon all men, unto condemnation.*"—Rom. v. 8. "*For all have finned, and come ſhort of the glory of God.*"—Rom. iii. 25. It is evident hence, that in Adam's offence all offended ; which ſuppoſes ſuch a *union* between Adam and his offſpring, that his ſin was their ſin, and his ruin their ruin : thus by his offence were they made ſinners ; whilſt they included in him were in paſſivity, and he the active conſciouſneſs of the whole. And that his ſin has corrupted the whole maſs of mankind, both the ſcriptures and common experience evidently declare. If it be granted that there was ſuch a *union* between *Adam* and his offspring, as rendered his ſin their's, why ſhould it be thought a thing incredible, that the like *union* ſubſiſting between *Jeſus* and his ſeed, renders his condition their's ? eſpecially, as the apoſtle has ſtated the matter thus ; "*As by one man's diſobedience, many were made finners ; ſo by the obedience of one, ſhall many be made righteous.*" Rom. v. 19. The ſcriptures here ſhowing the method of ſin in *Adam*, and of grace in *Chriſt*, take an occaſion to illuſtrate the latter by the former : intimating, that as ſin came upon all *Adam's* poſterity by his ſingle act, before they had any capacity of ſinning, after the ſimilitude of his tranſgreſſion, or of perſonal concurrence with him in his iniquity; it muſt have been from ſuch a *union* to him, as rendered

his

his condition their's, in whatever state he was.————
Thus " *by one man's disobedience, many were made
sinners.*"   In like manner *Christ's righteou'ness* is upon all his seed ; by his single act, before they had
any capacity of obeying, after the similitude of his
obedience ; or of assenting to what he did, or suffered : this manifests such a *union* to him, as renders
his condition theirs, in every state which he passed
through, insomuch that his righteousness, with all
the blessings and fruits thereof, is theirs, before they
were conscious of existence : Thus " *by the obedience of one, are many made righteous.*"

To prove that the atonement was satisfactory for
the whole *human race*, they alledge, that the scriptures abound with positive declarations to this effect :
" *The restitution of all things is preached by the
mouth of all God's holy prophets ever since the world
began.*"   It is said that " *Christ died for all,*" that
" *he is the propitiation for our sins, and not for ours
only, but for the sins of the whole world.*"

This denomination admit of no punishment for
sin, but what *Christ* suffered ; but speak of a punishment which is consequent upon sin, as *darkne's,
distress*, and *misery*, which, they assert, are ever
attendant upon *transgression*.   But as the scriptures
assure us, the *blood of Jesus cleanseth from all sin,*
" *that mystery of iniquity,*" which is so predominant at present in the human heart, will finally " *be
consumed by the spirit of his mouth, and be destroyed
by the brightness of his coming.*"   As " *to know the
true God, and Jesus Christ is life eternal ;*" and as
" *all shall know him from the least to the greatest.*"
That knowledge, or belief, will consequently dispel
or save from all that *darkne's, distress* and *fear* which

is ever attendant on *guilt* and *unbelief* : and being perfectly holy we shall consequently be perfectly and eternally happy.

*Relly's Union* p 7. 8 13. 14 22. 26. 36.
*Townsend's Remarks.* p. 16, 17.
*Female Catechism*, p. 13.

# W

**W**ALDENSES, Many authors of note make the antiquity of this denomination coeval with the apostolic age.*. The following is an extract from their *confession of faith*, which is said to have been copied out of certain manuscripts, bearing date near four hundred years before the time of *Luther*, and twenty before *Peter Waldo*.

I. That the scriptures teach, that there is one GOD *Almighty*, *all wise*, and *all good*, who has made all things by his *goodness* ; for he formed Adam in his own *image* and *likeness* ; but that by the *envy* of the Devil, and the *disobedience* of Adam, *sin* entered into the world, and that we are sinners in and by Adam.

II. That CHRIST was promised to our *fathers*, who received the *law*, that so knowing by the *law*
their

---

* The learned Mr. Allix, in his history of the churches of Piedmont, gives this account : That for three hundred years or more, the Bishop of Rome attempted to subjugate the church of Milan under her jurisdiction, and at last the interest of Rome grew too potent for the church of Milan, planted by one of the disciples ; insomuch, that the Bishop and the people, rather than own their jurisdiction, retired to the vallies, and from thence were called *Vallenses Wallenses*, or *the People in the Vallies*. [See Allix's History of the Churches of Piedmont, and Perrin's History of the Waldenses]

On the other hand, the Papists derive their origin from Peter Waldo. [See *Dupin's Church History*, and *Dufresnoy's Chronological Tables*]

their *unrighteousness* and *insufficiency*, they might desire the coming of CHRIST to satisfy for their *sins*, and accomplish the *law* by himself.

III. That CHRIST was born in the *time* appointed by GOD the Father ; that is to say, in the *time* when all *iniquity* abounded, that he might shew us *grace* and *mercy*, as being faithful.

IV. That CHRIST is our *life, truth, peace* and *righteousness*; as also our *Pastor, Advocate* and *Priest*, who died for the *salvation* all who believe ; and is risen for our *justification*.

V. That there is no *Mediator* and *Advocate* with GOD the Father, save JESUS CHRIST.

VI. That after this life, there are only two *places*, the one for the *saved*, and the other for the damned.

VII. That the *feasts*, the *vigils of saints*, the *water* which they call *holy* ; as also to abstain from *flesh* on *certain days*, and the like ; but especially the *masses*, are the inventions of men, and ought to be rejected.

VIII. That the *sacraments* are *signs* of the *holy thing*, visible forms of the *invisible grace* ; and that it is good for the faithful to use those *signs*, or *visible forms* ; but they are not essential to *salvation*.

IX. That there are no other *sacraments* but *baptism* and the *Lord's supper*.

X. That we ought to honour the *secular powers* by *subjection*, ready *obedience*, and paying of tributes.

*Perrin's Hist. of the Waldenses,* p. 226.
*Athenian Oracle,* vol. i. p. 224.

# WICLIFFITES,

**WICLIFFITES,** A ſect which ſprang up in England in the fourteenth century.    They took their
name from John Wicliff, *Doĉtor* and *Profeſſor of
Divinity* in the Univerſity of Oxford, a man of an
enterpriſing genius, and extraordinary learning.

He began with attacking the juriſdiĉtion of the
*Pope* and the *Biſhops* ; and declared, that *penance*
had no ſort of merit in the ſight of God, unleſs
followed with a reformed life.    He was a warm
oppoſer of *abſolution* :  for he alledged, that it
belonged to God alone to *forgive ſins* ; but
inſtead of aĉting as God's miniſters,  the *Romiſh*
clergy took upon them to *forgive ſins* in their
own names.   He alſo taught, that *external confeſſion* was not neceſſary to ſalvation ; exclaimed
againſt *indulgences, prayers* to the *ſaints,* the *celibacy
of the clergy,* the doĉtrine of *tranſubſtantiation,
monaſtic vows* ; and other praĉtices in the *Romiſh
Church.*

He not only exhorted the laity to ſtudy the ſcriptures, but alſo tranſlated into *Engliſh* theſe divine
books, in order to render the peruſal of them more
univerſal.

The followers of Wickliff were alſo called
Lollards.

*Moſheim's Eccleſiaſtical Hiſt. vol* iii *p.* 166.
*Gilpin's Life of Wickliff, p* 67  68  73
*Bailey's Diĉtionary, vol.* ii  [*See Wickiffites*]

**WILHELMINIANS,** A ſeĉt which aroſe in the
thirteenth century ; ſo called from *Withelmina,* a
Bohemian woman, who reſided in the territory of
Milan.    She perſuaded a large number, that the
*Holy Ghoſt* was become *incarnate* in her perſon, for
the ſalvation of a great part of mankind.

According

According to her doctrine, none were faved by the blood of JESUS, but true and pious Chriftians ; while the *Jews, Saracens,* and unworthy Chriftians, were to obtain falvation through the Holy Spirit which dwelt in her ; and that, in confequence thereof, all which had happened to CHRIST, during his appearance upon earth in the human nature, was to be exactly renewed in her perfon, or rather in that of the *Holy Ghoft,* which was united to her.

*Mofheim's Ecclef. Hift. vol.* iii. *p.* 131.

## Z

ZACHEANS, Difciples of Zacheus, a native of *Paleftine* ; who, about the year 350, retired to a mountain near the city of *Jerufalem,* and there performed his devotions in fecret ; pretending that prayer was only agreeable to *God* when it was performed fecretly and in filence.

*Broughton's Hiftorical Library, vol.* ii. *p.* 516.

ZANZALIANS. [See Jacobites]

ZUINGLIANS, A branch of the ancient *Proteftants* ; fo called from *Ulric Zuinglius,* a Divine of Switzerland, who received the Doctor's cap at Bafil, in 1505. He poffeffed an uncommon fhare of penetration and acutenefs of genius.

Zuinglius declaimed againft *indulgences,* the *mafs,* the *celibacy of the clergy,* and other doctrines of the Romifh Church. He differed both from *Luther* and *Calvin* in the following point, viz. He fuppofed only a *fymbolical* or *figurative* prefence of the body and blood of Chrift in the *Euchariff,* and reprefented a pious remembrance of Chrift's death, and of the benefits it procured to mankind, as the only fruits which arofe from the celebration of the Lord's fupper.*

He was alfo for removing out of the churches, and abolifhing in the ceremonies of public worfhip, many things which Luther was difpofed to treat with toleration and indulgence, fuch as images, altars, wax tapers, the form of exorcifm, and private confeffion.

The religious tenets of this denomination were, in moft other points, fimilar to thofe of the Lutherans. [See Lutherans]

*Mofheim's Ecclefiaftical Hiftory, vol. iv p 66, 79.*
*Broughton's Hiftorical Library vol. ii. p 519.*

* Luther held *confubftantiation*; and Calvin acknowledged a *real* though *fpiritual prefence* of Chrift in the *facrament*: fo that they all three entertained different fentiments upon this fubject.

APPENDIX.

# APPENDIX.

THE religions which are not included in the foregoing work, are the *Pagans*, *Mahometans*, *Jews* and *Deists*. Of these, the *Pagans* are the most extensive; and the worship of the *Grand Lama* is the most extensive and splendid mode of *Paganism*.

The *Grand Lama* is a name given to the Sovereign Pontiff, or High Priest of the *Thibetian Tartars*, who resides at *Patoli*, a vast palace on a mountain, near the banks of *Barampooter*, about seven miles from *Lahassa*. The foot of this mountain is inhabited by twenty thousand *Lamas*, or *Priests*, who have their separate apartments round about the mountain; and according to their respective quality are placed nearer, or at a greater distance from the *Sovereign Pontiff*. He is not only worshipped by the *Thibetians*, but also is the great Object of adoration for the various tribes of heathen *Tartars*, who roam through the vast tract of continent which stretches from the banks of the *Wolga* to *Correa* on the sea of *Japan*. He is not only the Sovereign Pontiff, the Vicegerent of the *Deity* on earth, but the more remote *Tartars* absolutely regard him as the Deity himself; and call him *God, the everlasting Father of Heaven*. They believe him to be immortal, and



endowed

endowed with all knowledge and virtue. Every year they come up from different parts to worship and make rich offerings at his shrine : even the Emperor of *China*, who is a *Manchou Tartar*, does not fail in acknowledgments to him in his religious capacity ; and actually entertains, at a great expence, in the palace of *Peking*, an inferior *Lama*, deputed as his nuncio from *Thibet*. The *Grand Lama* is never to be seen but in a secret place of his palace, amidst a great number of lamps, setting cross-legged upon a cushion, and decked all over with gold and precious stones ; where at a distance the people prostrate themselves before him, it being not lawful for any so much as to kiss his feet. He returns not the least sign of respect, nor ever speaks, even to the greatest Princes ; but only lays his hand upon their heads, and they are fully persuaded they receive from thence a full forgivness of all their sins.

The *Sunniasses*, or *Indian* pilgrims, often visit *Thibet* as a holy place ; and the *Lama* always enter-tains a body of two or three hundred in his pay. Besides his religious influence and authority ; the *Grand Lama* is possessed of unlimitted power thro'-out his dominions, which are very extensive. The inferior *Lamás*, who form the most numerous as well as the most powerful body in the state, have the priesthood entirely in their hands ; and besides, fill up many monastic orders, which are held in great veneration among them. The whole country, like *Italy*, abounds with Priests ; and they entirely sub-sist on the great number of rich presents which are sent them from the utmost extent of *Tartary*, from the empire of the *Great Mogul*, and from almost all parts of the *Indies*.

The

The opinion of thofe who are reputed the moft orthodox among the *Thibetians*, is, that when the *Grand Lama* feems to die either of old age, or of infirmity, his foul in fact only quits a crazy habitation to look for another younger or better, and is difcovered again in the body of fome child, by certain tokens known only to the *Lamás*, or Priefts, in which order he always appears. In 1774 the *Grand Lama* was an infant which had been difcovered fome time before by the *Tayfhoo Lama* ; who, in authority and fanctity of character, is next to the *Grand Lama*, and during his minority acts as chief.

Almoft all the nations of the Eaft, except the *Mahometans*, believe the *Metempfychofis* as the moft important article of their faith ; efpecially the inhabitants of *Thibet* and *Ava*, the *Peguans*, *Siamefe*, the greateft part of the *Chinefe* and *Japanefe*, and the *Monguls* and *Kalmucks*, who changed the religion of *Schamanifm* for the worfhip of the *Grand Lama*.

According to the doctrine of this *Metempfychofis*, the foul is always in action, and never at reft : for no fooner does fhe leave her old habitation, but fhe enters a new one. The *Dailai Lama* being a divine perfon, can find no better lodging than the body of his fucceffor ; or the *Foe* refiding in the *Dailai Lama* which paffes to his fucceffor : and this being a God to whom all things are known ; the *Dailai Lama* is therefore acquainted with every thing which happened during his refidence in his former body.

This religion is faid to have been of three thoufand years ftanding ; and neither time, nor the influence of men has had the power of fhaking the
authority

authority of the *Grand Lama*.   This *theocracy* extends as fully to temporal, as to fpiritual concerns.

The *Eaſt-India* Company made a treaty with the *Lama* in 1774.

Guthrie's Geogr. Gram. Edition printed 1783  p. 596 597.
Middleton's New Syſtem of Geography, vol. 1. p 33.
Ann. Reg. 1780  p. 62.
Oeconomy of Human Life, p 5.
Dr. Stile's Election Sermon, p. 76.

The Mohammedans, or Mahometans, derive their name and doctrine from *Mohammed*, or *Mahomet*, who was born in *Arabia* in the fixth century.   He was endowed with a fubtle genius, and poſſeſſed an enterprize and ambition peculiar to himfelf.   He pretended to receive revelations ; and declared,  that God fent  him into the world not only to teach his will, but to compel mankind to embrace it.   The magiftrates of *Mecca* were alarmed at the progreſs of his doctrines, and *Mohammed* being apprifed of their defign to deftroy him, fled to *Medina* : from this flight, which happened in the 622d year of *Chriſt*, his followers compute their time.   This æra is called in *Arabic*, *Hegira*.

The book in which the *Mahometan* religion is contained is called the *Korân*, or *Alcoran*, by way of eminence, as we fay the *Bible*, which means the *Book*.*   Its doctrines made a moft rapid progreſs over *Arabia*, *Syria*, *Egypt* and *Perſia* ; and *Mohammed*

---

* The generality of the *Mohammedans* believe, that the firſt manufcript of the *Koran* has been from everlaftig by God's throne written on a table of vaft bigneſs, called the *Preſerved Table*, in which are recorded the Divine decrees : that a copy from this table, in one volume on paper, was, by the miniftry of the angel Gabriel, fent down to the loweſt Heaven in the month of *Ramadan*.

*hammed* became the moft powerful monarch in his time. His fucceffors fpread their religion and conquefts over the greateft part of *Afia*, *Africa* and *Europe*; and they ftill give law to a very confiderable part of mankind.

The great doctrine of the *Korân* is the *unity of God*: to reftore which point, *Mohammed* pretended was the chief end of his miffion; it being laid down by him as a fundamental truth, that there never was nor ever can be more than one true orthodox religion. For though the particular laws or ceremonies are only temporary, and fubject to alteration according to the Divine direction, yet the fubftance of it being *eternal truth*, is not liable to change, but continues immutably the fame. And he taught, that whenever this religion became neglected, or corrupted in effentials, *GOD* had the goodnefs to reinform and readmonifh mankind thereof by feveral prophets, of whom *Mofes* and *Jefus* were the moft diftinguifhed till the appearance of *Mohammed*. The *Korân* afferts *Jefus* to be the true *Meffias*, the *word* and *breath* of God, *Worker of Miracles, Healer of Difeafes, Preacher of Heavenly Doctrine*, and *exemplary Pattern of a perfect Life*; denying that he was crucified, but affirming that he afcended into *Paradife*; and that his religion was mended by *Mohammed*, who was the *feal* of the prophets, and was fent from *God* to reftore the *true religion*, which was corrupted in his time, to its primitive fimplicity; with the addition, however, of peculiar laws and ceremonies, fome of which had been ufed in former times, and others were now firft inftituted.

The *Mohammedans* divide their religion into two general parts—*faith or theory*, and *religion or practice*.

*tice.* Faith or theory is contained in this confeſſion of faith,—*There is but one God, and Mohammed is his prophet.* Under theſe two propoſitions are comprehended ſix diſtinct branches.—

1. Belief *in God.*
2. *In his* angels.
3. *In his* ſcriptures.
4. *In his* prophets.
5. *In the* reſurrection and judgment.
6. *In* God's abſolute decrees.

They reckon four points relating to practice.—

1. Prayer, *with* waſhings, &c.
2. Alms.
3. Faſting.
4. Pilgrimage to Mecca.

The idea which *Mohammed* taught his diſciples to entertain of the *Supreme Being*, may be ſeen from a public addreſs he made to his countrymen, which is as follows :

" Citizens of *Mecca !*

" The hour is now come when you muſt give an account of your reaſon and your talents. In vain have you received them from an Almighty Maſter, liberal and beneficent—in caſe you uſe them negligently, or if you never reflect. in the name of this Maſter, I muſt tell you, he will not ſuffer you to abuſe his ineſtimable gifts by waſting life away unprofitably, and imploying them only in unworthy amuſements. No more permit deluſive pleaſures to diſtract your hearts ! Open your minds and receive the truth ! Woe to you for the unworthy notion you have entertained of *God !* The heaven and the earth are his own ! and there is nothing in all their copious furniture but what invariably obeys him ! The ſun and ſtars with all their glory, have never

diſdained

difdained his fervice ! and no being can refift his will, and the exercife of his omnipotence ! He will call men to an account, and require of them the reafon for all thofe gods they have invented in defiance of reafon ! *There is no other God but GOD, and him only we muſt adore !"*

The belief of the exiftence of *Angels* is abfolutely required in the *Koran* : the *Mohammedans* fuppofe they have pure and fubtil bodies, created of fire ; and that they have various forms and offices ; fome being employed in writing down the actions of men, others in carrying the throne of God, and other fervices. They reckon four angels fuperior to all the reft : Thefe are, *Gabriel*, who is employed in writing down the divine decrees ; *Michael*, the friend and protector of the Jews ; *Azrael*, the angel of death ; and *Ifrafil*, who will found the trumpet at the refurrection. They likewife affign to each perfon two guardian angels.

The *Devil*, according to the *Koran*, was once one of the higheft angels, but fell for refufing to pay homage to *Adam* at the command of *God*.

Befides Angels and Devils, the *Mohammedans* are taught by the *Koran* to believe an intermediate order of Creatures, which they call *Jin*, or *Genii*, created alfo of fire; but of a groffer fabric than angels ; and are fubject to death. Some of thefe are fuppofed to be good, and others bad, and capable of future falvation or damnation as men are ; whence *Mohammed* pretended to be fent for the converfion of *Genii*, as well as men.

As to the *fcriptures*, the *Mohammedans* are taught by the *Korán*, that *God*, in divers ages of the



world,

world, gave revelations of his will in writing to several prophets. The number of these sacred books, according to them, are one hundred and four; of which ten were given to *Adam*, fifty to *Seth*, thirty to *Enoch*, ten to *Abraham*; and the other four, being the *Pentateuch*, the *Psalms*, the *Gospel*, and the *Korân*, were successively delivered to *Moses*, *David*, *Jesus*, and *Mohammed*; which last being the *seal* of the prophets these revelations are now closed. All these divine books, excepting the four last, they agree to be entirely lost, and their contents unknown. And of these four, the *Pentateuch*, *Psalms* and *Gospels*, they say, have undergone so many alterations and corruptions, that very little credit is to be given to the present copies in the hands of the *Jews* and *Christians*.

The number of *prophets* which have been from time to time sent into the world amounts to two hundred and twenty-four thousand; among whom three hundred and thirteen were apostles, sent with special commissions to reclaim mankind from infidelity and superstition; and six of them brought new laws or dispensations, which successively abrogated the preceding. These were 1. *Adam*, 2. *Noah*, 3. *Abraham*, 4. *Moses*, 5. *Jesus*, 6. *Mohammed*.

The next article of faith required by the *Koran*, is the belief of a general *resurrection* and a future *judgment*. But before these they believe there is an intermediate state, both of the soul and of the body after death. When a corps is laid in the grave, two angels come and examine it concerning the *unity of God* and the mission of *Mohammed*. If the body answers rightly it is suffered to rest in peace,

and

and is refreshed by the air of *Paradise* : if not, they
beat it about the temples with iron maces ; then
press the earth on the corps, which is gnawed and
stung by ninety-nine dragons with seven heads each.

As to the souls of the faithful, when they are
separated from the body by the *angel of death*, they
teach, that those of the *prophets* are admitted into
*Paradi e* immediately. Some suppose the souls of
*believers* are with *Adam* in the lowest Heaven ; and
there are various other opinions concerning their
state. Those who are called the most orthodox
hold, that the souls of the wicked are confined in a
dungeon under a green rock, to be there tormented
till their re-union with the body at the *general resurrection*.

●That the *resurrection* will be general, and extend
to all creatures, both angels, genii, men and animals,
is the received opinion of the *Mohammedans*, which
they support by the authority of the *Koran*.

Mankind, at the *resurrection*, will be distinguished
into three classes ; the first, of those who go on foot ;
the second, of those who ride ; and the third, of
those who creep grovelling with their faces on the
ground. The first class will consist of those believers whose good works have been few ; the second,
of those who are more acceptable to *God* ; whence
*Ali* affirmed that the pious, when they come forth
from their sepulchres, shall find ready prepared for
them white-winged camels, with saddles of gold.
The third class will be composed of the infidels,
whom *God* will cause to make their appearance
with their faces on the ground. When all are af-
sembled together, they will wait, in their ranks and

orders, for the judgment ; ſome ſay forty years, others ſeventy, others three hundred, and ſome no leſs than fifty thouſand years. During which time they will ſuffer great inconveniences, the good as well as the bad,* from their thronging and preſſing upon each other, and the unuſual approach of the ſun, which will be no farther off them than the diſtance of a mile ; ſo that the ſkulls of the wicked will boil like a pot, and they will be all bathed with ſweat. At length GOD will come in the clouds ſurrounded by the angels, and will produce the books wherein every man's actions are written. Some explaining thoſe words ſo frequently uſed in the *Koran, God will be ſwift in taking an account*, ſay, that he will judge all creatures in the ſpace of half a day ; and others, that it will be done in leſs time than the twinkling of an eye. At this tribunal, every action, thought, word, &c. will be weighed in a balance held by the angel Gabriel, of ſo vaſt a ſize, that its two ſcales are capacious enough to contain both Heaven and Earth.

The trials being over, and the aſſembly diſſolved, thoſe who are to be admitted. into Paradiſe, will take the right-hand way ; and thoſe who are deſtined to hell fire, the left : but both of them muſt firſt paſs the bridge called in *Arabic, Al Sirat*, which is laid over the middle of Hell, and is deſcribed to be finer than a hair, and ſharper than the edge of a ſword. The wicked will miſs their footing and fall headlong into Hell.      In

* Yet they make a manifeſt difference between the ſufferings of the righteous and the wicked : for the limbs of the former, particularly thoſe parts they uſed to waſh before prayer, ſhall ſhine gloriouſly, and their ſuffering ſhall laſt no longer than the time neceſſary to ſay their prayers : and they ſhall be protected from the heat of the ſun by the ſhade of God's throne.

In the *Koran* it is said that *Hell* has seven gates ; the first for the *Musselmans*, the second for the *Christians*, the third for the *Jews*, the fourth for the *Sabians*, the fifth for the *Magicians*, the sixth for the *Pagans*, the seventh and worst of all, for the *Hypocrites of all religions*. The inhabitants of Hell will suffer a variety of torments, which shall be of eternal duration, except with those who have embraced the true religion, who will be delivered thence, after they have expiated their crimes by their sufferings.*

The righteous, after having surmounted the difficulties in their passage, will enter *Paradise*, which they describe to be a most delicious place, whose earth is the finest *wheat*, or *musk* ; and the stones *pearls*, or *jacinths*. It is also adorned with flowery fields, beautified with trees of gold, enlivened with the most ravishing musick, abounding with rivers of *milk*, *wine* and *honey*, and watered by lesser springs, whose pebbles are *rubies*, *emeralds*, &c. Here the faithful enjoy the most exquisite sensual delights, free from the least alloy.†

The sixth great point of *faith* which the *Mohammedans* are taught to believe is, *GOD's absolute decree*, and predetermination both of good and evil. The doctrine, which they call orthodox, is, that whatever doth or shall come to pass in the world,

whether

* Between *Paradise* and *Hell* they imagine there is a *wall* or *partition*, in which, some suppose, those were placed whose good and evil works exactly counterpoised each other. These will be admitted to *Paradise* at the last day, after they have performed an act of adoration, which will make the scale of their good works to over-balance.

† Some of the most refined *Mahometans* understand their prophet's description of *Paradise* in an *allegorical sense*.

whether it be good or bad, proceedeth entirely from the Divine will, and is irrevocably fixed and recorded from all eternity in the *preserved table* ; and that God hath secretly predetermined not only the adverse and prosperous fortune of every person in the world, in the most minute particulars, but also his obedience or disobedience, and consequently his everlasting happiness or misery after death ; which fate or predestination it is impossible by any foresight or wisdom to avoid. *

Of the four practical duties required by the Koran, *prayer* is the first. *Mohammed* used to call *prayer the pillar of religion and key of Paradise.* Hence he obliged his followers to pray five times every twenty-four hours, and always wash before prayers.

*Circumcision* is held by the Mohammedans to be of Divine institution.

The giving of *alms* is frequently commanded in the *Koran*, and often recommended therein jointly with prayer ; the former being held of great efficacy in causing the latter to be heard with God.

*Fasting* is a duty enjoined by *Mohammed* as of the utmost importance. His followers are obliged by the express command of the *Koran*, to fast the whole month of *Ramadan.* ; during which time they are obliged to fast from day-light to sun-set. The
reason

* Of this doctrine *Mohammed* made great use for the advancement of his designs ; encouraging his followers to fight without fear, and even desperately, for the propagation of their faith, by representing to them that all their caution could not avert their inevitable destiny, or prolong their lives for a moment  Hence some of his followers carry this matter so far as to take no care to avoid the *plague,* which is common in *Eastern* countries.

reafon of the month of *Ramadan* is pitched upon for that purpofe is, they fuppofe that at that time the *Koran* was fent down from Heaven.

The *pilgrimage to Mecca* is fo neceffary a point of practice, that, according to a tradition of *Moham-med*, he who dies without performing it, may as well die a *Jew* or a *Chriftian* ; and the fame is expreffly commanded in the *Koran*.

The negative precepts of the *Koran* are, to abftain from *ufury*, *gaming*, drinking of *wine*, eating of *blood* and *fwines flefh*.

The *Mohammedans* are divided and fubdivided in-to an endlefs variety of fects : as it is faid there is as great a diverfity in their opinions as among the Chri-ftians, it is impoffible to give a particular account of their divifions in the compafs of this work ; which will admit only of noticing a few of their principal denominations.

The divinity of the *Mohammedans* may be divided into *fcholaftic* and *practical*. Their *fcholaftic divinity* confifts of *logical, metaphyfical, theological,* and *philo-fophical* difquifitions ; and is built on principles and methods of reafoning very different from what are ufed by thofe who pafs among the *Mohammedans* themfelves for the founder divines, or more able phi-lofophers. This art of handling religious difputes was not known in the infancy of *Mohammedifm*, but was brought in when fects fprang up, and articles of religion began to be called in queftion.

As to their *practical divinity* or *jurifprudence*, it confifts in the knowledge of the decifions of the law which regard practice gathered from diftinct proofs. The principal points of faith fubject to the
examination

examination and difcuffion of the fchoolmen are, the *unity* and *attributes* of GOD ; the *divine decrees,* or *preaeftination* ; the *promiffes* and *threats* contained in the *law* ; and matters of *biftory* and *reafon.*

The fects among the Mohammedans who are efteemed *orthodox,* are called by the general name of *Sonnites,* or *Traditionarifts,* becaufe they acknowledge the authority of the *Sonna,* or collection of moral traditions of the fayings and actions of their prophet.

The *Sonnites* are fubdivided into four chief fects, viz.

1ft. The *Hanifites.* 2d. The *Malekites.* 3d. The *Shafeits.* 4th. The *Hanbalites.*

The difference between thefe fects confifts only in a few indifferent ceremonies.

The fects whom the generality of the *Mohammedans* fuppofe entertain erroneous opinions are numerous ; the following are felected from a large number, in order to give fome ideas of the difputes among *Mohammedan* divines.

Firft, the *Montazalites,* the followers of *Wafel Ebn Ata.* As to their chief and general tenets, 1ft. They entirely rejected all eternal attributes of God to avoid the diftinction of perfons made by the Chriftians. 2d. They believed the word of God to have been created in *fubjecto,* as the fchoolmen term it, and to confift of letters and founds ; copies thereof being written in books to exprefs and imitate the original. They alfo affirmed, that whatever is created in *fubjecto* is alfo an accident, and liable to perifh. 3d. They denied *abfolute predeftination* ; maintaining, that God was not the author of evil, but

but of good only ; and that man was a free agent.
4th. They held, that if a profeſſor of the true religion be guilty of a grievous ſin, and die without
repentance, he will be eternally damned, though his
puniſhment will be lighter than that of the infidels.
5th. They denied all viſion of God in Paradiſe by
the corporeal eye, and rejected all compariſons or
ſimilitudes applied to God.

This ſect are ſaid to have been the firſt inventors
of *ſcholaſtic divinity*, and are ſubdivided, as ſome
reckon, into twenty different ſects.

Secondly, the *Haſhemians* ; who were ſo named
from their maſter *Aba Haſham Abel al Salem*  His
followers were ſo much afraid of making God the
author of evil, that they would not allow him to be
ſaid to create an *infidel*, becauſe an *infidel* is a compound of *infidelity* and *man*, and God is not the creator of *infidelity*.

Thirdly, the *Nohámians*, or followers of *Ibráhim
al Nedhám*, who imagined he could not ſufficiently
remove God from being the author of evil, without
diveſting him of his power in reſpect thereto, taught
that no power ought to be aſcribed to God concerning evil and rebellious actions : but this he affirmed
againſt the opinion of his own diſciples, who allowed that God could do evil, but did not becauſe of
its turpitude.

Fourthly, the *Jahedhians*, or followers of *Amru
Ebn Bahr*, a great doctor of the *Montazalites*, who
differed from his brethren in that he imagined the
damned would not be eternally tormented in hell,
but would be changed into the nature of fire, and
that the fire would of itſelf attract them without
any neceſſity of their going into it.

E e

Fifthly,

Fifthly, the *Kodarians*, or followers of *Mahad al Johni*. This sect deny *absolute predestination* ; saying, that evil and injustice ought not to be attributed to GOD, but to man who is a free agent, and may therefore be rewarded or punished for his actions, which GOD has granted him power either to do or omit.

Sixthly, the *Jabarians*, who are the direct opponents of the *Kadarians*, denying free agency in man, and ascribing his actions wholly to GOD. The most rigid of this sect will not allow man to be said either to act or have any power at all, either *operative* or *acquiring* ; asserting, that man can do nothing, but produces all his actions by *necessity*, having neither *power*, nor *will*, nor *choice*, any more than an inanimate agent : they declare that *rewarding* and *punishing* are also the effects of *necessity*, and the same they say of the imposing of commands.

Seventhly, the *Jamians*, the followers of *Jam Ebn Safwan*, who held the same doctrine with the *Jabarians* ; and likewise maintained, that *Paradise* and *Hell* will vanish, or be annihilated after those who are destined thereto respectively shall have entered them, so that at last there will remain no existing Being besides GOD ; supposing those words of the *Korán*, which declare that the inhabitants of *Paradise* and of *Hell* shall *remain therein forever*, to be *hyperbolical* only, and intended for corroboration, and not to denote an eternal duration in reality.

Eighthly, the *Schites :* this name is used peculiarly to denote those who maintain *Ali Ebn Ali Taleb* to be their lawful *Khalif*, or *Iman*, and that the supreme authority both in spirituals and temporals, of right belongs to his descendants.

Some

Some of thefe affirm, that GOD appeared in the form of *Ali*, and with his tongue proclaimed the moft hidden myfteries of religion ; and fome have gone fo far as to afcribe Divine honours to him, and to expect his return in the clouds ; and having fixed this belief as an article of their faith, they keep a fine horfe ready faddled &c. for him in the mofque of Cufa.

Others believe that he is concealed in a grotto near Cufa, where he will continue till the day of judgment, and then come forth to convert all people to the *Koran*.

*Sale's Koran, vol* i. *p* 83 93. 94 95 96 97 99 100,
111. 112. 114 117, 120, 122. 126, 128, 137, 138, 141,
142. 146. 148. 150 152 153. 201, 202, 203, 204, 205,
211, 212, 213. 214, 216, 227.
*Turkifh Spy vol.* vii *p.* 205.
*Guthrie's Geographical Grammar, p.* 580 581.
*Boulainvilliers Life of Mahomet.*
*Bayley's Dictionary. vol.* ii.  [*See Schites*]

The *modern Jews* are difperfed over every king-dom in the world ; and in fpite of the miferies they have fuffered, ftill overlook all nations, and confider themfelves as the favourites of Heaven.

The *Jews* commonly reckon but thirteen articles of their faith. *Mamonides, a famous Jewifh Rabbi,* reduced them to this number when he drew their confeffion about the end of the eleventh century ; and it was generally received. All the *Jews* are obliged to live and die in the profeffion of thefe thir-teen articles.

I.   That GOD is the creator of all things ; that he guides and fupports all creatures ; that he has done every thing ; and that he ftill acts, and fhall act during the whole eternity.

E e 2

II. That

II. That *GOD is one.* There is no unity like his. He alone hath been, is, and shall be eternally our God.

III. That GOD is incorporeal, and cannot have any material properties ; and no corporeal essence can be compared with him.

IV. That GOD is the beginning and end of all things, and shall eternally subsist.

V. That GOD alone ought to be worshipped, and none but him is to be adored.

VI. That whatever has been taught by the *prophets* is true.

VII. That *Moses* is the father and head of all cotemporary doctors, and those who lived before, or shall live after him.

VIII. That the *law* was given by *Moses.*

IX. That the *law* shall never be altered, and GOD will give no other.

X. That GOD knows all the thoughts and actions of men.

XI. That GOD will regard the works of all those who have performed what he commands, and punish those who have transgressed his laws.

XII. That the *Messiah* is to come, though he tarry a long time.

XIII. That the resurrection of the dead shall happen when GOD shall think fit.

The *modern Jews* adhere still as closely to the *Mosaic* dispensation, as their dispersed and despised condition will permit them. Their service consists chiefly in reading the law in their synagogues, together

with

with a great variety of prayers. They use no facrifices fince the deftruction of the temple. They re-
peat bleffings and particular praifes to God, not only
in their prayers, but on all accidental occafions, and
in almoft all their actions. They go to prayers three
times a day in their fynagogues. Their fermons are
made not in Hebrew, which few of them now perfectly underftand, but in the language of the country
where they refide. They are forbidden all vain fwearing, and pronouncing any of the names of God without neceffity. They abftain from meats prohibited
by the Levitical law ; for which reafon whatever
they eat muft be dreffed by *Jews*, and after a manner peculiar to themfelves. As foon as a child can
fpeak, they teach him to read and tranflate the *bible*
into the language of the country where they live.
In general they obferve the fame ceremonies which
were practifed by their anceftors in the celebration
of the *Paffover*. They acknowledge a two-fold law
of God, a written and an unwritten one. The former is contained in the *Pentateuch*, or five books of
Mofes : the latter, they pretend, was delivered by
God to Mofes, and handed down from him by *oral
tradition*, and now to be received as of *equal authority* with the former. They affert the perpetuity of
their *law*, together with its perfection. They deny
the accomplifhment of the prophecies in the perfon
of *Chrift* ; alledging, that the *Meffiah* is not yet
come, and that he will make his appearance with
the greateft worldly pomp and grandeur, fubduing
all nations before him, and fubjecting them to the
houfe of Judah. Since the prophets have predicted
his mean condition and fufferings, they confidently
talk of two *Meffiahs* : one, *Ben-Ephraim*, whom
they

they grant to be a perfon of a mean and afflicted condition in the world ; and the other, *Ben-David,* who fhall be a victorious and powerful Prince.

Almoft all the *modern Jews* are *Pharifees,* and are as much attached to tradition as their anceftors were ; and affert, that whoever rejects the *oral law* deferves death.   Hence they entertain an implacable hatred to the *Caraites,* a fect among the *Jews,* who adhere to the text of Mofes and the word of God ; rejecting the *Rabbiniftical* interpretation and *cabala.*   The number of the *Caraites* is fmall in comparifon with the *Rabbins :* and the latter have fo great an averfion to this fect, that they will have no alliance or even converfation with them.   And if a *Caraite* would turn *Rabbinift,* the other Jews would not receive him.

The *modern Pharifees* are lefs ftrict than their anceftors with regard to food, and other aufterities of the body.   They formerly fafted the fecond and fifth day of the week ; and put thorns at the bottom of their robes, that they might prick their legs as they went along : they lay upon boards covered with flint ftones, and tied thick cords about their waifts : but thefe mortifications were not obferved always, nor by all.   They paid tithes as the law prefcribed, and gave the thirtieth and fiftieth part of their fruits ; adding voluntary facrifices to thofe which were commanded, and fhewing themfelves very exact in performing their vows.   As to their doctrine, with the *Effenes,* they held *abfolute predeftination,* and with the *Sadduces, free will.*   They believed with *Pythagoras,* the *tranfmigration of fouls ;* efpecially thofe of people of virtue ; efteeming thofe who were notorioufly wicked to be eternally miferable.

rable. As to lefs ciimes, they held they were punifhed in the bodies which the fouls of thofe who
committed them were next fent into. According
to this notion it was, thatChrift's difciples afked him
concerning the blind man, *Who did fin, this man or
his parents, that he was born blind?* John ix. 2.
And when the difciples told Chrift that *fome faid
he was Elias,* and others *Jeremias, or one of the prophets,* the meaning only can be, that they thought
he was come into the world animated with the foul
of *Elias, Jeremias,* or fome of the old prophets *tranf-
migrated* into him.

There are ftill fome of the *Sadduces* in *Africa* and
in feveral other places ; but they are very few in
number ; at leaft, there are but very few who declare
openly for thefe opinions.

There are to this day fome remains of the ancient fect of the *Samaritans,* who are zealous for the
*law* of *Mofes,* but are defpifed by the *Jews,* becaufe
they receive only the *Pentateuch,* and obferve different ceremonies from theirs. They declare they
are no *Sadduces,* but acknowledge the *fpirituality*
and *immortality* of the foul. There are of this fect
at *Gaza, Damafcus, Grand Cairo,* and in fome other
places of the *Eaft,* but efpecially at *Sichem,* now called *Naploufe,* which is rifen out of the ruins of the
ancient *Samaria,* where they facrificed not many
years ago, having a place for this purpofe on Mount
*Gerizim.*

With regard to the *ten tribes,* the learned Mr. *Baf-
nage* fuppofes they ftill fubfift in the *Eaft* ; and gives
the following reafons for this opinion.—1ft. *Salma-
naffar* had placed them upon the banks of the *Chaboras,*

*ras*, which emptied itfelf into the *Euphrates*. On the Weft was *Ptolemy's Chalcitis* and the city *Carra*. And therefore God has brought back the *Jews* to the country from whence the patriarchs came. On the Eaft was the province of *Ganzan* betwixt the two rivers *Chaboras* and *Saocoras*. This was the firft fituation of the *tribes* : but they fpread into the neighbouring provinces, and upon the banks of the *Euphrates*. 2d. The *ten tribes* were ftill in being in this country when *Jerufalem* was deftroyed, fince they came in multitudes to pay their devotions in the temple. 3d. They fubfifted there from that time to the eleventh century, fince they had their heads of the captivity and moft flourifhing academies. 4th. Though they were confiderably weakened by perfecutions, yet travellers of that nation difcovered abundance of their brethren and fynagogues in the twelfth and fourteenth centuries. 5th. No new colony has been fent into the *Eaft* ; nor have thofe which were there been driven out. 6th. The hiftory of the *Jews* has been deduced from age to age, without difcovering any other change than what was caufed by the different revolutions of that empire—the various tempers of the governors—or the inevitable decay in a nation, which only fubfifts by toleration. We have therefore reafon to conclude, that the *ten tribes* are ftill in the *Eaft*, whether God fuffered them to be carried. If the families and tribes are not diftinguifhable, it is impoffible it fhould be otherwife in fo long a courfe of ages and afflictions which they have paffed through. In fine, fays this *learned author*, if we would feek out the remains of the *ten tribes*, we muft do it only on the banks of *Euphrates*, in *Perfia*, and the neighbouring provinces.

It is impoſſible to fix the number of people the *Jewiſh nation* is at preſent compoſed of: but yet w have reaſon to believe, there are ſtill near three millions of people who profeſs this *religion,* and, as their phraſe is, are *witneſſes of the unity of God in all the nations in the world.*

They always are expecting a glorious return, which ſhall raiſe them above all the nations of the earth. They flatter themſelves this deliverance will ſpeedily arrive, though they dare not fix the preciſe time.

*Baſnage's Hiſt of the Jews, p, 110. 115, 227,*
*274, 467. 746. 747 748.*
*Broughton's Hiſt Library. vol. i p. 205. 221,*
*522 —vol. ii. p 226 245. 329.*
*Collier's Hiſt. Dictionary, vol. ii. [See Pha-*
*riſees and Samaritans]*

The *Deiſts* are ſpread all over *Europe,* and have multiplied prodigiouſly among the higher rank in moſt nations ; but the ſentiments which are diſtinguiſhed by this title, are rarely embraced among the common people.

The name of *Deiſts* is ſaid to have been firſt aſſumed about the middle of the ſixteenth century, by ſome gentlemen in *France* and *Italy,* in order to avoid the imputation of *Atheiſm.* One of the firſt authors who made uſe of this name was *Peter Viret,* a celebrated Divine ; who, in a work which was publiſhed in 1563; ſpeaks of ſome perſons in that time who were called by a new name, that of *Deiſts.* Theſe, he tells us, profeſſed to believe a *God,* but ſhewed no regard to *Jeſus Chriſt,* and conſidered the doctrines of the *apoſtles* and *evangeliſts* as fables and dreams.

F f

The

The *Lord Edward Herbert*, *Baron of Cherbury*, who flourished in the seventeenth century, has been regarded as the most eminent of the *Deistical* writers, and appears to be one of the first who formed *Deism* into a system ; and asserted the *sufficiency, universality*, and *absolute perfection* of *natural religion*, with a view to discard all extraordinary revelation as useless and needless. He reduced this *universal religion* to five articles, which he frequently mentioned in his works.

I.　That there is one supreme GOD.

II.　That he is chiefly to be worshipped.

III.　That *piety* and *virtue* are the principal parts of his worship.

IV.　That we must repent of our sins ; and if we do so God will pardon us.

V.　That there are rewards for good men, and punishments for bad men, in a future state.

The *Deists* are classed by some of their own writers into two sorts—*mortal* and *immortal Deists*.— The latter acknowledge a *future state*—the former deny it, or at least represent it as a very uncertain thing.

The learned *Dr. Clark*, taking the denomination in the most extensive signification, distinguishes *Deists* into four sorts.—The first are, such as pretend to believe the existence of an infinite, eternal, independent, inttelligent Being ; and who, to avoid the name of *Epicurean Atheists*, teach also, that this *supreme Being* made the world ; though at the same time they agree with the *Epicureans* in this, that they fancy God does not at all concern himself in

the

the government of the world, nor has any regard to, or care of, what is done therein.

The fecond fort of *Deifts* are thofe who believe not only the being, but alfo the providence of *God,* with refpect to the natural world ; but who not allowing any difference between moral good and evil, deny that God takes any notice of the morally good and evil actions of men : thefe things depending, as they imagine, on the arbitrary conftitution of human laws.

A third fort of *Deifts* there are, who believe in the natural attributes of God, and his all-governing providence, and have fome notion of his moral perfections alfo ; yet deny the immortality of the foul, believing that men perifh entirely at death, and that one generation fhall perpetually fucceed another, without any future reftoration or renovation of things.

A fourth, and the laft fort of *Deifts* are, fuch as believe the exiftence of a *fupreme Being,* together with his providence in the government of the world, as alfo all the obligations of natural religion ; but fo far only as thefe things are difcoverable by the light of nature alone, without believing any Divine revelation.

Many of the *modern Deifts* in *Europe* are faid to be of that clafs who deny the immortality of the foul, and any future ftate of exiftence.

*Leland's View of Deiftical Writers, vol. i. p. 2, 3.*
*Broughton's Hift Library, vol. i. p. 316.*
*Voltaire's Univerfal Hiftory, vol. ii. p. 259.*

*A short View of the different Religions of the several People and Kingdoms of the habitable World.*

## 1st. RELIGIONS of EUROPE.

EAST AND WEST GREENLAND. The *Greenlanders* believe the immortality of the soul, and the existence of a spirit called Thorngarsuk: the *Angukuts*, or Priests, who are supposed to be his immediate successors, form very different opinions with regard to his nature, form, and place of residence: they suppose all the elements are filled with spirits, from which every *Angukut* is supplied with a familiar spirit called *Thorngak*, who is always ready when summoned to their assistance.

They pretend to cure diseases by spells and charms, to converse with their God *Thorngarsuk*, and to promulgate his commands.*

DENMARK, The *Lutheran religion* is uni-
NORWAY, versally embraced in these king-
SWEDEN. doms; excepting that at *Livonia* in *Sweden*, there are a number of *Papists*, and at *Copenhagen* in *Denmark*, there is a church allowed for the French refugees; and at *Glukstat* a few Popish families have been permitted the use of a chapel.†

LAPLAND. The *Laplanders* believe in a good and evil Principle, which they suppose to be at constant variance, and the prevalence of either, productive of the happiness or misery of mankind.

They

* Jones's Universal Grammar. Vol. i. p. 134.
† Broughton. Vol. ii. p. 323.

They believe a *Metemphycosis*, or transmigration of souls, and pay their adoration to certain *Genii*, who they suppose inhabit the air, mountains, lakes, &c. They also place an implicit faith in magic ; and their magicians, who are a peculiar set of men, make use of what they call a drum, made of the hollowed trunk of a fir, pine or birch tree, one end of which is covered with a skin ; on this they draw, with a kind of red colour, the figures of their own gods, as well as of *Jesus Christ*, the *apostles*, the sun, moon and stars, birds, and rivers : on these they place one or two brass rings, which, when the drum is beaten with a little hammer, dance over the figures ; and, according to their progress the sorcerer prognosticates.*

RUSSIA. The established religion is that of the *Greek Church*. This church, according to its original constitution, is governed by four Patriarchs, viz. those of Alexandria, of Jerusalem, of Antioch, and of Constantinople ; the latter of which, assumes to himself the title of *universal* or *œcumenical* Patriarch, on account of his residing in the imperial city, and having a larger jurisdiction than the rest.†

The conquered provinces retain the exercise of their own religion ; and such is the extent of this vast empire, that many of its inhabitants are *Mahometans*, and there are many *Pagans* in the uncultivated provinces.‡

SCOTLAND. The established religion is the *Presbyterian*, which was introduced into this country by *John Knox*, a disciple of *Calvin*, in the year 1561,

* Guthrie, p. 96.  † History of Religion, Number iv. p. 250.
‡ Guthrie, p. 124,

1561,* and ſtill continues, being moſt agreeable to the genius and inclination of the people.†

The Diſſenters in *Scotland* conſiſt of the *Epiſcopalians*, a few *Quakers*, *Roman Catholics*, and other ſects, who are denominated from their preachers.‡

ENGLAND. The eſtabliſhed religion in this kingdom is that of a *Proteſtant Epiſcopacy*. The ſovereigns of England, ever ſince the reign of Henry the Eighth, have been ſtiled, the Supreme Heads of the Church. And the Church of England under the monarchical power over it, is governed by two Archbiſhops, and twenty-four Biſhops. The Archbiſhops are dignified with the addreſs of Your Grace. The Archbiſhop of Canterbury is the firſt peer of the realm, as well as metropolitan of all England. The Biſhops are addreſſed, Your Lordſhips ; and ſtiled, Right Reverend Fathers in God ; and precede as Barons, on all public occaſions.

The dignitaries of the Church of England, ſuch as Deans, Prebends, and the like, have generally large incomes. England contains about ſixty Arch-deacons, whoſe buſineſs it is to viſit the churches twice or thrice every year. Subordinate to them are the rural Deans, formerly ſtiled Arch-preſbyters, who ſignify the Biſhop's pleaſure to his clergy, the lower claſs of which conſiſts of Prieſts and Deacons.

The thirty-nine articles of the Church of England are *Calviniſtical* ; yet there are not many of the eſtabliſhed church who think they are ſtriſtly and conſcientiouſly bound to believe the doctrinal parts

of

---

of thefe articles, which they are obliged to fubfcribe before they can enter into holy orders.

TheDiffenters in England are very numerous ; the principal denominations are the *Prefbyterians, Independents, Baptifts, Quakers,* and *Methodifts.* The *Methodifts* are divided into different parties, and form large focieties. There is alfo a large number of *Arians, Socinians, Deifts,* and other fubordinate denominations. And many families in *England* ftill profefs the *Roman Catholic* religion ; and its exercife is under very mild and gentle reftrictions.*

WALES. The eftablifhed religion is that of the Church of England ; but fome ancient families are *Roman Catholics.*†

IRELAND. The eftablifhed religion is fimilar to that of England ; and there are as many denominations, particularly *Prefbyterians, Quakers, Baptifts,* and *Methodifts.*

FRANCE. The eftablifhed religion in this kingdom is *Roman Catholic,* in which their Kings have been fo conftant that they have obtained the title of *Moft Chriftian ;* and the Pope, in his bull, gives the King of *France* the title of *Eldeft Son of the Church.* The *Galacian* clergy are, however, more exempt than others who profefs the Romifh religion from the Papal authority ; their church confines the Pope's power entirely to things relating to falvation ;‖ and has feveral antient rights, which they have taken care never to relinquifh. The Pope never can excommunicate the *King* of *France,* or abfolve

* ‡ Guthrie, p. 211, 212, 213.   † *ibid.* p. 377.   ‖ *ibid.* p. 415

folve any of his fubjects from their allegiance : he is not allowed to be fuperior to an œcumienical or general Council : and they affert, that infalibility is lodged, not in the Pope, but in a general Council only.*

The *Hugonots* in *France*, who were formerly oppreffed with heavy perfecutions, enjoy a good degree of religious liberty at prefent. ‡

The *Roman Catholics* in this kingdom are divided into feveral denominations ; among whom the Janfenifts; Quietifts, and Borigno nifts are chief.||

*Deifm* prevails greatly among thofe of high rank.

UNITED PROVINCES. The *Dominant* fect of Chriftians in thefe *Provinces* are thofe who are called the *Reformed Church.* They are fevere *Calvinifts*, who maintain the doctrine of the *Synod of Dort.*

*Roman Catholics*, amongft whom are the *Janfénifts.* They are in proportion to the inhabitants of the *Provinces* as two to three.

The *Remonftrants* or *Arminians*, who only have churches in *Holland, Utrecht* and *Friefland.* The greateft part of them are inhabitants of *Holland*, principally *Amfterdam, Rotterdam* and *Geuda.*

*Lutherans*, are a very great and increafing number.

*Baptifts*, divided into feveral fects, are mighty and numerous. Thofe who are called *Menonites* approach nigh to the *Reformed Church.* The *Baptifts* are generally *Unitarians*, loving and practifing *univerfal toleration.*

*Collegiants*,

* Hift. Religion, Nnmber vi. p. 256.    ‡ Stile's Sermon, p. 58;
|| Jones.    Vol. i; p. 577;

*Collegiants*, formed by the persecution of the *Remonstrant* ministers in 1619. They have no peculiar minister, but every one learns and preaches what he thinks useful : at present they are only in *Holland*.

*Quakers*, with us are a small number.

*Hernhutters*, and at Amsterdam, *Perhans*, and members of the Grecian church ; to which add many thousand *Jews*.

There is at present, notwithstanding the rigid *Placards* against the *Roman Catholics* and *Socinians*, a prevailing spirit of candor and Catholicism among the different denominations.

The ministers of the gospel belonging to the *Dominant church*, are maintained by the civil magistrate ; those of the *Dissenters*, by their own churches, who have acquired funds for various purposes, by gifts, testaments, legacies, and donations of private men.

*Deism*, in the worst sense of the word is not common in this country. Few men, who love to be called philosophers ; some profligates, and boys, constitute this class. *

**AUSTRIAN & FRENCH NETHERLANDS.** The established religion here is the *Roman Catholic* ; but *Protestants* and other denominations are not molested.†

**GERMANY.** The *Roman Catholic, Lutheran,* and *Calvinistical* religions, are professed in this empire.

G g

pire.

* Extract of a letter from a Gentleman of character in *Holland* to his friend in *America*.          † Guthrie, p. 444.

pire. The inhabitants of Auſtria, Barbaria, and the Spiritual Electorates, and ſome other places, are *Roman Catholics.* Thoſe of Mecklenburgh, Holſtein, Brandenburgh, Saxony and Pomerania, *Lutherans.* The Heſſians, and the people in the ſouth of Franconia, *Calviniſts.* The reſt of the empire is a mixture of all theſe denominations. ☩

The preſent Emperor of Germany has granted a moſt liberal religious toleration, and ſuppreſſed moſt of the religious orders of both ſexes, as uſeleſs to ſociety.*

PRUSIA. The eſtabliſhed religions in this kingdom are the *Lutheran* and *Calviniſtic*—chiefly the former ; but *Roman Catholics*, *Baptiſts,* and other denominations are here tolerated. ☩

BOHEMIA. Though *Popery* is the eſtabliſhed religion of this place, yet there are many *Proteſtants,* who are now tolerated in the free exerciſe of their religion ; and ſome of the *Moravians* have embraced the doctrines of Count *Zinzindorf,* which have been propagated in ſeveral parts of the globe.‡ In order to extend this denomination, the *Count* ſent his fellow-labourers thro'out the world. He himſelf has been over all *Europe,* and at leaſt twice to *America.* ‖

HUNGARY. The eſtabliſhed religion of the Hungarians is the *Roman Catholic,* though the major part of the inhabitants are *Proteſtants* and *Greeks,* who now enjoy the full exerciſe of their religious liberties.§

TRANSYLVANIA,

☩ Jones, vol. i. p. 465.   * Guthrie, 476   ☩ *Ibid.* p. 476.
‡ 480.        ‖ Riauus's Hiſt. of the Moravians, p. 25.
§ Guthrie, 484.

TRANSYLVANIA, SCLAVONIA, and CROATIA. *Roman Catholics, Lutherans, Calvinists, Socinians, Arians, Greeks, Mahometans,* and other fects, enjoy their feveral religions in *Tranfylvania.*

The *Sclavonians* are zealous *Roman Catholics*; though *Greeks* and *Jews* are tolerated.*

The religion of the *Croats* is fimilar to that of the *Tranfylvanians* and *Sclavonians,* who are their neighbours.†

POLAND. The number of *Proteftants,* confifting of *Lutherans* and *Calvinifts,* in their republic, is very confiderable; and when thefe are joined to the *Greek Church,* the whole are called *Diffidents.* At the fame time, the *Polifh* nobility and the bulk of the nation, are tenacious of the *Roman Catholic* religion.

The *monafteries* in this country are, by fome writers, faid to be five hundred and feventy-fix, and the *nunnaries* one hundred and feventeen, befides two hundred and forty-fix feminaries or colleges, and thirty-one abbeys.

No country has bred more *Deifts* and *Freethinkers* in religious matters than *Poland.*‡

SWITZERLAND. *Calvinifm* is faid to be the religion of the *Proteftant Swiffes:* but this muft chiefly be underftood with refpect to the mode of church government; for in fome doctrinal points they are far from being *Calvinifts.*

*Zuinglius* was the apoftle of Proteftanifm in *Switzerland.*‖        G g 2        SPAIN.

* Guthrie, p. 486.   † P. 486.   ‡ P. 491.   ‖ P. 507.

SPAIN.    The *Spaniards* are ſtrict *Roman Catholics*, and their King is diſtinguiſhed with the epithet
of *Moſt Catholic.* *

The *Inquiſition*, a tribunal which it is ſaid was e-
rected about the year 1212, by *Dominic*, a *Spaniard*,
and intended for the extirpation of thoſe who were
ſuppoſed to entertain erroneous opinions, formerly
reigned here in all its horrors.†    At preſent its pe-
nalties are greatly leſſened ; but though diſuſed it is
not abrogated. It appears, however, that the power of
the clergy has been greatly leſſened of late years.‡
A royal edict has been iſſued to prevent the admiſſion
of noviciates into the different convents without
ſpecial permiſſion ; which has a great tendency to
reduce the monaſteries in this kingdom : for which
purpoſe the King has publiſhed an ordinance, containing twenty-five articles ; to which is added, a
liſt of the convents to be ſuppreſſed, or united to
others.‖

Before the ſuppreſſion of the *Jeſuits*, the King of
*Spain*, as well as the King of *France* and the government of *Naples*, threatned to take ſome ſteps fatal
to the Court of *Rome*. *Venice* propoſed to reform
their religious communities, without paying any attention to the *Holy See* ; ſo that no *Pope* was ever
elected in more tempeſtuous times than the late *Pontiff Ganganelli* ; but after he had ſuppreſſed this religious order, the Kings and the Venetian ſtate immediately accommodated the diſputes which had ſub-
ſiſted ſo long between them and the Cour: of Rome.§

PORTUGAL.

---

* Guthrie. p. 517.    † Limborch'sHiſt. of the Inquiſition, p. 60.
‡ Guthrie, p. 517.    ‖ London Town and Country Magazine,
1784, p. 49.    § Ganganelli's Letters, vol. i. p. 19. 44.

PORTUGAL. The eftablifhed religion of this country is the *Roman Catholic*, in the ftricteft fenfe. But the *Pope's* authority in Portugal, has been of late fo much curtailed, that it is difficult to defcribe the religious ftate of this country.

The royal revenues are greatly increafed at the ex-pence of the religious inftitutions in this kingdom.*

Before the election of the late *Pontiff Ganganelli*, Portugal was about to choofe a Patriarch, and lay afide all communication with the *Pope* ; but he took the firft fteps to an accommodation with Portugal, and fucceeded in re-eftablifhing the antient friend-fhip which had fubfifted between the two Courts.†

ITALY. The religion of the *Italians* is the *Roman Catholic* ; from hence it fpread over *Europe*. The *ecclefiaftical* government of the Papacy has em-ployed many volumes in defcribing it.‡ The *Car-dinals*, who are next in dignity to the *Pope*, are fe-venty, in allufion to the feventy difciples of our Saviour, and are chofen by the *Roman Pontiff*.— Thefe Cardinals elect the *Pope* ; which election is determined by the plurality of voices. The election of a *Pope* is followed by his coronation ; and this ceremony is performed in the *Lateran* church, where they put a *triple crown* upon his head. The provin-ces which depend on the *Holy See* are governed by *Legates* ; and there are few countries where the *Pope* has not ambaffadors, who are ftiled *Nuncios*.

The title given to the *Pope* is, *His Holinefs*, and the *Cardinals* have that of *Emminence*.

All

* Guthrie, p. 530. † Ganganelli's Letters, p. 19, 21.
‡ Guthrie, p. 563.

All the numerous ecclefiaftics, and religious orders who profefs the *Roman Catholic* religion, are under the *Pope* ; and every one of thefe orders has its General at Rome ; by whom, the *Pope* is acquainted with every thing which paffes in the world. *

At prefent the *Papal* authority is evidently at a low ebb, † and is not refpected as it was formerly. The celebrated *Pope Ganganelli*, who has been ftiled the *Phænix of Ages*, ‡ after the matureft deliberation, figned a brief on the 21ft July, 1773, which fuppreffed the famous order of the *Jefuits*, who have been the warmeft affertors of the Papal power, and whofe cabals and intrigues have made them formidable for ages to every Court in *Europe*, and enabled them to eftablifh a powerful, well-regulated fovereignty in another hemifphere. ‖

As the *Jefuits* had a great fhare in the education of youth, the fhutting up their fchools might have proved of bad confequences if this Pontiff had not prevented it. After having fketched out a plan of education, worthy of the greateft mafter, he caft a rapid eye upon fome *Priefts* and *Friars*, who by their talents and example were capable of replacing the *Jefuit* teachers, and immediately inftituted them Profeffors ; fo that, to the aftonifhment of *Rome*, there feemed to be fcarce an interval between the departure of the *Jefuits* and the coming of their fucceffors. §

In the *Roman Catholic* kingdoms, *Rome* has no adminiftration but what is purely fpiritual : it is only

in

* Barclays Dictionary.     [See Pope]
† Guthrie, p 563.          ‡ Stiles's Sermon, p. 18,
‖ Paraguay, in South America.
§ Ganganelli's Letters, vol. i. p. 2, 43. 44.

in the ecclefiaftical ftate that fhe has any temporal authority.[*]

Perfons of all denominations live unmolefted in *Italy*, provided no grofs infult is offered to their worfhip.[†]   Even the Jews are allowed the full exercife of their religion in the heart of Rome ;[‡] and the profeffors of a religion which once ftigmatifed all others as unworthy the facred rights of humanity, now openly avow the liberal fentiments of mildnefs, forbearance, and moderation.[||]   The famous Pontiff above-mentioned obferves in his letters, " That every impetuous zeal which would bring down fire from Heaven excites only hatred. A good caufe fupports itfelf; fo that religion needs only produce its proofs, its traditions, its works, and its gentlenefs, to be refpected. Chriftianity of itfelf overthrows every fect which may be inclined to fchifm, or which breathes a fpirit of animofity."[§]

*Deifm* prevails greatly among the politer part of the inhabitants of this country.[**]

## TURKEY *in* EUROPE.

<table>
<tr><td rowspan="4">Containing</td><td>DANUBIAN PROVINCES, LITTLE TARTARY, GREECE.</td><td>The eftablifhed religion in thefe parts is the *Mahometan* ; the *Turks* profefs that of the fect of *Omar.*—</td></tr>
</table>

There is no ordination among their clergy :—Any perfon may be a Prieft who pleafes to take the habit,

and

---

* Ganganelli's Letters, vol. ii. p. 208.       † Guthrie, p. 563.
‡ Ganganelli's Letters, vol. ii. p. 138.
|| London Magazine, 1784. p. 8.
§ Ganganelli's Letters, vol. i. p. 130. 131.
** Hiftory of Religion, No. iv. p. 176.

and perform the functions of his order; and may lay
down his office when he pleases.   Their chief Priest
or *Mufti* seems to have great power in the state.*
He is stiled by the *Mahometans* the *Maker of Laws,
Giver of Judgments,* and *Prelate of Orthodoxy.*†
*Friday* is the day set apart by *Mahomet* for the ob-
servance of religious worship.   This day was pitched
upon in order to distinguish his followers from
the *Jews* and *Christians.*‡

There are large numbers of the *Greek Church*
in the *Turkish* dominions; and also some *Armenians*
and *Jews.*

## EUROPEAN ISLANDS.

ICELAND.   The only religion which is tolerated in this *Island* is the *Lutheran.*‖

ORCADES,        The religion of these Islands is
HEBRIDES, &       *Protestant,* according to the
SHETLAND.         discipline of the Church of
                  *Scotland :* but the *Roman Ca-*
*tholic* religion prevails among some of the natives of
the *Hebrides.*§

SCANDINAVIAN ISLANDS.   These Islands
being peopled either from *Sweden, Denmark,* or
*Norway,* profess the *Lutheran* religion.**

MAJORCA,        The inhabitants of these *Islands*
MINORCA,         profess the *Roman Catholic* reli-
and YVICA.       gion.

                                 CORSICA,

* Guthrie, p. 579.        † Broughton, vol. ii. p. 147.
‡ Sale's Koran, vol. i. p. 199.
‖ Guthrie, p. 71.        § ibid. 141, 142.
** Broughton, vol. ii. p. 326.

CORSICA,          The inhabitants of thefe *Iſlands*
SARDINIA.          are *Roman Catholics* ; and it is
                   faid, that in *Sardinia*, the peo-
ple will dance, and fing profane fongs in their churches, immediately after divine worſhip.

SICILY,          The *Roman Catholic* religion is pro-
MALTA.          feſſed in thefe Iſlands, and is fo ef-
                 fential to the order of the Knights
of Malta, that no perfon of a different perfuafion
can be admitted into it.

AZORES.    Thefe Iſlands being inhabited by the
Portuguefe, profefs the *Romiſh* religion, as eſtabliſhed
in the kingdom of *Portugal*.

CANDIA,          The eſtabliſhed religion of thefe
CYPRESS,          and the other Iſlands under the
RHODES.          *Turks*, is *Mahometaniſm* ; but
                  there are numbers of Chriſtians
who profefs the tenets of the *Greek Church*.*

                  H h          2d, RELIGIONS

* Broughton. Vol. ii. p. 327.

## 2d. RELIGIONS OF ASIA.

### TURKEY in ASIA.

Containing { PART OF ARABIA, SYRIA, PALESTINE, NATOLIA, MESOPOTAMIA, TURCOMANIA, GEORGIA,

The *Mahometan* is the eſtabliſhed religion of theſe countries ; but there a number of *Jews* (eſpecially in Paleſtine) intermixed : and many Greek Chriſtians, Armenians, Jacobites, Maronites, Neſtorians and Melchites. All denominations are tolerated in many parts of the Turkiſh dominions.*

TARTARY. { RUSSIAN, CHINESE, MOGULIAN, INDEPENDENT.

The religion of this country partakes of the *Mahometan*, the *Gentoo*, the *Greek*, and even the *Popiſh*. Some of them worſhip little rude images dreſſed up in rags. Each has a deity, with whom they make very free when matters do not go according to their own mind.

The inhabitants of *Tibet*, a large tract of *Tartary*, worſhip the *Grand Lama*. Another religion which is very prevalent among the Tartars is that of *Schamaniſm*.—The profeſſors of this religious ſect believe in one ſupreme God, the creator of all things. They believe that he loves his creation, and all his creatures ; that he knows every thing, and is all powerful ; but that he pays no attention to the particular actions of men, being too great for them to be able

to

* Broughton, Vol. ii. p. 329.

to offend him, or to do any thing which can be meritorious in his fight. They are all firmly perfuaded of a future exiftence :—They alfo maintain, that the fupreme Being has divided the government of the world, and the deftiny of men among a great number of fubaltern Divinities under his command and controul, but who, neverthelefs, generally act according to their own fancies ; and, therefore, mankind cannot difpenfe with ufing all the means in their power for obtaining their favour. They likewife fuppofe, that, for the moft part, thefe inferior Deities abominate and punifh premeditated villainy, fraud and cruelty.*

A band of *Tartars* in *Siberia*, have in every hut a wooden idol termed, in their language, *Shetan*, to which they addrefs their prayers for plenty of game in hunting, promifing to give it, if fuccefsful, a new coat or bonnet.†

KAMTCHATKA. The inhabitants of this peninfula acknowledge many malevolent Deities, having little or no notion of the good Deity. They believe the air, the water, the mountains, and the woods to be inhabited by malevolent Spirits, whom they fear and worfhip.‡

The method which the *Emprefs of Ruffia* takes to convert her Pagan fubjects in *Kamtchatka*, is to exempt from taxes, for ten years, fuch as profefs the Chriftian religion. The *Pagan Kamtjchodales* believe the immortality of the foul.§

H h 2

CHINA.

---

* Guthrie. p. 596.    † Kaim's Sketches, vol. iv. p. 176.
‡ P. 142.    § P. 275.

CHINA. Befides the worſhip of the *Grand La-ma*, the religion of China is divided into three ſects. 1ſt. The foilowers of *Laokium*, who lived five hun-dred years before *Chriſt*, and taught, that *God* was corporeal. They pay divine honours to the philo-ſopher *Laokium*; and give the ſame worſhip, not only to many Emperors who have been ranked with the Gods, but alſo to certain Spirits under the name of *Xamte*, who preſide over every element. They call this ſect that of the *Magicians*, becauſe the learned of it addict themſelves to *Magic*, and are believed to have the ſecret of making men immortal.

2d. The worſhippers of *Foe*, who flouriſhed a thouſand years before our *Saviour*, and who became a God at the age of thirty years. He is repreſented ſhining in light, with his hands hid under his robes, to ſhew that he does all things inviſible. The Doc-tors of this ſect teach a double law, the one *exter-nal*, the other *internal*. According to the *external law*, they ſay, that all the good are recompenſed, and the wicked puniſhed, in places deſtined for each. They enjoin all works of mercy; and forbid cheat-ing, impurity, wine, lying and murder, and even the taking life from any creature whatever.

The *interior* doctrine of this ſect, which is kept ſecret from the common people, teaches a pure, un-mixed *atheiſm*, which admits neither rewards nor puniſhments after death,—believes not in a Provi-dence, or the immortality of the ſoul,—acknow-ledges no other *God* but the *Void* or Nothing,—and which makes the ſupreme happineſs of mankind to conſiſt in a *total inaction*, an *intire inſenſibility*, and a *perfect quietude*.*         3d. A

---

* Hiſtory of Ignatius, vol. ii. p. 98, 99, 100.

3d. A sect which acknowledges the philosopher *Confucius* for its master, who lived five hundred years before our *Saviour*. This religion, which is professed by the *literati* and persons of rank in *China* and *Tonquin*, consists in a deep inward veneration for the *God* or *King of Heaven*, and in the practice of every *moral virtue*. They have neither temples nor Priests, nor any settled form of external worship: every one adores the supreme Being in the way he himself thinks best.*

The *Chinese* also honour their dead ancestors; burn perfumes before their images; bow before their pictures; and invoke them as capable of bestowing upon them all temporal blessings.†

MOGUL's EMPIRE. The original inhabitants of *India* are called *Gentoos*, or, as others call them, *Hindoos*. They pretend that *Brumma*, who was their legislator both in politics and religion, was inferior only to God; and that he existed many thousand years before our account of the creation. The *Bramins*—for so the Gentoo Priests are called—pretend, that he bequeathed to them a book, called the *Vidam*, containing his doctrines and instructions;— and that though the original is lost, they are still possessed of a commentary upon it, called the Shah-stah, which is wrote in the Shanscrita language, now a dead language and known only to the Bramins, who study it. The foundation of *Brumma's* doctine consisted in the belief of a supreme Being, who has created a regular gradation of beings, some superior, and some inferior, to man;—in the immortality of the soul, and a future state of rewards and punishments,

* Kæm. Vol. iv. p. 189. † Hist. of Ignatius, vol. ii. p. 103.

punishments, which is to consist of a transmigration into different bodies, according to the lives they have led in their pre-existent state. From this it appears more than probable, that the *Pathegorian Metamp-sychesis* took its rise in *India*.*

The necessity of inculcating this complicated doctrine among the lower ranks, induced the *Bramins* to have recourse to sensible representations of the *Deity* and his attributes ; so that the original doctrines of *Brumma* were changed into idolatry : and though the established religion in the *Mogul's Empire* is *Mahometanism*, there are various sects of *Pagans*—as the *Banians*, the *Perjees*, and the *Faquirs*. The *Banians* believe a transmigration of souls ; and therefore have hospitals for beasts, and will by no means deprive any animal of life. But of all living creatures they have the greatest veneration for the Cow, to whom they pay a solemn address every morning. Of these *Banians* there are reckoned in *India* about twenty-four different sects. The *Perjees* are the posterity of the antient *Persians*, and worship the element of fire : besides which they have a great veration for the Cock. The *Faquirs* are a kind of *Monks*, and live very austere, performing many severe acts of mortification. Some continue for life in one posture ; some never lie down ; some have their arms always raised above their heads ; and some mangle their bodies with knives and scourges. Most of the Indians believe the river Ganges has a sanctifying quality, for which reason they often wash themselves in it. There are many *Jews* and *European Christians* in the *Mogul's* dominions.‡

THE

---

* Guthrie, p. 313.   † Kaim, vol. iv. p. 19.
‡ Broughton, vol. ii. p. 328.

THE PENINSULA OF INDIA WITHIN THE GANGES. The inhabitants of this tract of land are generally *Mahometans* ; but the natives of the inland parts worship the sun, moon and other idols. In some parts, they look upon the first creature they meet in the morning as the proper object of worship for that day, except it be a Crow, the very sight of which is enough to confine them to their houses for the whole day. In the sea-port towns there are a number of *Jews* and *European Christians*. ||

THE PENINSULA OF INDIA BEYOND THE GANGES. The inhabitants of this *peninsula* are generally *Pagans*. The *Siamites* hold, all nature is animated by a rational soul ; that the soul transmigrates through many states, and is then confined to a human body to be punished for its crimes. They hold nine degrees of felicity and punishment. *

In the kingdom of Pegu, they have a kind of religious veneration for Apes and Crocodiles, believing those persons very happy who are devoured by them. *Mahometanism* prevails in some parts, but mixed with many *Pagan* rites and ceremonies. +

When the Kings of this part of India are interred, a number of animals are buried with them, and such vessels of gold and silver as they think can be of use to them in a future state. ‡

ARABIA, *(That part which is not included in Turkey.)* The wandering tribes in the southern and inland parts acknowledge themselves as the subjects of no foreign power ; but have preserved their independence

‖ Broughton, vol. ii. p. 328.    * Middleton, vol. i. p. 155.
+ Broughton, vol. ii. p. 328.    ‡ Guthrie, p. 618.

dependence from the earlieſt ages. Many of the wild *Arabs* ſtill continue *Pagans*, though the people in general are *Mabometans.* *

PERSIA. The Perſians are ſtrict Mahometans, but of the ſect of *Ali*. They differ from the *Turks* concerning the ſucceſſion of *Mobammed*. The Turks reckon them thus : *Mobammed, Abubeker, Omar, Oſman, Ali*. But the Perſians reckon *Ali* to be the immediate ſucceſſor of *Mobammed*. The *Gaurs*, who pretend to be the poſterity of the ancient *Magi*, and ſtill worſhip the fire, are ſaid to be numerous in *Perſia*, though tolerated in but few places. A combuſtible ground, about ten miles diſtant from Baku, a city in the north of *Perſia*, is the ſcene of their devotions. It muſt be admitted, that this ground is impregnated with very ſurpriſing inflamatory qualities ; and contains ſeveral old little temples ; in one of which the *Gaurs* pretend to preſerve the ſacred flame of the univerſal fire, which riſes from the end of a large hollow cane ſtruck into the ground, reſembling a lamp burning with pure ſpirits. ‡

## The ASIATIC ISLANDS.

THE JAPAN ISLANDS. The worſhip of the *Japaneſe* is *Paganiſm*, divided into ſeveral ſects : 1. The *Sinto*, who believe that the ſouls of good men are tranſlated to a place of happineſs next to the habitation of their Gods : But they admit no place of torment ; nor have they any notion of a Devil, but what animates the Fox, a very miſchievous animal of that country. They believe the ſouls of the wicked, being denied entrance into Heaven, wander about to expiate their ſins.      II. Thoſe

II. Thofe of the *Bubfdo* religion believe, that in the other world there is a place of mifery as well as of happinefs, and that there are different degrees of both, proportioned to the different degrees of virtue and vice. When fouls have expiated their fins, they are. fent back to animate fuch vile animals as refembled them in their former ftate of exiftence : from thefe they pafs into the bodies of more innocent animals ; and at laft are again fuffered to enter. human bodies : after the diffolution of which, they run the fame courfe of happinefs or mifery as at firft. †

III. The *Siutto*, who admit of no ceremonies in religion. There are innumerable temples and idols in this ifland ; one temple in particular, contains thirty-three thoufand three hundred and thirty-three idols. *

THE LADRONE ISLANDS,
and FORMOSA.

The inhabitants of thefe *iflands* are all *Pagans*. Thofe of *Formofa* recognife two Deities in company ; the one a male, god of the men ; the other a female, goddefs of the women. The bulk of their inferior Deities are the fouls of upright men, who are conftantly doing good, and the fouls of wicked men, who are conftantly doing ill. §

The inhabitants of the *Ladrone Iflands* believe Heaven is a region under the earth, filled with cocoa-trees, fugar-canes, and a variety of other delicious fruits ; and that Hell is a vaft furnace conftantly red hot ; thofe who die a natural death go ftrait to Heaven : They may fin freely if they can, but pre-

I i

ferve

---

† Kaim, vol. iv, p. 130.     * Middleton, vol. i. p. 392.
§ Kaim, vol. iv. p. 153.

ferve their bodies againſt violence ; but war and bloodſhed are their averſion.*

THE MOLUCCA ISLANDS.   The inhabitants of theſe Iſlands, who believe the exiſtence of malevolent inviſible Beings, ſubordinate to the ſupreme benevolent Being, confine their worſhip to the former, in order to avert their wrath : and one branch of their worſhip is, to ſet meat before them, hoping, that when the belly is full, there will be leſs inclination to miſchief.†

PHILLIPINE ISLANDS.   The inhabitants of theſe Iſlands are generally *Mahometans* ‡

CELEBES.   The inhabitants of this Iſland are profeſſed *Mahometans*, who retain many *Chineſe* ceremonies.§

## *The SUNDA ISLES.*

BORNEO, SUMATRA, JAVA, &c.   The inhabitants of theſe Iſlands, who reſide on the ſea-coaſt, are generally *Mahometans* ; but the natives who reſide in the inland parts are *Pagans.*‖   The *Iduans*, a people in the Iſland of *Borneo*, believe, that every perſon they put to death muſt attend them as a ſlave in the other world.   The worſhip of the inhabitants of *Java* is ſimilar to that of the *Molucca* Iſlands.+

CEYLON.

* Kaim. vol. iv. p. 235.          † *ibid* p. 190.
‡ Middleton. [See Phillipines]   § *ibid.*   [See Celebes]
‖ Broughton, vol. ii. p. 330.     + Kaim, vol. iv. p. 152.

CEYLON. The inhabitants of this Island ac-
k ..wledge an all powerful Being, and imagine their
D ....es of a second and third order are subordinate
to him, and act as his agents. Agriculture is the
peculiar province of one, navigation of another.
*Budæw* is revered as the mediator between God
and man. Another of their favourite Deities is the
tooth of a *Monkey.**

MALDIVE ISLANDS. The inhabitants of
these islands are *Mahometans*, who retain many
*Pagan* ceremonies.†

I i 2        3d. RELIGIONS

* K..m, vol. iv; p. 152.      † Middleton.  [See Ma'dives]

## 3d. RELIGIONS of AFRICA.

EGYPT. The prevailing religion of this country is *Mahometanism.* There are also a number of *Jews,* and many Christians called *Coptics,** who are subject to the *Alexandrian* Metropolitan. He has twelve *Bishops* under him, but no *Archbishops.* They have seven sacraments, viz.——*Baptism,* the *Eucharist, Confirmation, Ordination, Faith, Fasting,* and *Prayer.* They circumcise their children before *baptism,* and ordain Deacons at seven years of age. They follow the doctrine of the *Jacobites* with regard to the *nature of Christ,* and *baptism by fire.*†

## BARBARY.

Containing: {
MOROCCO,
FEZ,
ALGIERS,
TRIPOLI,
BARCA.
}

The inhabitants of these states are *Mahometans.* Many subjects of *Morocco* follow the tenets of *Hamet* one of their Emperors, who taught, that the doctrines of *Hali* and *Omar,* and other interpreters of the law, were only human traditions. There are also many persons in and about *Algiers,* who differ from the other *Mahometans* in divers particulars. Some of them maintain, that to fast seven or eight months merits eternal happiness ; and that idiots are the elect of God. ‡

BILDULGERID, ZAARA, OR THE DESART.

The religion professed in these countries is *Mahometanism* ; but there is scarce any sign of religion among

* Guthrie, p. 665. † Barclay's Dictionary. [See Coptics]
‡ Guthrie, p. 672.

among many of the people. There is a number of *Jews* scattered up and down in the best inhabited places in *Biidulgerid* *

NEGROLAND. The inhabitants of this vast country are either *Mahometans* or *Pagans*. And some in the midland parts live altogether without any sign of religion. †

GUINEA. *Paganism* is the religion of this country. The *Negroes* on the Gold Coast believe a *supreme Being*, and have some ideas of the immortality of the soul ; they address the Almighty by a fetish, or charm, as mediator, and worship two days in a week. They ascribe evil in general, and all their misfortunes to the Devil, whom they so fear, as to tremble even at the mention of his name. ‡ Those of the kingdom of *Benim* acknowledge a supreme Being, whom they call *Orifa* ; but they think it needless to worship him, because being infinitely good, they are sure he will not hurt them. On the contrary, they are very careful in paying their devotions to the *Devil*, who they think is the cause of all their calamities. They do not think of any other remedy for their most common diseases, but to apply to a forcerer to drive him away. Such Negroes as believe in the Devil paint his image white. §

NUBIA. The inhabitants of this spacious country are either strict *Mahometans* or *Pagans*. ||

ETHIOPIA

---

* Broughton, vol. ii. p. 331.          † ibid.
‡ Middleton, vol. i. p. 320.
§ Kaim, vol. iv. p. 142.
|| Broughton, vol. ii. p. 331.

**ETHIOPIA SUPERIOR, or ABYSSINIA.**
This fpacious empire contains a great mixture of people, of various nations, as *Pagans, Jews,* and *Mahometans:* but the main body of the natives are *Chriftians,* who hold the fcriptures to be the fole rule of faith. Their Emperor is fuprome, as well in ecclefiaftical as civil matters. They ufe different forms of *baptifm,* and keep both Saturday and Sunday as a *Sabbath.* They are circumcifed, and abftain from fwines flefh, not out of any regard to the *Mofaic* law, but purely as an ancient cuftom of their country. Their divine fervice confifts wholly, in reading the *fcriptures,* adminiftering the *Eucharift,* and hearing fome *Homilies* of the fathers.*

**ETHIOPIA INFERIOR.** The numerous inhabitants of thefe countries are *Pagans,* excepting thofe of *Zanguebar, Ajan,* and *Abex,* who profefs *Mahometanifm.*†

## LOWER GUINEA.

Containing, { LOANGO, CONGO, ANGOLO, BENGULA, MANTAMAN.

The inhabitants of thefe countries are *Pagans.* In the kingdom of *Loango,* the people entertain a faint notion of *God,* whom they call *Sambian Pongo.*‡

**CAFFRARIA.** The *Hottentots* believe in one fupreme Being, called *Goanya Tequon,* or *God of Gods.* They place his refidence beyond the moon, and fuppofe him a humane and benevolent Being; but they have no mode of worfhiping him, for which
they

---

‡ Broughton, vol. ii. † 322. ‡ Ibid. ‡ Ibid.

they give this reason, that he cursed our first parents for having offended him ; and on this account they never paid him adoration since.   They worship the *Moon* at full and change, and the *Gold Beetle,* which makes a saint of all he lights upon.   Their evil Deity, whom they call *Tongoa,* is a crabbed, malicious, mischievous Being,  to whom they ascribe all their misfortunes.*

## AFRICAN ISLANDS.

MADAGASCAR;   The inhabitants of this Island believe *God* to be the author of all good,  and the Devil the author of all evil †   There are also some *Mahometans* in this Island ; but here are no mosques, temples, nor any stated worship, except some of the inhabitants of this place offer sacrifices of beasts on particular occasions ; as,  when sick ; when they plant yams  or rice ; when they hold their assemblies ; circumcise their children ; declare war ; enter into new-built houses ; or bury their dead.   Many of them observe the *Jewish Sabbath,* and give some account of the sacred history, the creation and fall of man, as also of *Noah, Abraham, Jacob,* and *David* ; from whence it is conjectured they are descended of *Jews,* who formerly settled here, though none knows how or when.‡

CAPE VERD ISLANDS,  The inhabitants of
CANARY  ISLANDS,  these  islands  are
MADERAS.  *Roman Catholics.*‖

ZOCOTRA;

* Middleton, vol. i. p. 384.     † P 535
‡ Guthrie, p. 680.     ‖ Broughton, vol. ii. p. 332.

ZOCOTRA.   The inhabitants of this ifland are *Mahometans* of *Arab* extraction.

COMORA.   The inhabitants of this ifland are Negroes of the *Mahometan* perſuaſion. *

4th. RELIGIONS

* Guthrie. p. 6, 83.

## 4th. RELIGIONS OF AMERICA.

## UNITED STATES.

## *NEW-ENGLAND.*

*PREVIOUS to an account of the present denominations in this part of America, a short sketch of the Aborigines will not perhaps, be unentertaining to some readers.*

**MASSACHUSETTS, NEW-HAMPSHIRE, RRODE-ISLAND, CONNECTICUT;** The natives of *New-England* believed not only a plurality of *Gods*, who made and govern the several nations of the world, but they made Deities of every thing they imagined to be great, powerful, beneficial, or hurtful to mankind : yet, they conceived one Almighty Being, who dwells in the *southwest* region of the Heavens, to be superior to all the rest : this Almighty Being they called *Kichtan*, who at first, according to their tradition, made a man and woman out of a stone, but upon some dislike destroyed them again ; and then made another couple out of a tree, from whom descended all the nations of the earth ; but how they came to be scattered and dispersed into countries so remote from one another they cannot tell. They believed their supreme God to be a *good Being*, and paid a sort of acknowledgement to him for plenty, victory, and other benefits.

K k

But

But there is another power which they called *Hob-bamocko*, in English the *Devil*, of whom they stood in greater awe, and worshipped merely from a principle of terror.

The immortality of the soul was universally believed among them ; when good men die they said their souls went to *Kichtan*, where they meet their friends, and enjoy all manner of pleasures ; when wicked men die, they went to *Kichtan* also, but are commanded to walk away ; and so wander about in restless discontent and darkness forever.*

At present the Indians in *New-England* are almost wholly extinct.†

MASSACHUSETTS.   There are various denominations in this state, but the *Congregationalists* predominate.  Those of *New-England*, generally regulate themselves according to the *Congregational Platform*.  This *Platform* leaves the scripture to be the sole rule of faith, ordinances and discipline, as to what relates to authority and polity.  It leaves each church with plenary unceded power ; making the Councils and Synods advisory only.  It was passed and received as the plan of public confederacy, which united the *Presbyterians* and *Independents* under the one common title of *Congregationalists*.

It was a fundamental principle of this union, that every voluntary assembly of Christians had power to form, organize and govern themselves ; and in imitation of the apostolic churches, to gather and incorporate themselves by a public covenant, and to elect and ordain all their public officers.‡        There

* Neal's History of New-England, vol. i. p. 33, 34, 35.
† Belknap's History of New-Hampshire, vol. i. p. 124.
‡ Stiles's Christian Union, p. 56, 65.

There are also in this state a number of *Episco-palians, Presbyterans, Baptists, Quakers, Hopkinsians, Universalists, Shakers, Deists,* &c.

NEW-HAMPSHIRE. The prevailing religion of this state is similar with that of the *Massachusetts.* And the other denominations are nearly the same ; only it is said, there is a larger proportion of *Quakers.*

RHODE-ISLAND. This state was settled by some of the Antinomian exiles, on a plan of *entire religious liberty* : men of every denomination being equally protected and countenanced, enjoying all the honours and offices of government.

Many of the *Quakers* and *Baptists* flocked to this new settlement ; and there never was an instance of persecution for conscience sake countenanced by the Governors of this state. *

There are at present in this state, a large number of *Quakers* and *Baptists* of different denominations ; a few *Congregationalists, Moravians, Universalists, Hopkinsians,* &c.

The *Jews* have a synagogue in this state.

There are also a few in *Rhode-Island* who adhere to *Jemima Wilkinson,* who was born in *Cumberland.* It is said by those who are intimately acquainted with her, that she asserts, that in October 1776, she was taken sick and actually died, and her soul went to Heaven, where it still continues. Soon after, her body was re-animated with the spirit and power of *Christ,* upon which she set up as a public teacher, and declares she has an immediate revelation for all she delivers ; and is arrived to a state of absolute perfec-

K k 2                                      tion.

* Belknap's History of New-Hampshire, vol. i. p. 39.

tion. It is also said she pretends to foretel future events, to discern the secrets of the heart, and to have the power of healing diseases : and if any person who makes application to her is not healed, she attributes it to their want of faith. She asserts, that those who refuse to believe these exalted things concerning her, will be in the state of the unbelieving *Jews*, who rejected the counsel of God against themselves ; and she tells her hearers, this is the eleventh hour, and this is the last call of mercy that ever shall be granted them : for she heard an enquiry in Heaven, saying, " Who will go and preach to a dying world ?" or words to that import : and she says she answered, " Here am I, send me ;" and that she left the realms of light and glory, and the company of the heavenly host, who are continually praising and worshipping God, in order to descend upon earth, and pass through many sufferings and trials for the happiness of mankind. She assumes the title of the *Universal Friend of Mankind* ; hence her followers distinguish themselves by the name of *Friends*.*

CONNECTICUT. *Congregationalism* is the predominant religion of this state ; but a number of the *Connecticut* churches have formed themselves on the *Presbyterian* model according to *Scotland*.†

There is also a number of *Episcopalians, Baptists, Quakers, Hopkinsians, Universalists, Sandemanians, Deists*, &c.

NEW-YORK. The inhabitants of this state are generally *Protestants* of different persuasions,

as

---

* Brownell's Enthusiastical Errors, p. 5, 7, 9, 14.
† Stiles' Christian Union, p. 68.

as *Lutherans, Quakers, Baptists, Episcopalians, Dutch, Gallic* and *German Calvinists, Moravians, Methodists,* &c. who have all their respective houses of worship.

The *Jews* have a synagogue in this state.

It is ordained in the constitution of *New-York,* that the free exercise of religious worship, without discrimination or preference, shall forever be allowed to all mankind.

There is also a number of *Shakers* at *Nisquiunia* in this state.‡

A gentleman of *New-York,* who lately visited a society of *Shakers* in *Acquakanoch,* whose congregation consisted of about ninety persons, was astonished at the facility with which they performed almost incredible actions : one woman, in particular, had acquired such an understanding in the principle of balance as to be able to turn round on her heel a full half hour, so swiftly, that it was difficult to discriminate the object. They are extremely reluctant to enter into conversation upon the principles of their worship, but content themselves with declaring, that they have all been very great sinners, and therefore it is that they mortify themselves by painful exercises. ‖

NEW-JERSEY. After the coming of the white people, the *Indians* in *New-Jersey,* who once held a plurality of Deities, supposed there were only three, because they saw people of three kinds of complexions, viz.—*English, Negroes,* and themselves.

It

‡ Guthrie, p. 729. ‖ Boston Gazette, October 25, 1784.

It is a notion pretty generally prevailing among them, that it was not the fame God made them who made us ; but that they were created after the white people : and it is probable they fuppofe their God gained fome fpecial fkill by feeing the white people made, and fo made them better : for it is certain they look upon themfelves, and their methods of living, which they fay their God exprefsly prefcribed for them, vaftly preferable to the white people, and their methods.

With regard to a future ftate of exiftence, many of them imagine that the *chichung*, i. e. the fhadow, or what furvives the body, will, at death, go fouthward, and in an unknown but curious place—will enjoy fome kind of happinefs, fuch as hunting, feafting, dancing, and the like. And what they fuppofe will contribute much to their happinefs in the next ftate is, that they fhall never be weary of thofe entertainments.

Thofe who have any notion about rewards and punifhments in a future ftate, feem to imagine that moft will be happy, and that thofe who are not fo, will be punifhed only with privation, being only excluded from the walls of the good world where happy fpirits refide.

Thefe rewards and punifhments, they fuppofe to depend entirely upon their behaviour towards mankind ; and have no reference to any thing which relates to the worfhip of the fupreme Being.*

According

* This account is extracted from the Journal of the late pious Mr. Brainard, who formed a fociety of Chriftian Indians at Crofweekfang, in *New Jerfey*. [See Brainard's Life, p. 448. 449, 450.]

According to the prefent conftitution of this ftate, all perfons are allowed to worfhip God in the manner which is moft agreeable to their own confciences. There is no eftablifhment of any one religious fect, in preference to another ; and no Proteftant inhabitants are to be denied the enjoyment of any civil rights, merely on account of their religious fentiments.*

There are *Dutch, Gallic,* and *German Calvinifts* in this ftate.† There is alfo a number of *Epifcopalians, Prefbyterians, Baptifts, Quakers,* &c.

PENNSYLVANIA. The inhabitants of this ftate are of different religious denominations, efpecially *Quakers* ; it was from *William Penn, a celebrated Quaker,* that this place received its name. Civil and religious liberty in their utmoft latitude, was laid down by this great man, as the only foundation of all his inftitutions. Chriftians of all denominations might not only live unmolefted, but have a fhare in the government of this colony.‡

At prefent the *Quakers* have at leaft four places of worfhip in the city of *Philadelphia.* A number feparated from the reft on account of political principles, maintaining defenfive war, and have built an elegant plain meeting-houfe in *Arch-ftreet.* They call themfelves *free Quakers* ; but it is thought fince the peace, they will reunite with the other *Friends.*

There are alfo in this city, three *Epifcopal* churches, two *Roman-Catholic* chapels ; feveral *German* and *Dutch* churches, fome of which are *Lutheran,* others *Calviniftical* ; one *Moravian* chapel ; one *Methodift*

meeting ;

* Guthrie, p. 728.    † Stiles' Election Sermon, p. 54.
‡ Guthrie, p. 733.

meeting ; three *Prefbyterian* or *Congregational* ; one *Baptift* church, *Ca.vinifts* ; part of this church who feparated from the other, call themfelves *Univer- falifts*.

There is alfo a number of *Jews* in this ftate. †

. DELAWARE. The religious denominations in this ftate, are faid to be fimilar with thofe of *Penn- fylvania*.

. MARYLAND. The firft European fettlers of this ftate were chiefly, if not wholly, *Roman-Catho- lics*, and, like the fettlers of New-England, their fettlement was founded upon a ftrong defire of the unmolefted practice of their own religion.*

Lord *Baltimore*, one of the moft eminent of the fettlers, eftablifhed a perfect toleration in all religious matters, fo that Diffenters of all denominations flock- ed to this colony.§

At prefent there is here a larger proportion of *Roman Catholics* than in any of the other ftates.‖ Among the Proteftants, *Epifcopacy* is the predomi- nant religion ; but there are various other denomi- nations.

VIRGINIA. The predominant religion in this ftate, is that of the *Church of England* ; but all other denominations are tolerated.

*Virginia* contains fifty-four parifhes and churches, thirty or forty of which have minifters, with cha- pels of eafe in thofe of larger extent.‡

NORTH

† Extract of a letter from a Lady, who fometime refided in Philadelphia.    * Univerfal Hift. vol. xl. p 466    § Guthrie. ‖ Barclay's Dict. [fee Maryland]    ‡ *Ibid.* [See Virginia]

NORTH AND SOUTH CAROLINA. The predominant religion in thefe ftates, is *Epifcopacy*; but there are various other perfuafions; liberty of confcience being univerfally allowed.*

GEORGIA. According to the beft account, the *Indian* natives of *Georgia* had fome notion of an omnipotent Being, who formed man, and inhabited the fun, the clouds, and the clear fky. They like-wife had fome idea of his providence and power over the human race. It is even faid, that they be-lieved fomewhat of a future ftate; and that the fouls of bad men walk up and down the place where they died; but, that God, or, as they call him, the *Beloved*, choofes fome from children, whom he takes care of, and refides in and teaches.†

At prefent *Epifcopacy* is the predominant religion of this ftate.

There is a confiderable number of *Dutch, Gallic,* and *German Calviniftical* churches, at *Ebenezer*, in *Georgia*.

There is alfo a number of *Methodifts*. Here the Rev. Mr. *George Whitefield* founded an orphan-houfe, which is now converted into a college for the education of young men defigned chiefly for the miniftry; and through his zeal and pious care, this favourite feminary is at prefent in a thriving con-dition.‡

## BRITISH AMERICA.

NOVA-SCOTIA. The eftablifhed religion of this province is the church of *England*; but all

L l                              fects

---

* Broughton.    † Univerfal Hift. vol. xi. p. 464.    ‡ Guthrie.

sects of Christians are tolerated, and government so far encourages them as to render contracts between ministers and people binding. *Nova-Scotia* is settled by people from *New-England, Old-England,* and *Ireland.* These different people bring their peculiar modes and local attachments with them.—The greatest part of them were originally of the *Congregational,* or *Presbyterian* persuasion : but being scattered round the shores of this province in small villages, they have been unable to support the establishments of the gospel. Hence a number of illiterate men have stepped forth as the ministerial instructors of this people, and have proselyted many.

At the head of this class was the late Mr. *Henry Allen,* a man of natural good sense, and warm imagination. This man has journeyed nearly through the province, and by his popular talents made many converts. He has also published several treatises and sermons, in which he declares he has advanced some new things. He says, that the souls of all the human race are emanations, or rather parts of the one Great Spirit ; but that they individually originally had the powers of moral agents ; that they were all present with our first parents in *Eden,* and were actual in the first transgression. He supposes, that our first parents in innocency were pure spirits, without material bodies ; that the material world was not then made ; but in consequence of the fall man being cut off from God, that they might not sink into immediate destruction, the world was produced, and they cloathed with hard bodies ; and that all the human race will in their turns, by natural generation, be invested with such bodies, and in them enjoy a state of probation for happiness of

immortal

immortal duration. He fays, that the body of our Saviour was never raifed from the grave, and that none of the bodies of men ever will be : but when the original number of fouls have had their courfe on earth, they will all receive their reward or punifhment in their original unembodied ftate. He fuppofed *baptifm*, the *Lord's fupper*, and *ordination*, matters of indifference.

Thefe are his moft diftinguifhing tenets, which he and his party endeavour to fupport by alledging, that the fcriptures are not to be underftood in their literal fenfe, but have a fpiritual meaning. He has had fuch influence over his followers, that fome of them pretend to remember their being in the garden of *Eden*. The moment of their converfion, they are fo well affured of that, it is faid fome of them even calculate the age of their *cattle* by it.

Mr. *Allen* begun to propagate his fentiments about the year 1778 : he died 1783 ; and fince his death his party much decline.

There is a confiderable number of *Methodifts*, or difciples of Mr. *Wefly*, in this province, and one or two focieties of *Baptifts*, who do not much differ from thofe of their name among us.

The number of *Epifcopalian* clergy in this province, may be about nine ; *Prefbyterians* and *Congregationalifts*, feven.*

CANADA. The Indians of this continent have an idea of the fupreme Being ; and they all in general agree in looking upon him as the Firft Spirit,

L l 2

and

---

* This account was given by an ingenious young Clergyman, who refided at *Nova-Scotia*, in the years 1782, 178_.

and the Governor and the Creator of the world. It is said, that almost all the nations of the *Algonquin* language, give this *sovereign Being* the appellation of the Great *Hare*. Some again call him *Michabou*, and others *Atahocan*. Most of them hold the opinion, that he was born upon the waters, together with his whole court, entirely composed of four-footed animals, like himself; that he formed the earth of a grain of sand, which he took from the bottom of the ocean, and that he created man of the bodies of the dead animals. There are likewise some who mention a God of the waters, who opposed the designs of the Great *Hare*, or at least refused to be assisting to him. This God is according to some, the great *Tyger*. Lastly, they have a third called *Matcomek*, whom they invoke in the winter season.

The *Areskoui* of the *Horons*, and the *Agreskoufé* of the *Iroquois*, is in the opinion of these nations, the sovereign Being, and the God of war. These Indians do not give the same original to mankind with the *Algonquins*; they do not ascend so high as the first creation.—According to them there were in the beginning six men in the world, and if you ask them who placed them there, they answer you, they don't know.

The Gods of the Indians have bodies, and live much in the same manner with us, but without any of those inconveniences to which we are subject. The word *Spirit*, among them, signifies only a Being of a more excellent nature than others.

According to the *Iroquois*, in the third generation there came a deluge, in which not a soul was saved, so that in order to re-people the earth, it was necessary to change beasts into men. Besides

Besides the First Being, or the Great Spirit, they hold an infinite number of genii or inferior spirits, both good and evil, who have each their peculiar form of worship.

They ascribe to these Beings a kind of immensity and omnipresence, and constantly invoke them as the guardians of mankind. But they never address themselves to the evil genii, except to beg of them to do them no hurt.

They believe the immortality of the soul, and say that the region of their everlasting abode lies so far westward, that the souls are several months in arriving at it, and have vast difficulties to surmount. The happiness which they hope to enjoy, is not believed to be the recompense of virtue only ; but to have been a good hunter, brave in war, &c. are the merits which entitle them to this Paradise, * which they and the other American natives figure as a delightful country, blessed with perpetual spring, whose forests abound with game, whose rivers swarm with fish, where famine is never felt, and uninterrupted plenty shall be enjoyed without labour or toil. ‡

Many of the Indian natives have been converted to Christianity ; and no accounts could be procured to ascertain how far some of their tribes now retain the sentiments above described.

The predominant religion in this province, at present, is the *Roman Catholic ;* but there are *Protestants* of different denominations.

*SPANISH*

* Charlevoix's Voyage to North-America, vol. ii. p. 141, 142, 143, 144, 145, 152, 153, 154, 155.
‡ Robertson's History of South-America, vol. i. p. 387.

## SPANISH AMERICA.

**LOUISANIA.** The natives of this part of *America*, moſt of them, have an idea of a ſupreme Being, whom they call the *Grand Spirit*, by way of excellence ; and whoſe perfections are as much ſuperior to all other Beings, as the fire of the ſun is to elementary fire. They believe this omnipotent Being is ſo good, that he could not do evil to any one, even if he inclined. That though he created all things by his will, yet he had under him ſpirits of an inferior order, who, by his power, formed the beauties of the univerſe ; but that man was the work of the Creator's own hands. Thoſe ſpirits are, by the *Natches*, termed free ſervants or agents ; but at the ſame time they are as ſubmiſſive as ſlaves. They are conſtantly in the preſence of God, and prompt to execute his will. The air, according to them, is full of other ſpirits of more miſchievous diſpoſitions, and theſe have a chief, who was ſo eminently miſchievous, that God Almighty was obliged to confine him ; and ever ſince, thoſe ærial ſpirits do not commit ſo much miſchief as they did before, eſpecially if they are entreated to be favourable. For this reaſon the ſavages always invoke them when they want either rain or fair weather.

They give this account of the creation of the world, namely.—That GOD firſt formed a little man of clay, and breathed upon his work, and that he walked about, grew up, and became a perfect man ;—but they are ſilent as to the creation of women.*

The

* Modern Univerſal Hiſtory, vol. xl. p. 374.

The greateſt part of the natives of *Louiſania* had formerly their temples as well as the *Natches*, and in all theſe temples a perpetual fire was preſerved.§

The Chriſtians inhabiting this place are *Roman Catholics.*

EAST AND WEST FLORIDA. The natives of this country believe a ſupreme benevolent Deity, and a ſubordinate Deity who is malevolent ; neglecting the former who they ſay does no harm ; they bend their whole attention to ſoften the latter, who they ſay torments them day and night.*

The *Apalachites* bordering on *Florida*, worſhip the ſun, but ſacrifice nothing to him which has life : they hold him to be the parent of life, and think he can take no pleaſure in the deſtruction of any living creature : their devotion is exerted in perfumes and ſongs.†

The Spaniſh inhabitants of this country are *Roman Catholics.*

NEW MEXICO, INCLUDING CALIFORNIA. The inhabitants of this country are chiefly *Indians*, whom the *Spaniſh* miſſionaries have in many places brought over to Chriſtianity.‡

In the courſe of a few years after the reduction of the *Mexican* empire, the ſacrament of baptiſm was adminiſtered to more than four millions. Many of theſe proſelytes, who were adopted in haſte, either retained their veneration for their ancient religion in its full force,

§ Charlevoix Voyages, vol. ii. p. 273:
* Kaim's Sketches, vol. iv. p. 155. † *Ibid.* p. 216:
‡ Guthrie, p. 763.

force, or mingled an attachment to its doctrines and rites, with that slender knowledge of Christianity which they acquired. These sentiments the new converts transmitted to their posterity, into whose minds they have sunk so deep, that the Spanish ecclesiastics, with all their industry, have not been able to eradicate them. The religious institutions of their ancestors are still remembered, and held in honour by the Indians both in *Mexico* and *Peru*, and whenever they think themselves out of reach of inspection by the Spaniards, they assemble and celebrate their Pagan rites.*

OLD MEXICO, or NEW SPAIN. The divinities of the native inhabitants of *Mexico* were cloathed with terror, and delighted in vengeance. The figures of serpents, of tygers, and of other destructive animals decorated their temples. Fasts, mortifications and penances, all rigid, and many of them excrutiating to an extreme degree, were the means which they employed to appease the wrath of their Gods. But of all offerings, human sacrifices were deemed the most acceptable.†

Notwithstanding the vast depopulation of *America*, a very considerable number of the native race still remains both in *Mexico* and *Peru*. Their settlements in some places are so populous as to merit the name of cities. In the three audiences into which *New Spain* is divided, there are at least two million of Indians; a pitiful remnant indeed of its ancient population! but such as still form a body of people superior in number to that of all the other inhabitants of this vast country.‡    In

---

* Robertson's Hist. S. America, vol. ii. p. 384, 385.
† *Ibid.* vol. ii. p. 302, 303.    ‡ P. 351.

In confequence of grants beftowed upon *Ferdi-
nand* of *Spain* by Pope *Alexander* VI. and *Julius* II.
the Spanifh Monarchs have become, in effect, the
heads of the *Roman Catholic* American church. In
them the adminiftration of its revenues is vefted.—
Their nomination of perfons to fupply vacant bene-
fices, is inftantly confirmed by the Pope. Papal
bulls cannot be admitted into America ; nor are they
of any force there, until they have been previoufly
examined and approved of by the Royal Council of
the Indies : and if any bull fhould be furreptitioufly
introduced, and circulated in *America,* without obtaining that approbation, ecclefiaftics are required,
not only to prevent it from taking effect, but to feize
all the copies of it, and tranfmit them to the Council of the Indies.*

The hierarchy is eftablifhed in *America* in the
fame form as in Spain, with its full train of Arch-
bifhops, Bifhops, Deans, and other dignitaries.—
The inferior clergy are divided into three claffes,
under the denomination of *Curas, Doctrineros,* and
*Miffioneros.*—The firft are parifh Priefts, in thofe
parts of the country where the Spaniards have fettled.
The fecond have the charge of fuch diftricts as are
inhabited by Indians fubjected to the Spanifh government, and living under its protection. The
third are employed in converting and inftructing
thofe fiercer tribes, which difdain fubmiffion to the
Spanifh yoke, and live in remote or inacceffible regions to which the Spanifh arms have not penetra-
ted. So numerous are the ecclefiaftics of all thofe
various orders, and fuch the profufe liberality with
M m which

* R_bertfon's Hiftory of South America, vol. ii. p. 376.

which many of them are endowed, that the revenues of the church in *America* are immenfe.  The
worſhip of *Rome* appears with its utmoſt pomp in
the *New World.*—Churches and convents there are
magnificent and richly adorned ; and on high feſtivals, the difplay of gold and filver, and precious
ſtones, is fuch as exceeds the conception of an *European.**

There are four hundred monaſteries in *New Spain.*

PERU.  The Sun, as the great ſource of light,
of joy and fertility in the creation, attracted the
principal homage of the native *Peruvians.*  The
moon and ſtars, as co-operating with him, were entitled to fecondary honours.  They offered to the
fun a part of thofe productions, which his genial
warmth had called forth from the boſom of the
earth, and reared to maturity.  They facrificed, as an
oblation of gratitude, fome of the animals who were
indebted to his influence for nouriſhment.  They
prefented to him choice fpecimens of thofe works of
ingenuity which his light had guided the heart of
man in forming.  But the Incas never ſtained his
altars with human blood ; nor could they conceive
that their beneficent father, the Sun, would be delighted with fuch horrid victims.†

At prefent there are feveral diſtricts in *Peru*, particularly in the kingdom of Quito, occupied almoſt
entirely by Indians ‡

Notwithſtanding fome of the native Peruvians ſtill
practife in fecret their Pagan rites, the *Roman Catholic* is the prevailing religion in this place.  From
the

---

* Robertſon's Hiſt. vol. ii. p. 377.  † P. 309, 310.  ‡ 351.

the fond delight the American Spaniards take in the external pomp and parade of religion, and from their reverence for ecclefiaftics of every denomination, they have beftowed profufe donatives on churches and monafteries ; †  and have conceived fuch an high opinion of monaftic fanctity, that religious houfes have multiplied to an amazing degree in the Spanifh colonies.

It was obferved in the year 1620, that the number of convents in Lima covered more ground than all the reft of the city.

The fecular Priefts in the New World are lefs diftinguifhed than their brethren in Spain, for literary accomplifhments of any fpecies.  But the higheft ecclefiaftical honours are often in the hands of the monaftic orders, and it is chiefly to them that the Americans are indebted for any portion of fcience which is cultivated among them.*

The Spaniards form fuch an idea of the incapacity of the Indians, that a Council held at Lima decreed that they ought to be excluded from the facrament of the Eucharift.  And though Paul IIId. by his famous bull, iffued in the year 1537, declared them to be rational creatures, entitled to all the privileges of Chriftians ; yet after the lapfe of two centuries, during which they have been members of the church, very few are deemed worthy of being admitted to the holy communion.

From the idea which was entertained of their incapacity, when Philip the IId. eftablifhed the Inquifition in America, in the year 1570, the Indians

M m 2

were

---

† Robertfon's Hiftory, vol. ii, p. 365.          * 381.

were exempted from the jurifdiction of that tribunal, and ftill continue under the infpection of their diocefans. Though fome of them have been taught the learned languages, and have gone through the ordinary courfe of academic education with applaufe, their frailty is ftill fo much fufpected, that no Indian is either ordained a Prieft, or received into any religious order.*

CHILI. The mountainous part of this country is ftill poffeffed by tribes of its original inhabitants. That part of Chili, which may properly be deemed a Spanifh province, is a narrow diftrict, extending along the coaft from the defart of Atacamas to the ifland of Chiloe, above nine hundred miles.†

The *Roman Catholic* inhabitants have eftablifhed divers feminaries in this place for the converfion of the natives; who, it is faid, paid religious worfhip to the Devil.‡

TERRA FIRMA. The *Roman Catholic* is the eftablifhed religion of this place, as well as in the other Spanifh fettlements in South America.

PARAGUAY. The Jefuits entered this country in the year 1586, they began by gathering together about fifty wandering families, who they perfuaded to fettle; and they united them in a little townfhip. When they had made this beginning, they laboured with fuch indefatigable pains, and with fuch mafterly policy, that they prevailed upon thoufands of various difperfed tribes to embrace their religion; and thefe foon induced others to follow their example,

magnifying

---

* Robertfon's Hift. vol. II. p. 386.   † P 333
‡ Burke, vol. II. p. 254

magnifying the peace and tranquility they enjoyed under the direction of the fathers.

It is said that above three hundred and forty thousand families, several years ago, were subject to the Jesuits, living in obedience, and an awe bordering upon adoration, yet procured without any violence or constraint.*

It is said that nothing can compare with the procession of the Blessed Sacrament in this place; and that, without any display of riches and magnificence, it yields in nothing to the richest and most magnificent procession in any other part of the world.

A Spanish gentleman describes it in the following manner :——" It is attended with very fine dancing, and the dancers are all neatly dressed. Over the greens and flowers which compose the triumphal arches, under which the Blessed Sacrament passes, there appear flocks of birds of every colour, tied by the legs, to strings of such a length, that a stranger would imagine they enjoyed their full liberty, and were come of their own accord to mix their warblings with the voices of the musicians and the rest of the people; and bless, in their own way, him whose providence carefully supplies all their wants.

" All the streets are hung with carpets very well wrought, and separated by garlands, festoons, and compartments of verdure, disposed with the most beautiful symmetry. From distance to distance, there appear lions and tygers very well chained, that they may not disturb the solemnity instead of adorning it; and even very fine fishes sporting and

playing

---

* Guthrie, p. 775.

playing in large bafons of water.   In a word, every fpecies of living creatures affift at the folemnity,  as it were by their  deputies, to do homage to the  incarnate word, in his auguft facrament ;  and acknowledge  the fovereign dominion his father ha* given him  over all living.   Wherever  the proceffion paffes  the ground is  covered with  mats,  and ftrewed with flowers and odoriferous herbs.   All, even the fmalleft children,  have a hand  in thefe decorations, amongft which,  are likewife to be feen  the flefh of the animals newly killed for  food ;  every thing the Indians regale themfelves with  at their greateft rejoicings ;  and  the firft fruits  of their labours ;  all, in  order  to make an offering of  them  to the Lord ; the grain  particularly they  intend to  fow, that he may give it a bleffing.   The warbling of the birds, the roaring of  the lions and tygers, the voices of  the muficians, the plain  chaunt of  the choir,  all intermix without confufion,  and confpire to form a concert  not  to  be  equalled in  any  other  part of the world.

"  The  great royal ftandard is carried behind the Bleffed Sacrament.   The Cacique,  the Corregidor, the Regidors and  the Alcades fupport the canopy. The militia, both horfe and foot, with their colours and ftandards flying,  affift likewife, at the proceffion, in good  order.   But however ftriking this fpectacle may be, the greateft beauty of it confifts in the piety, the modefty, and refpect, and even the air of holinefs vifible in  every countenance.

"  As foon as the Bleffed Sacrament is returned to the church, the Indians prefent  the miffionaries all the feveral kinds  of eatables which have been expofed in the proceffion ;  and the fathers, after fending

the

the beſt of every thing to the ſick, diſtribute what remains, among the reſt of the inhabitants. The evening concludes with the moſt curious fire-works."*

In 1767 the Jeſuits were ſent out of *America* by royal authority, and their ſubjects were put upon the ſame footing with the reſt of the inhabitants of this country.†

## PORTUGUESE AMERICA.

**BRAZIL.** Though the natives of America in general acknowledge the being of a GOD, and the immortality of the ſoul, yet ſeveral tribes have been diſcovered which have no idea whatever of a ſupreme Being, and no rites of religious worſhip. ‡

The natives of Brazil had no temples nor Prieſts ; but they were ſo much affrighted by thunder, that it was not only the object of religious reverence ; but the moſt expreſſive name in their language for the Deity was *Toupan*, the ſame by which they diſtinguiſh thunder.§

The eſtabliſhed religion at preſent in this place, is the *Roman Catholic*.

## DUTCH AMERICA.

**GUIANA.** The ſavage tribes in this place believe the exiſtence of one ſupreme Deity, whoſe chief attribute is benevolence ; and to him they aſcribe every good which happens. But as it is againſt his nature to do ill, they believe in ſubordinate

dinate

---

* Charlevoix Hiſt. of Paraguay. vol. i, p. 286, 287, 288.
† Guthrie, p 776.
‡ Robertſons Hiſtory, vol. i, p. 381.    § p. 488.

dinate malevolent Beings like our Devil, who occafion thunders, hurricanes and earthquakes, and who
are the authors of death and difeafes, and of every
misfortune.*

The religion of the Chriftian inhabitants of this
place is fimilar with the *United Provinces*.

## *P A G A N   A M E R I C A.*

AMAZONIA: The inhabitants of this country
are faid to worfhip images made of wood, fet up in
their houfes, for they have no temples, their Priefts
teaching them, that thefe pieces of timber are really inhabited by certain divinities from Heaven.†

## *A M E R I C A N   I S L A N D S.*

NEWFOUNDLAND. The natives of this ifland
when firft difcovered, had fome knowledge of a fupreme Being, and believed that men and women were
originally created from a certain number of arrows
ftuck faft in the ground. They generally believe
the immortality of the foul, and that the dead go into
a far country, there to make merry with their friends.‡

The prefent religion of this place is fimilar with
Nova-Scotia.

JAMAICA,      The religion of thefe iflands
BARBADOES,    is univerfally of the *Church*
BERMUDAS,     *of England*.

The *Negroes* on thefe and the other *Weft-India*
iflands believe, that they fhall return to their native
country

---

* Kaim, vol. iv, p. 150.
† Broughton. vol. ii, p. 334.
‡ Broughton, vol. ii, p. 335.

country after death. This thought is so agreeable, that it chears the poor creatures, and renders the burden of life easy, which otherwise to many of them would be quite intolerable. They look upon death as a blessing, and some of them meet it with surprising courage and intrepidity. They are quite transported to think their slavery is near an end—that they shall revisit their native shores, and see their old friends and acquaintance. When a *Negro* is about to expire, his fellow-slaves kiss him, wish him a good journey, and send their hearty good wishes to their relations in *Guinea*. They make no lamentations, but with a great deal of joy inter his body, believing he is gone home and happy. *

The original inhabitants of the *West-India* islands are now almost extirpated.†

CUBA,
HISPANIOLA. The inhabitants of these and the other islands belonging to *Spain* are *Roman Catholics* ‡

MARTINICO. The predominant religion in this and the other islands belonging to *France* is the *Roman Catholic.*

OTAHEITE, AND THE OTHER SOCIETY ILANDS, THE FRIENDLY ISLES, THE SANDWICH ISLES, &c. The inhabitants of these and the other islands lately discovered in the South Sea, in general acknowledge an almighty, invisible Lord and Creator of the universe, who executed the various parts of the creation by various



subordinate

* Guthrie, p. 704.
† Barclay's Dictionary. ‡ Broughton, vol. i. p. 335.

ſubordinate powerful Beings.   They are of opinion,
that he is good and omniſcient ; that he ſees and
hears all human actions ; and is the giver of all good
gifts.   They feel their own wants, and therefore
apply for redreſs to the ſupreme Being, and offer
him, with a grateful heart, the beſt gifts of their
lands.   They acknowledge to have a Being within
their bodies, which ſees, hears, ſmells, taſtes, and
feels, which they call *E-tee-heĕ* ; and they believe,
that after the diſſolution of the body, it hovers about
the corps ; and laſtly, retires into the wooden re-
preſentations of human bodies, erected near the burying-places.   They are convinced of the certainty
of a happy life in the *Sun*, where they ſhall feaſt on
*bread-fruit*,* and meat which requires no dreſſing :
and they think it their duty to direct their prayers
to this ſupreme Divinity, or *Eatooa Rahʌi*.   Thoſe
who have leiſure among theſe people, are very deſirous of learning what is known relative to this and
all other inferior Divinities, and to practiſe ſuch virtues, as by the general conſent of mankind, conſti-
tute good actions.   Theſe are briefly the general
outlines of their religious worſhip.

The name *Eatooa*, admits a very great latitude in
its interpretation : however, they admit a Being
which they call *Eatooa-Rahai*, which is the ſupreme
                                                Deity

---

* The tree which bears this fruit, is about the ſize of a mid-
ling oak, with large leaves deeply ſituated, and when broken
from the branch, exudes a white milky juice.  The fruit is about
the ſize of a child's head, and nearly ſhaped like it.  It is covered
with a ſkin, the ſurface of which is reticulated, and it has a ſmall
core.  I. is quite white ; and when roaſted or boiled, has the con-
ſiſtence of new wheat bread, and reſembles it in taſte ; only it is
ſweeter.   There are large foreſts of this fruit on moſt of the iſlands
in the South Sea.  [See Cook's laſt Voyage, p. 48]

Deity above all. Each of the islands surrounding *Thaitee* has its principal God, or tutelar Deity.——
This is always the Divinity whom the High-Priest
of each isle addresses in his prayers at the grand *Marai* of the Prince of that island.

The great *Deity* they think to be the prime cause
of all divine and human Beings; and suppose the inferior Deities, and even mankind are descended from
him and another Being of the female sex; and in
this respect, they call the great Deity *Ta-rou-tiay
Etō mou*, the great procreating stem: but his wife
is not of the same nature with him.——They imagine
a coexisting hard substance necessary, which they
call *O tē pa pa*. These procreated *O-Heē-naà*, the
Goddess who created the moon, and presides in that
black cloud, which appears in that luminary;—*Te-whetto-ma-tarai*, the creator of the stars;—*Oo-már-rico*, the God and creator of the seas; and *Orre-or-re*, who is God of the winds. But the sea is under
the direction of thirteen Divinities, who have all
their peculiar employment. The great God lives in
the sun, and is tho't to be the cause of earthquakes.
They have one inferior Genius, or Divinity, of a malignant disposition, residing near the *morai*, or burying-places, and in or near the chest including the
heads of their deceased friends, each of which is
called the house of the Evil Genius. The people
are of opinion, that when a Priest invocates this evil
Genius, he will kill, by a sudden death, the person
on whom they intend to bring down the vengeance
of this Divinity. They have another inferior Divinity, who had the same power of killing men, with
this difference only, that he was not addressed by
prayer, but is only worshipped by hissing. This last



kind

kind of Genius, is called *Tēē-bēē*: this, they fay, is
the Being which hears, fmells, taftes and feels within
us, and after death exifts feparately from the body,
but lives near burying-places, and hovers round
the corpfe of their friends; and is likewife an object
of their reverence, though addreffed only by hiffing.
Thefe *Tēē-bēēs* are likewife feared: for, according
to their belief, they creep during night into the houfes, and eat the heart and entrails of the people fleep-
ing therein, and this caufes their death.*

The inhabitants of thefe iflands honour their Divinities—firft, by prayers; fecondly, by fetting a-
part a certain order of men to offer up thefe prayers;
thirdly, by fetting apart certain days for religious
worfhip; fourthly, by confecrating certain places
for that purpofe; fifthly, by offering human facrifices
to the God of war.† They preferve a condemned
malefactor, of an interior clafs, for a facrifice; provided they are not poffeffed of any prifoner of war.
The *Otaheiteans*, and the other Iflanders, prepare
thofe oblations on their morafs.

We have plain proofs that the Otaheiteans have
notions of a *metemphichofis*.‡

NEW HOLLAND. The people inhabiting
this vaft ifland appear to be all of one race.‖ But
no account can yet be procured which indicate their
entertaining any ideas of religion. The *New-Hol-
lander* is a mere favage; nay, more, he poffeffes
the loweft rank in the clafs of Beings.§

From

* Fofter's Geog. Obfervations, p. 533, 534.    † Ibid.
‡ C ok's laft Voyage, p 76, 131, 136.
‖ Roberfon, vol. i. p 472.
§ Cook's laft Voyage, p. 12.

*From the foregoing view of the various religions of the different countries of the world, it appears, that the Christian Religion is of very small extent, compared with those many and vast countries overspread with Paganism or Mohammedism. This great and sad truth may be further evinced by the following calculation, ingeniously made by some, who, dividing the inhabited world into thirty parts, find, that*

| | | | | |
|---|---|---|---|---|
| XIX | | | Pagans, | |
| VI | | | Jews and Mohammedans, | |
| II | Of them are pos- sessed by | | Christians of the Greek Church, | |
| III | | | Those of the | Church of Rome, Protestant Commu- nion. |

*If this calculation be true, Christianity, taken in its largest latitude, bears no greater proportion to the other religions than five to twenty five.* *

---

* It is worthy our observation, that the above calculation was made before the late discoveries of the north-west part of America, the north-east part of Asia, the vast tract of New-Holland, New-Guinea and the numerous other islands in the Pacific Ocean : how much greater then must the numerical difference appear at the present day, between that part of mankind, who enjoy the light of Christianity, and that part who are now groping in Pagan dark- ness !

## THE END.

# ERRATA.

| Page. | line. | | for | read. |
|---|---|---|---|---|
| 9 | 5 from top, | | take, | took. |
| 11 | 15 from bottom, | | to, | no. |
| 18 | 16 from top, | | names, | name. |
| 29 | 16 | | centur, | century. |
| 43 | 11 from bottom, | | Camufars, | Camifars. |
| ibid. | 8 | | diftinguifh, | diftinguifhed. |
| 66 | 9 from top | | Frates, | Fratres. |
| 67 | 8 | | Dauphing | Dauphiny. |
| 83 | 17 | | manners, | manner. |
| 86 | 16 | | perfelfly, | perfectly. |
| 87 | 5 from bottom, | | Janfenites, | Janfenius. |
| 104 | 12 from top, | | entities, | entities. |
| 135 | 16 | | choir, | chair. |
| 140 | 2 | | difpofes, | difpenfe. |
| 191 | 12 | dele | ex-. | |
| 194 | 9 from bottom, | | by parallel, | by a parallel, |

## APPENDIX.

| 6 | 10, 11 | for | reflect in the name of this Mafter : I muft tell you, | read | reflect. In the name of this Mafter, I muft tell you, |
|---|---|---|---|---|---|
| 17 | 8 from bottom, | | feventh, | | eleventh. |
| 30 | 10 from top, | | Borignomifte, | | Borigoonifts. |
| 36 | 4 from bottom, | | of Jefuits, | | of the Jefuits. |
| 64 | 1 at top, | | Bhriftians, | | Chriftians. |

[Other fmaller errors the candid reader will excufe.]

# I N D E X,

## TO THE

## ALPHABETICAL COMPENDIUM, &c.

INDEX

# I N D E X,

## T O   T H E

## A P P P E N D I X.

---

# A CHRONOLOGICAL TABLE.

**CENTURY I.**

**C**Erinthians,
Docetae,
Ebionites,
Gnoftics,
Menanderians,
Nazareans,
Nicolatans,

Offenians,
Simonians.

**CENTURY II.**

Adamites,
Alogians,
Ammonians,
Apellæans,

Aquarians,
Archonticks,
Artemonites,
Arcotyrites,
Afcodrogites,
Bardefanifts,
Bafalidians,
Cainians,
Carpocratians,

# A CHRONOLOGICAL TABLE.

Carpocratians,
Cerdonians,
Elcefaites,
Encratites,
Florinians,
Helfaites,
Heracleonites,
Hermogenians,
Marcofians,
Melitonians,
Monarchians,
Montanifts,
Ophites,
Quartodecimani,
Saturnians,
Secundians,
Serverians,
Sethians,
Valentinians.

## CENTURY III.

Apocaritæs,
Arabici,
Afclepidotæans,
Beryllians,
Bonofians,
Eutuchites,
Hieracites,
Manichæans,
Melchizedichians
Myftics,
Noetians,
Novations,
Originifts,
Paulians,
Quintilians,
Sabellians.

## CENTURY IV.

Aerians,
Aetians,
Agnoites,
Amomæans,
Apollinarians,
Arians,
Affuritans,
Audæans,
Colluthians,
Collyridians,
Donatifts,
Eudoxians,
Eufebians,
Euftathians,
Luciferians,
Marcedonians,
Marcellians,
Maffalians,
Patricians,
Photinians,
Prifcillianifts,
Pfatyrians,
Sacophori,
Satanians,
Selucians,
Triformiani.

## CENTURY V.

Acephali,
Angelites,
Armenians,
Eutychians,
Maronites,
Monophyfites,
Neftorians,
Pelagians,
Semi-Pelagians,
Soldins,
Stilites,
Theopafchites.

## CENTURY VI.

Aphtharpodocites
Cononites,
Corrupticola,
Damianifts,
Gacianitæ,
Jacobites,
Melecians,
Tritheifts.

## CENTURY VII.

Abyffinians,
Aginians,
Chazinzarians,
Eicetæ,
Gnofimachi,
Lampetians,
Monothelites,
Paulicians.

## CENTURY VIII.

Adoptians,
Albanenfes,
Albanois,
Ethnophrones,
Greek-Chruch.

## CENTURY IX.

Abrahamians,
Predeftinarians.

CENTURY

# A CHRONOLOGICAL TABLE.

**CENTURY X.**

Anthopomor-
phites.

**CENTURY XI.**

Azymites,
Berengarians.

**CENTUTY XII.**

Apostolics,
Arnoldists,
Bogomiles,
Capuati,
Catharists,
Eonites,
Gazares,
Henricians,
Joachimites,
Paſſaginians,
Petrobruſſians,
Tanquelians.

**CENTURY XIII.**

Almaricians,
Brethren and Siſ-
ters of the Free
Spirit,
Flagellants,
Fratricelli,
Wilhelminians.

**CENTURY XIV.**

Dancers,
Dulcinists,
Turlupins.

**CENTURY XV.**

Calixtins,
Diggers,
Fratres Albati,
Huſſites,
Men of Under-
standing,
Taborites,
Wicliffites.

**CENTURY XVI.**

Amſdorfians,
Antinomians,
Baptists,
Barlaamites,
Brownists,
Budneians,
Calvinists,
Davidists,
Energici,
Equinians,
Eraſtians,
Familists,
Farvonians,
Illuminati,
Inviſibles,
Jeſuits,
Libertines,
Lutherans,
Mennonites,
Molinists,
Oſiandrians,
Schewenkfeldians
Servetians,
Socinians,
Stancarians,
Synergiſts,

Ubiquitarians,
Zuinglians.

**CENTURY XVII.**

Arminians,
Behmenists,
Biddelians,
Borignomists,
Calixtins,
Cocceians,
Fifth Monarchy-
Men,
French Prophets,
Hattemists,
Janſenists,
Keithians,
Labbadiſts,
Philadelphian So-
ciety,
Quakers,
Quietiſts,
Ranters,
Roſecrucians,
Seekers,
Traſkites,
Uckewalliſts,
Verſchoriſts.

**CENTURY XVIII.**

Dunkers,
Hopkinſians,
Methodists,
Moravians,
Sandemanians,
Shakers,
Univerſaliſts.

## A

REVEREND *Mr.* Thomas Abbott, Brooklyn,
   *Mr.* Samuel Abbot, *jun.* Andover,
*Rev. Mr.* Zabdiel Adams, Lunenburgh,
*Rev. Mr.* Moses Adams, Acton,
*Rev. Mr.* Jedediah Adams, Stoughton,
*Mr.* Samuel Adams, *jun.* Boston, 2 *Copies.*
*Mr.* Elijah Adams, Medfield, 2 *Copies.*
*Deacon* Enoch Adams, ditto,
*Mr.* Joseph Adams, ditto,
*Mr.* Ward Adams, Franklin,
*Mr.* John Adams, Roxbury,
*Mr.* George Whitefield Adams, Newton,
*Mr.* Thomas Adams, Pepperrell,
*Miss* Sukey Adams, Boston, 2 *Copies.*
*Miss* Eunice Adams, Medfield,
*Miss* Sally Adams, Pepperrell,
*Miss* Silence Adams, Medway,
*Capt.* Silas Alden, Needham,
*Col.* John Allen, Passamagudda,
*Miss* Polly Allen, Boston,
Ebenezer Allen, *A. M.* Stoneham,
*Mr.* John Allen, Barnstable,
*Mr.* Eleazer Allen, *jun.* Dedham,
*Mr.* James Ames, Bridgewater,
*Mr.* Robert Anan, Rhode-Island College,
Nathaniel Appleton, *Esq;* Boston, 2 *Copies.*
Welcome Arnold, *Esq;* Providence,
*Mr.* John Ayres, Needham,

Andrew.

## B

Andrew Bacchus, *Esq*; Plainfield, *Connecticut*,
*Rev. Mr.* Ifaac Backus, Middleborough,
*Mr.* Jofiah Bacon, Springfield,
*Mr.* Jofeph Bacon, Winchendon,
*Rev. Mr.* Benjamin Balch, Danvers,
*Mr.* Thomas Bancroft, *Student*, Harvard-College,
Aaron Bancroft, *A. M.* Reading, 2 *Copies*,
*Mr.* James Bancroft, Bofton,
Nathaniel Barber, *Esq*; ditto,
*Mr.* Beriah Baftow, Wrentham,
*Capt.* John Baxter, *jun.* Medfield,
*Mr.* Stephen Baxter, *Student*, Harvard College,
*Mr.* Silas Beaman, Shrewfbury,
*Mr.* George Benfon, Providence,
*Dr.* Amariah Bigelow, Shrewfbury,
*Mifs* Olive Bigelow, ditto,
*Mr.* William Bigelow, Natick,
*Mr.* William Billings, Bofton,
*Mr.* Nathan Blake, Wrentham,
Caleb Blake, *A. B.* ditto, 2 *Copies*.
*Mr.* Samuel Blodget, Bofton,
*Rev. Mr.* Caleb Blood, Newton,
*Mr.* Jonathan Bowdrick, Franklin, 2 *Copies*.
*Hon.* Jabez Bowen, *Esq*; Providence, *Lieut. Governor*
*Capt.* John Boyd, Franklin,             (*of* Rhode-Ifland,
*Mr.* Benjamin Boyden, Walpole,
John Bradford, *A. M.* Bofton,
*Mr.* Luther Brick, Sherburne,
*Mr.* Daniel Brick, ditto,
*Mr.* John Bridge, Lexington,
*Mr.* Antipas Brightman, Waldoborough,
Jofeph Brown, *Esq*; Providence,
*Rev. Mr.* Elijah Brown, Sherburne,
*Mr.* William Brown, Bofton,
*Mr.* Jofiah Brown, ditto,
Nicholas Brown, *Esq*; Providence,
*Mifs* Polly Brown, ditto,

*Rev.*

*Rev. Mr.* Joseph Brown, Winchendon,
*Mr.* William Brown, Fitchburgh,
*Rev. Mr.* Nathan Buckman, Medway,
*Mr.* John Buckminster, Barre,
*Major* Seth Bullard, Walpole,
*Mr.* Benjamin Bullard, Sherburne,
*Rev. Mr.* John Bullard, Pepperrell,
Moses Bullen, *Esq;* Medfield,
*Mr.* Samuel Butler, Providence,
*Mr.* Joshua Butters, Boston.

## C.

*Mr.* Seth Capron, Norton,
*Rev. Mr.* Benjamin Caryl, Dedham,
*Rev.* Charles Chauncy, *D. D.* Boston,
*Mr.* Nathaniel Champney, Cambridge,
*Rev. Mr.* Daniel Chaplin, Groton,
*Mr.* Elisha Cheney, Newton,
*Mr.* Ephraim Chenery, Medfield,
*Rev. Mr.* Jabez Chickering, Dedham,
*Mr.* Daniel Chickering, Needham,
*Rev. Mr.* John Clark, Boston,
*Mr.* Dyer Clark, Franklin,
*Mr.* Stephen Clark, Wrentham,
*Mr.* Jacob Clark, Medfield,
*Mr.* Pitt Clark, ditto,
*Mr.* Phillips Clark, ditto,
*Miss* Sibel Clark, ditto,
*Mr.* Roland Clark, *jun.* Sturbridge,
*Mr.* Zimri Cleaveland, Medfield,
*Mr.* John Coburn, Boston,
*Rev. Mr.* Curtis Coe, Durham, *New-Hampshire,*
*Mr.* Jonathan Colburn, Dedham,
*Mr.* James Foster Condy, Boston,
*Mr.* Ezra Conant, *jun.* Concord, 2 *Copies.*
*Mr.* Jacob Cooper, Boston, 2 *Copies.*
*Mr.* Peter Coolidge, *jun.* Medfield,
*Mr.* Jacob Corey, Sturbridge,

Mr.

*Mr.* Ebenezer Corey, Roxbury,
Thomas Cowden, *Efq;* Fitchburgh,
Ebenezer Crafts, *Efq;* Sturbridge,
Richard Cranch, *Efq;* Braintree, 2 *Copies.*
Abraham Cummings, *A. M.* ditto,
*Major* James Cunningham, Medfield,
*Rev. Mr.* Phillips Curtifs, Sharon,
*Mifs* Sally Curtifs, Newton.

### D

Stephen Dana, *Efq;* Cambridge,
*Mr.* Jeremiah Daniels, *jun.* Medway,
David Daniels, *A. M.* ditto,
*Mr.* Daniel Davis, Harvard,
Robert Davis, *Efq;* Bofton,
*Mr.* Nathaniel Davis, ditto,
*Hon.* Caleb Davis, *Efq;* ditto,
*Mr.* Jofeph Day, Walpole,
*Mifs* Eunice Day, Wrentham,
*Hon.* Samuel Dexter, *Efq;* Dedham,
*Rev. Mr.* Jordan Dodge, Sturbridge,
*Mr.* Thomas Doggett, Attleborough,
*Hon.* Jofeph Dorr, *Efq;* Mendon,
*Dr.* Philip Draper, Dedham,
Solomon Drowne, *M. B.* Providence,
*Mr.* Eliphalet Dyer, *jun.* Windham, *Connecticut.*

### E

*Rev. Mr.* Jofeph Eckley, Bofton,
John Eddy, *A. M.* Newton,
*Mr.* Richard Eddy, Providence,
*Mr.* George Ellis, Medfield,
*Mr.* Oliver Ellis, ditto, 3 *Copies.*
*Mr.* Jonathan Ellis, Needham,
*Mr.* Samuel Emerfon, Hollis,
*Rev. Mr.* Nathaniel Emmons, Franklin, 6 *Copies.*
*Rev. Mr.* Mofes Everett, Dorchefter,

*Rev.*

Rev. *Mr.* Oliver Everett, Boston,
*Miss* Tryphena Everett, Foxborough.

## F

Rev. *Mr.* Eleazer Fairbanks, Shrewsbury, 2 *Copies.*
*Mr.* Jonathan Felt, Wrentham,
*Mr.* John Fenno, Boston,
*Hon.* Jabez Fisher, *Esq;* Franklin,
*Mr.* Daniel Fisher, ditto,
Elias Fisher, *A. M.* Wrentham,
*Mr.* Nathaniel Fisher, Needham,
*Mr.* Simon Fisher, Sturbridge,
*Mr.* John Flagg, Shrewsbury,
*Mr.* Nehemiah Flanders, Newbury-Port,
Theodore Foster, *Esq;* Providence,
*Mr.* Nathaniel Foster, Boston,
*Mr.* John Foster, Western,
*Mr.* Joseph Fox, Fitchburgh,
Rev. *Mr.* James Freeman, Boston,
*Mr.* Benjamin Freeman, Sturbridge,
*Mr.* Edmund Freeman, Rhode-Island-College,
*Mr.* Nehemiah Fuller, Fitchburgh,
*Mr.* Henry Fullerton, Boston.

## G

Rev. *Mr.* Thomas Gair, Medfield, 3 *Copies.*
Rev. *Mr.* Francis Gardner, Leominster,
*Mr.* Jotham Gay, Dedham,
*Mr.* Calvin Gay, Walpole,
*Mr.* Benjamin Goldthwait, Boston,
*Miss* Finis Gookin, Dedham,
Rev. William Gordon, *D. D.* Roxbury,
*Hon.* Nathaniel Gorham, *Esq;* Charlestown,
*Mr.* Jonathan Gould, Rhode-Island-College,
*Mrs.* Catharine Macaulay Graham, Boston,
Rev. *Mr.* Nathaniel Green, Charlton,
*Mr.* Timothy Green, Rhode-Island-College,

Rev.

*Rev. Mr.* William Greenough, Newton,
*Dr.* Daniel Greenleaf, Boston,
Benjamin Guild, *A. M.* ditto, 2 *Copies.*
*Mr.* Moses Guild, Dedham,

## H

*Deacon* Moses Hales, Winchendon,
*Mr.* Josiah Hall, Newton,
Mr. Charles Hamant, Medfield,
Mr. Francis Hamant, ditto,
*Capt.* William Hammond, Newton,
Mr. Nicholas Harris, Walpole,
Mr. Samuel Hartshorne, ditto,
Mr. Ebenezer Hartshorn, Rindge, *New-Hampshire,*
Mr. Oliver Hastings, Weston,
*Rev. Mr.* Jason Haven, Dedham,
David Haven, *Esq;* Framingham, 2 *Copies.*
Moses Haven, *A. B.* ditto,
Mr. Abijah Hawes, Wrentham,
Mr. James Hawes, ditto,
*Miss* Mary Hawes, Franklin,
James Hawes, *Esq;* Westborough,
Mr. Lemuel Hedge, Hardwick, 3 *Copies.*
*Miss* Elizabeth Herriman, Rowley,
Benjamin Hichborn, *Esq;* Boston,
*Miss* Jane Hill, ditto,
*Capt.* John Hiwell, ditto,
Mr. Josiah Holbrook, Wrentham,
*Miss* Martha Holbrook, Medfield,
Mr. David Holbrook, Sherburne,
*Capt.* David Holbrook, Wrentham, 2 *Copies.*
Mr. John Holbrook, Sturbridge,
Mr. Edward Holyoke, Boston,
*Dr.* Abraham Holland, Walpole, *New-Hampshire,*
*Rev.* Mr. Jonathan Homer, Newton,
*Rev.* Mr. William Hooper, Dover, *New-Hampshire,*
*Capt.* Caleb Hopkins, Boston,
Samuel Hunt, *A. M.* ditto,

*Dr.*

*Dr.* Edward Hunt, Shrewsbury,
*Rev.* Mr. Afa Hunt, Middleborough,
William Hyflop, *Efq;* Brooklyn, 4 *Copies.*
*Hon.* David Howell, *Efq;* Providence,
Mr. John Howland, ditto.


I


Mr. John Jackfon, Bofton,
Mr. John Jenkins, ditto, 2 *Copies.*
*Dr.* James Jerauld, Medfield,
Daniel Jones, *Efq;* Bofton, 3 *Copies.*
John Jones, *Efq;* Dedham,
Mr. Eleazer Jones, Cambridge,
*Dr.* John Joy, Bofton.


K


Mr. Jonathan Kendrick, Newton,
Mr. Ebenezer Kingfberry, Dedham,
Mr. Enoch Kingfberry, ditto,
Mr. Benjamin Kingfberry, *jun.* Walpole,
Mr. Seth Kingfberry, *jun.* ditto,
*Mifs* Abigail Kollock, Wrentham.


L


Mr. Seth Lawrence, Franklin,
Mr. Thomas Lawrence, Bofton,
Mr. Nathaniel Lawrence, Woburn,
*Rev.* Mr. Jófeph Lee, Royalfton,
Mr. Thomas Lee, Cambridge, 3 *Copies.*
Mr. Jofhua Leland, Sherburne,
Mr. Levi Lindfey, Walpole,
Mr. Abner Lincoln, Hingham,
Mr. Ezekiel Little, Haverhill,
*Dr.* Samuel Lock, Sherburne,
John Lucas, *Efq;* Bofton.

## M

*Rev.* James Manning, *President of* Rh. Island-College,
Mr. Rufus Man, Medfield, 2 *Copies.*
Mr. Ebenezer Man, Shrewsbury,
Mr. Nathan Man, Franklin,
Mr. Thomas Man, ditto,
*Col.* Sabin Mann, Medfield,
*Dr.* Bazaleel Mann, Attleborough,
*Dr.* Seth Mann, Walpole,
Mr. David Mann, Wrentham,
Mr. Joseph Martin, Providence,
*Lieut.* Henry Marble, Westborough,
*Col.* David Mason, Boston,
*Rev.* Samuel Mather, *D. D.* Boston,
Mr. Asahel Matthews, Southborough,
*Capt.* Ephraim May, Boston,
Mr. Daniel Mayo, Cambridge,
Mr. Jonathan Medcalf, Franklin,
Mr. Luther Medcalf, Medway,
Mr. John Messenger, Wrentham, 2 *Copies.*
Mr. Timothy Metcalf, ditto,
Mr. Thomas Miller, Charlestown,
Mr. Oliver Mills, Needham,
*Rev.* Mr. George Morey, Walpole,
*Dr.* Isaac Morrill, Natick,
Mr. Eliakim Morrill, ditto,
Mr. Samuel Morse, Franklin,
*Rev.* Mr. Ebenezer Morse, Shrewsbury,
Mr. Peletiah Morse, Natick,
Mr. Joseph Morse, Medfield,
*Miss* Abigail Morse, ditto,
*Miss* Hannah Morse, ditto,
*Dr.* Moses Mosman, Sudbury.


## N

Andrew Newell, *Esq;* Sherburne,
Mr. Samuel Nightingale, *jun.* Providence,

Mr.

### O

Mr. Daniel Oliver, *Student*, Dartm. College, 6 *Copies*,
Mr. Amos Ordway, Fitchburgh.

### P

Mr. Joseph Pierce Palmer, Boston,
Mr. Brick Parkman, Weftborough,
Rev. Mr. Seth Payfon, Rindge, *New-Hampfhire*.
Mr. George Payfon, Walpole,
Mr. Thomas Payfon, *jun.* Cambridge,
Mr. Elifha Peirce, Brattleborough,
Mr. Ebenezer Pemberton, Plainfield, *Connecticut*,
Daniel Perry, *Efq*; Medfield,
Mifs Efther Perry, Medway,
Mr. William Peters, Medfield,
Afa Piper, *A. M.* Acton,
Rev. Mr. John Pitman, Providence,
Mr. Gerfhom Plimpton, Sturbridge, 2 *Copies*.
Mr. Frederick Plimpton, ditto, 3 *Copies*.
Mr. Benjamin Plympton, Medfield,
Mr. Jofeph Plympton, ditto,
Mr. Elifha Pond, Franklin,
Mifs Kezia Pond, ditto,
Rev. Mr. E. Porter, Roxbury,
Mr. Nicholas Power, Providence,
Mr. John Pratt, Plainfield, *Connecticut*,
Mr. Allen Pratt, Bridgwater,
Mr. Seth Pratt, ditto,
Mr. Simeon Pratt, Medfield,
Rev. Mr. Thomas Prentice, ditto,
Mr. Stephen Prentice, Sherburne.

### Q

Edmund Quincy, *Efq*; Boston.

### R

Mr. Stephen Randel, Providence,

Rev.

*Rev. Mr.* Afaph Rice, Weſtminſter,
*Mr.* Moſes Richardſon, Medway,
*Mr.* Abijah Richardſon, ditto,
*Mr.* John Richardſon, Franklin,
*Rev. Mr.* George Robinſon, Killingly, *Connecticut,* 3
Aſher Robins, *A. M.* Rhode-Iſland,                   ( *Copies.*
*Rev. Mr.* William Rogers, Philadelphia, *Pennſylvania,*
*Mr.* John Rogers, Boſton,
*Lieut.* John Rogers, Newton,
*Mr.* John Rogers, Providence,
*Mr.* George Roulſtone, Boſton,
*Miſs* Betſey Ruſſell, Natick.

## S

*Rev. Mr.* Zedekiah Sanger, Duxbury,
*Mr.* Afa Sanger, Sherburne,
*Mr.* Daniel Sanger, Framingham,
*Hon.* Samuel Phillips Savage, *Efq;* Weſton,
*Mr.* Nathaniel Sawyer, Kingſton,
*Mr.* Samuel Scott, Bellingham,
*Rev. Mr.* Job Seamans, Attleborough,
*Dr.* Timothy Shepard, Sherburne,
*Mr.* Thomas Sherburne, Boſton,
*Mr.* Peter Sigourney, ditto,
*Rev. Mr.* Iſaac Skillman, ditto,
*Mr.* John Slack, Needham,
*Rev. Mr.* Iſaac Smith, Boſton,
Joſhua Smith, *Efq;* Southborough,
*Mr.* Lebbeus Smith, Medfield,
*Mr.* Timothy Smith, ditto,
*Mr.* Jonathan Smith, Hadley,
*Rev. Mr.* Joſeph Snow, Providence,
*Mr.* Benjamin Spear, Franklin,
*Mr.* Elias Stanley, Attleborough,
*Rev. Mr.* Samuel Stillman, Boſton,
*Dr.* Benjamin Stone, Shrewſbury,
*Mr.* Peter Stone, Southborough,
*Mr.* Joſeph Stone, Eaſt-Sudbury,

Mr.

*Mr.* Luther Stone, Fitchburgh,
William Story, *Efq;* Bofton,
*Hon.* James Sullivan, *Efq;* ditto, 2 *Copies.*
*Rev. Mr.* Jofeph Sumner, Shrewfbury;
Nathaniel Sumner, *Efq;* Dedham, 2 *Copies.*

### T

*Mr.* Jonathan Tay, Sherburne,
*Rev. Mr.* Ebenezer Thayer, Hampton, *N. Hampfhire,*
George Thacher, *A. B.* Biddeford,
*Rev. Mr.* Thomas Thacher, Dedham,
*Rev. Mr.* John Thomfon, Berwick,
*Rev. Mr.* Charles Thomfon, Swanzey,
*Capt.* Eliphalet Thorp, Dedham,
*Mr.* Edward Thurbur, Providence,
*Mr.* Daniel Thurfton, Franklin,
*Mr.* Shippie Townfend, Bofton,
Horatio Townfend, *A. B.* Medfield,
*Mifs* Sarah Townfend, ditto,
*Mr.* Thomas-H. Townfend, Needham,
*Dr.* Thomas Truman, Providence,
*Mr.* Jedediah Tucker, Stoughton,
*Hon.* Cotton Tufts, *Efq;* Weymouth,
*Mr.* Seth Turner, Medfield,
*Mr.* John Turuer, ditto,
*Mr.* Amos Turner, Medway,
*Mr.* Samuel Twifs, Franklin,
*Mr.* Royall Tyler, Uxbridge.

### U

*Mifs* Abigail Volney, Bofton,
*Mr.* Nathan Underwood, Needham,
*Mr.* John Upton, Fitchburgh,
*Mr.* Jacob Upton, ditto.

### W

*Mr.* Thomas Walcutt, Bofton,
*Mrs.* Elizabeth Walley, Roxbury,

Mr. Amos Walton, Wrentham,
Mr. Stephen Wardwell, Providence,
Mifs Rebecca Ward, Newton,
Mr. Jofeph Ware, Sherburne,
Mr. John Ware, ditto,
Mr. Elijah Ware, Wrentham,
B. Waterhoufe, *Profeffor of the Theory and Practice of*
Hon. Oliver Wendell, *Efq*; Bofton, 4 Copies. ( *Phyfic,*
*Rev.* Mr. Samuel Weft, Needham,
Mr. Eleazer Wheelock, Medfield,
*Rev.* Mr. Phinehas Whitney, Shirley,
Mr. Jofeph Whiting, Franklin,
Mifs Mehitable Whiting, Natick,
Daniel Whitney, *Efq*; Sherburne,
*Dr.* Ifrael Whiton, Winchendon,
Mr. John White, Shrewfbury,
*Rev.* Mr. Anthony Wibird, Braintree,
*Rev.* Mr. Ebenezer Wight, Bofton,
Mr. Jonathan Wight, Medfield,
Job Wight, *A. B.* ditto,
Henry Wight, *A. B.* ditto,
*Dr.* Aaron Wight, Medway,
*Rev.* Mr. William Williams, Wrentham,
Mr. Benjamin Wilfon, Weftminfter,
*Dr.* Jonathan Wild, Walpole,
*Capt.* Jofhua Witherlee, Bofton,
Mr. Silas Winchefter, Brooklyn,
Mr. Jonathan Winfhip, Cambridge,
Mr. Ebenezer Woodward, Newton,
Peter Wood, *Efq*; Marlborough,
Mr. Abijah Wyman, Afhby.

---

[☞ *Should the Titles of any of the foregoing Gentle-*
*men be omitted, 'tis defired that fuch Omiffion may be*
*excufed.*]

www.ingramcontent.com/pod-product-compliance
Lightning Source LLC
Chambersburg PA
CBHW031027120726
47905CB00007B/2070